Jainism and Ethical Finance

The financial crisis of 2008 has led to a re-evaluation of the role of financial institutions and their relationship with the wider economy and society. This process has meant an increased questioning of both the conduct of business itself and the principles behind commercial and financial activities. Yet non-western voices have been notably absent from this debate, as have alternatives to the dominant western-derived economic ideologies.

From the ancient spiritual wisdom or *Dharma* of the Jains, there emerges a practical modern philosophy fully in tune with the re-emergence of India as a global economic power. Jain individuals, businesses and charities have played a powerful role in India's rise and within the global Indian Diaspora. Jain communities are noted everywhere for their contributions to business, the professions and science. These successes are based on the principles of inter-dependence and co-operation, with an emphasis on long-term consolidation rather than short-term bursts of growth.

Researchers and students interested in the ethics of finance, accounting and economics will find *Jainism and Ethical Finance* a scholarly and illuminating evaluation of Jain Dharma as a non-western case study. In the light of current concerns about the way global finance and banking systems operate, this book offers a timely alternative perspective.

Atul K. Shah PhD ACA is an academic, senior lecturer at Suffolk Business School, chartered accountant and social entrepreneur. A Jain community leader in the UK, he is a founder of *Jain Spirit* magazine and Young Jains. Atul is author of *Celebrating Diversity* (2007) and contributes to numerous financial journals.

Aidan Rankin MA (Oxon) MSc (Econ.) PhD is a London-based independent scholar and property consultant. He has written three books on Jain thought: *The Jain Path: Ancient Wisdom for the West* (2006), *Many-Sided Wisdom: A New Politics of the Spirit* (2010) and *Living Jainism: An Ethical Science* (2013).

Jainism and Ethical Finance
A Timeless Business Model

Atul K. Shah and Aidan Rankin

Routledge
Taylor & Francis Group

LONDON AND NEW YORK

First published 2017
by Routledge
2 Park Square, Milton Park, Abingdon, Oxon OX14 4RN

and by Routledge
711 Third Avenue, New York, NY 10017

First issued in paperback 2018

Routledge is an imprint of the Taylor & Francis Group, an informa business

British Library Cataloguing in Publication Data
A catalogue record for this book is available from the British Library

Library of Congress Cataloging in Publication Data
Names: Shah, Atul K., 1973- author. | Rankin, Aidan, 1972- author.
Title: Jainism and ethical finance / Atul K. Shah and Aidan Rankin.
Description: Abingdon, Oxon ; New York, NY : Routledge, 2017. | Includes bibliographical references and index.
Identifiers: LCCN 2016044681 (print) | LCCN 2017001456 (ebook) | ISBN 9781138648869 (hardback : alk. paper) | ISBN 9781315626178 (eBook)
Subjects: LCSH: Finance--Religious aspects--Jainism. | Finance--Moral and ethical aspects.
Classification: LCC HG103 .S53 2017 (print) | LCC HG103 (ebook) | DDC 294.4/173--dc23
LC record available at https://lccn.loc.gov/2016044681

ISBN 13: 978-1-138-58963-6 (pbk)
ISBN 13: 978-1-138-64886-9 (hbk)

Typeset in Times New Roman
by Taylor & Francis Books

To all entrepreneurs and students aspiring to live and act fairly, honestly and with integrity.

Contents

Foreword

Jain teachings date back 5,000 years to Northern India. Today, these teachings support a nontheistic religion, offer a practical living philosophy, and provide a set of values that inform the lives of some ten million Jains worldwide. Atul Shah and Aidan Rankin explain how these teachings, particularly the Jain values of Anekant (respect for the views of others), Ahimsa (non-violence in action, speech, and thought), and Aparigraha (non-possessiveness) can offer a useful guide to responsible business and financial practices. The authors provide numerous examples drawn from the Jain business community. The examples are offered both as an anecdote to an overly arid and typically incomplete orthodox view of business activity and as a useful supplement to contemporary thought on sustainability and corporate social responsibly. The ideas are inter-disciplinary and holistic and should appeal to a wide audience, including sociologists, business ethics scholars, accountants, bankers, economists, and business people generally.

The book has two themes: one negative and one positive. On the dark side, one finds the notion that orthodox business training, especially in the field of finance, divorces business thinking from the culture in which business is conducted, inserting instead an artificial and misleading notion of individual autonomy and hyper-rationality. The authors suggest that orthodox financial training is not only misguided, but also harmful, as it contributes to environmental degradation and ultimately to human suffering. On the positive side, the authors suggest a remedy. Business thinking needs to embrace culture, including recognition of the central role played by ethical values in guiding business conduct. Once culture and ethics are brought to the fore, both environmental and social problems can be, and naturally will be, more coherently addressed.

The authors' criticisms of orthodox finance are neither new nor overly emphasized in the text. The criticisms are, however, central to their argument. The authors note that finance theory emerged as a unique discipline in the 1970s. It derived from economics, particularly the neoclassical theory of the firm. That theory *assumes* that firms maximize profits by responding to exogenously determined forces of supply and demand. Because profit maximization is axiomatic, and supply and demand are exogenous, there is no role for executive discretion. If culture and ethics play a role in business decisions, that role is hidden. It is embedded in the production functions that dictate supply and the utility preferences that generate demand.

Orthodox theory takes on normative connotations in several ways. First, couched in the rhetoric of science, it appeals to an ethos of rationality and objectivity. Second, employing the language of consumer sovereignty, it offers a libertarian appeal to freedom and choice. Third, the theory suggests that following the dictates of self-interest and profit maximization will generate bounty for the society as a whole. Combining appeals to science, freedom, and bounty gives orthodox theory a strong rhetorical momentum. People want the theory to be correct, which perhaps goes far to explain why it remains the dominant view among both business academics and practicing financiers of how the economy actually works.

Shah and Rankin are not convinced. Rather than being blinded by the rhetorical appeal of orthodox theory, they see an economic system that is in desperate need of repair. Of particular concern are environmental degradation, recurring financial scandals that periodically threaten economic collapse, income polarization, poverty, and white-collar crime. What is needed, the authors argue, is a reprioritizing between finance and ethics, or more precisely, the inculcation of ethics into financial decision-making. The authors recognize that there is nothing wrong with seeking a profit. Profit seeking encourages individual industry, and profit enables contributions to others. But profit must be achieved in an ethical way and then employed in an ethical fashion. After all, as humans, we have no moral authority to either seek or use profit in unethical ways. That is the primary contribution of this book.

For me, Jainism offers a relatively non-threatening way to introduce ethics, including insights from a nontheistic religion, into the business model. Jain teachings identify a universal law or cosmic order called Dharma. Dharma exists, but it can only be perceived in its entirety by one who has attained enlightenment. The last person to achieve enlightenment, Mahavira, lived about 2,500 years ago. Without enlightenment, one can only offer a perspective on Dharma, but one cannot see Dharma entirely. This limitation is embedded in the value of Anekant, or multi-sidedness. The idea is that each living being perceives a unique aspect of Dharma; therefore, the perspective of each being deserves respect.

Anekant suggests a deep humility, a profound tolerance, and an embrace of diversity. These attitudes can prove quite useful in the business world. Anekant can promote collaboration within an organization as mutual respect frees subordinates to contribute useful ideas. It can also sensitize decision-makers to the diverse demands and tastes found in the global marketplace, making the organization more responsive and open to change.

The humility of Anekant is completely consistent with the Jain value of Ahimsa that dictates non-violence to all living creatures. Life deserves respect, and it should not be harmed. Expressing Ahimsa, a Jain monk, or Muni, will wear a mask to avoid inhaling living microbes and use a broom to protect insects from the Muni's steps. Strict vegetarians, most Jains also avoid eating the roots of plants, preferring leaves, beans, and nuts so as to enable the plant to survive. Although each Jain strikes his or her own compromises – not everyone will carry a broom – the reverence for life is nonetheless profound. Ahimsa is entirely consistent with the notion of Deep Ecology found in western thought and with contemporary discussions of sustainability. For a Jain, financial decisions are always long term and always incorporate the environment and social cohesion as central stakeholders.

Jain teachings also highlight the value of Aparigraha, or non-possessiveness. According to Jain philosophy, we are stewards of our possessions and must use them for the long-term good of society. Ostentatiousness and self-pride through wealth is anathema to Jain values. As a corollary, Aparigraha suggests philanthropy. Shah and Rankin note that Jains constitute less than one-half-of-one-percent of India's population, but pay 24 percent of all taxes collected. Jain values tend to generate financial success, and many Jain families are quite wealthy. This success, in turn, enables sharing with others, and philanthropy is both common and highly valued in the Jain community. According to Aparigraha, possessions are means to an end, not ends in themselves.

Throughout the book, Shah and Rankin illustrate how an embrace of Anekant, Ahimsa and Aparigraha can improve financial decisions. They offer a score of case studies drawn from India, East Africa, Northern Europe and the United Kingdom. Most are quite memorable. Mr Bhavarlal Jain founded Jain Irrigation as a means to help rural farmers increase production. The family-owned business is now the second largest drip-irrigation firm in the world and contributes to the Indian community by supporting both small farmers and local schools. In Belgium, Jains have succeeded in the diamond-polishing business in large measure due to their reputation for honesty. In the United Kingdom, Jain values have supported small businesses such as a vegan catering firm in London, and larger organizations such as Sigma Pharmaceuticals. In each case, the Jain business is driven by ethical values and an orientation toward serving others, rather than a calculation of short-term pecuniary gain.

In sum, Shah and Rankin have offered a useful supplement to orthodox finance. Finance theory tends to ignore both ethics and culture. Yet, business decisions benefit from a more holistic approach. Perhaps environmental threats, financial scandals, persistent poverty, and income polarization will cause orthodox thinkers to finally seek alternatives. Jainism provides a provocative place to start. The authors have provided an excellent account of ethical finance from a Jain perspective. Their argument deserves reflection.

Daniel T. Ostas, JD, PhD
James G. Harlow, Jr. Chair in Business Ethics
Michael F. Price College of Business
University of Oklahoma
Norman, OK, USA

Acknowledgements

This book has been emerging for decades, but speaking honestly, it has taken me a long time to get the confidence to write about my culture to transform my profession. This is because in both the accounting and finance professions, there is little space to speak about culture as these are primarily technical disciplines which in their very construction deny culture. When the bias of the academy and its research is monocultural and rigidly secularist, there is no space to talk about diverse cultural theories or faiths. I certainly felt that, even though this may sound like an exaggeration. Aidan and I were doctoral colleagues at the London School of Economics where our friendship started, and it continued ever since, with him writing three excellent books about my Jain culture and its contemporary relevance. We have co-operated on a number of ethical projects and writings over nearly two decades, and work well together. I would like to thank Aidan for his excellent co-operation and collegiality in the writing of this book. I was also motivated by the fact that the act of writing this book was itself a cross-cultural experience and we hope that it will reach diverse audiences through its language and accessibility. My colleague at University of Suffolk, Stuart Agnew, gave us very encouraging and constructive comments at a timely stage in the book finishing process, for which I am most grateful. I know for a fact that what we have written about is only the tip of a profound ethical iceberg, and hope and pray that such stories and lived examples continue to inspire future generations.

My greatest thanks go to my late father Mr Keshavji Rupshi Shah (Bapuji), who was a community leader, pioneer and visionary extraordinaire. His life was a beautiful expression of the Jain spirit of unconditional love, charity and generosity, and he transformed the lives of thousands over his lifetime. Growing up in Mombasa, Kenya, I never imagined that one day I would become an academic and write many books and articles, but here I am, thanks to my beloved Bapuji. My family members Ba, Ritesh, Dipti, Nina, Jaina and Meerav have supported me lovingly on this journey. For my intellectual mentoring, I would like to thank Prem Sikka, Michael Tobias, Professor Padmanabh S. Jaini and the late Shashikant Mehta. Many people provided me with encouragement on my life journey – Tara and Rajni Shah, Dr Lynne

Sedgmore CBE, Dr Jim Harding, Prakash Shah, Professor Werner Menski, Atul Dhanani and Al Bhimani. Thank you for your support and guidance.

AS

Many of the names mentioned by Atul have featured prominently in my exploration of Jain ideas and thought, as well as encouraging me on my intellectual journey. Of the names on his list, I would especially single out Lynne Sedgmore, Werner Menski and as a guiding influence, Padmanabh Jaini, whose seminal study of Jain thought was one of the first books I read on the subject, and which I continuously re-read and use as a point of reference more than ten years later. I am also grateful to Anant Shah for his friendship and gentle encouragement over the years and especially for his open and positive responses to my early questions as a non-Jain interested in both the philosophy of the Jains and its practical application, not least in the commercial arena which is the subject of this book.

Professor Kanti Mardia of Leeds and Oxford universities, with whom I was privileged to collaborate on an earlier book, has inspired me to see connections between some of the earliest insights of Jain thinkers and seers and the cutting edge of modern physics. He and his wife Pavan are models of Jain hospitality. Most important of all has been Atul's friendship, and with it the support and rigorous argument which have guided me over many years in my continuing quest to appreciate Jain Dharma more fully. Bharat Shah, of Sigma Pharmaceuticals, was generous with his time and greatly increased my understanding of how Jain belief and practice impacts on the running of a successful commercial enterprise. I have also profoundly benefitted from Jyoti Kothari's extensive knowledge and fascinating exploration of the jewellery industry and its connections with Jain communities in India. Mahersh and Nishma Shah are exemplars of ethical business practice and values.

I would like to thank my mother, Anne Vannan Rankin, who was the first person to teach me to value the principle of Ahimsa, or compassion for all forms of life, and my father, Professor David Rankin, whose wise advice and inspiration has been valuable to me throughout my life. Brian Scoltock has listened to and supported me with great patience and tolerance while I have been engaged in this and many previous projects. As Jains throughout the world remind us, *Parasparopagraho Jivanam*: All life is bound together.

AR

The stories and examples in this book came from members of the Jain community, to whom we are both very much indebted. We are also indebted to Jacqueline Curthoys at Routledge for commissioning the book and encouraging us throughout the writing process, along with her assistants Sinead Waldron, Nicola Cupit and Laura Hussey. We are grateful to our production editor at Routledge, Alaina Christensen, to Mark Wells for his indispensable work as indexer, and to our copy editor at Bookbright Media, Ellen Graham, as well as her production manager, Jamie Vidich. Without Ellen's careful, painstaking work and Jamie's wise advice, our book would not have come to life. Dr Sulekh Jain, of Houston, Texas, provided us with encouragement and assisted with the preparation of the manuscript. We thank him for this and value his commitment to the promotion of Jain education. We would like to thank our reviewers, Professors Janette Rutterford and Daniel T. Ostas, who encouraged us to work on this book. Dan in particular we thank for his dedication and generosity in writing the Foreword.

As ever, we take full responsibility for any errors or omissions, and hope that this book will induce our readers to write their own stories and express their thoughts about ethical finance from diverse cultural perspectives.

A note on Jain names

There are a number of references to people in the examples analysed in this book. Many of the surnames are similar, for example Shah and Jain are common. This can appear confusing to a reader not versed in the Jain Diaspora – it may even appear as if all belong to one family! The truth is more complicated. The last name or surname Jain is not adapted by all Jains, although all who have that last name are Jain. We know that in Punjab, some groups decided to adapt Jain as a last name to make their culture and identity visible. Similarly, many Shahs are Jain, although not all Shahs are Jain – it is a very frequent surname, shared by one of the authors of this book. However it is not necessarily an indicator of Jain heritage, as many Muslims are also called Shah.

Jains in India come from all parts of the country, and have a wide variety of last names, based on family lineages, community membership, and sometimes town or locality of family. It is important to remember that when we speak of culture, there is an assumption of commonality, but the truth is often much more complex. As an example, Jains speak different languages depending on their origins. They belong to different sects and sub-sects, ally themselves with a variety of gurus, revere different deities, and also practice in a variety of differing festivals and rituals even though they belong to the same faith. In the field of business and entrepreneurship, the Gujaratis and Marvadis are respected as the most proficient: The Economist (2015) has described Gujaratis as the world's leading entrepreneurs. Among Jains, the Shah name is an indicator of Gujarati heritage. The culture of Gujarati Jains also has characteristics in common with Hindus from Gujarat, including shared historical experience and frequent philosophical convergence.

Perhaps, in the interests of false simplicity, we are too often tempted to classify and categorise people, languages and cultures. There has always been fluidity in such definitions, and whilst there may be convenient bases for discussions, we must never forget the contextual variety which also exists. Understatement, modesty, even humility remain powerful ingredients of Jain culture. They accompany, and contribute to, the remarkable capacity of Jains to assimilate with the majority cultures around them while retaining their distinctive beliefs and way of life. These characteristics are alluded to throughout our book. One of their consequences has been that Jain identity often seems almost invisible to outsiders. We hope that in these pages we have been able to shed a discreet light on this intricate and unique culture.

1 Introduction

Aidan Rankin

I adore so greatly the principles of the Jain religion that I would like to be reborn in a Jain community.

Attributed to George Bernard Shaw (1856–1950), playwright, thinker and co-founder of the London School of Economics and Political Science

Rationale

The philosophy, faith and way of life of the Jains has been known to the world for many centuries through cross-cultural encounters ranging from travellers' tales to the translation of texts to the experience of western colonialism and its aftermath. With the impetus of colonialism, trade and social change, Jain communities have expanded from their Indian base to many other regions of the world, East Africa in particular, but also South-East Asia and more recently Europe, North America and Australia. Nonetheless, with the exception of a relatively small community of scholars, knowledge of Jain culture is patchy outside the Indian sphere of influence. It is even limited within India itself, although Mahatma Gandhi (himself a Hindu) popularised many of Jainism's core precepts, such as the commitment to non-violence. Understanding of the Jains is hampered in part by stereotypes associated with their asceticism. From a global (and especially western) perspective, these can appear negative, although they are practised by a tiny fraction of the overall Jain population. Also, the bias of academic research and scholarship both in India and the west has inclined towards hermeneutics and history. Our purpose here is to redress the balance towards the practical implications of Jain philosophy for its adherents. We aim to show how an ancient spiritual tradition is adapted with imagination and flexibility to the challenges and creative opportunities of the modern world. Specifically, we explore the relationship between the spiritual lives of the Jains and an ethical system applied to business and finance that differs markedly from the prevailing western paradigm.

The literature on ethical finance is relatively sparse compared to the huge growth and influence of finance as an academic discipline equipped with scholars, professional bodies, university courses and learned journals. Despite the ethical groundings of the science of economics (see Chapter 2), the current emphasis tends towards a sense of ethical detachment in the name of an elusive 'objectivity'. With the notable exception of the growing body of literature on Islamic finance, the emphasis of most academic research leans towards current western philosophies. Often, an especially privileged position is accorded to themes associated with neo-liberal economics and other 'universalist' or 'value-free' approaches to financial and business management. This bias can appear especially acute to those who are approaching the discipline from the perspective and experience of non-western cultures.

There are, of course, exceptions, including some influential figures in this area of western academia. John Boatright's influential treatise on financial ethics (1999) seeks to apply concepts of reason and natural justice to the activities of financial services and markets. Robert J. Shiller of Yale University, a Nobel Laureate and leader in the field of financial studies expresses profound concerns about the current direction of global finance, arguing for an ethical sea change from neutrality and narrow self-interest towards social responsibility and investment in a 'good society'. Shiller examines the roles and responsibilities of professionals in the world of finance (and some aspects of modern finance theory) from the perspective of normative ethics: the quest for a framework based on moral properties which can be discerned and applied. However he does not examine the ideological limitations of much of finance theory, in particular its two-dimensional or mechanistic view of the individual and his or her economic interests and its failure to emphasise the importance of cultural diversity. These omissions make finance theory itself appear increasingly problematic (Frankfurter and McGoun 2002).

The 2008 global financial crash has inspired a number of books questioning the morality of modern finance (e.g. Das 2011; Santoro and Strauss 2013). Hendry (2013) develops a philosophical framework of normative ethics to analyse core financial activities such as lending and borrowing, trading and speculation. These works are not explicitly concerned with cultural approaches to financial ethics and nor do they consider non-western perspectives. The lack of diversity of thought and the trend towards conformity in financial studies is noted with regret by some observers, notably Gendron and Smith-Lacroix (2013). Many recent studies of ethical finance (again with the exception of analyses of Islamic banking) virtually ignore the role of faith-based philosophies in formulating approaches to economics. This is despite the well-known historical contributions of faith to financial ethics (Graeber 2014). Faith has often provided an ethical 'grounding' for business practice. In the context of Britain's Christian history, for example, we may consider the role of the Methodists, Quakers and Unitarians in ameliorating the effects of the industrial revolution, along with the provision of workers' housing and their promotion of educational and penal reform (Thompson 2013). We may also remember the role of devout Anglicans in opposing the slave trade and laying the foundations for a culture of human rights (Hague 2008). Such influences continue to exert a profound influence, direct and indirect, over a society that can appear predominantly secular in character. In a non-western society such as India (the home of Jain philosophy and so an important focus of this study), faith retains an important role in directing or guiding the behaviour and choices of individuals and communities. Ideas that have cultural roots stretching back uninterruptedly over millennia are being reinterpreted in the modern context of a re-emerging global power.

Our book therefore aims to fill an important gap in current discussion of financial institutions and practices by drawing from a successful non-western system of values and practice: that of the Jains of India and the Indian Diaspora. At the same time, we seek to re-unite financial questions with broader cultural and ecological issues. The language of our book and many aspects of its subject matter might seem initially unfamiliar within this discipline and its academic allies. For example, the connection between financial and ecological concerns is an important feature of our analysis. This is because Jain culture does not compartmentalise areas of human activity or interest. It is at times explicitly critical of material accumulation and even economic growth when they are pursued as ends in themselves, without a social context. This inclusive and interdisciplinary perspective forms the core of our book's underlying philosophy.

Restraint and long-term thinking lie at the heart of what might reasonably be termed Jain economics. Crucially, the concept of 'society' extends beyond human communities to other species and ecosystems. This approach combines sustainable economics with prosperity, ecological responsibility with wealth creation. It also connects well with concerns, inspired by the environmental movement, that the conduct of economics has been too anthropocentric, i.e., human-centred. The results of this imbalanced thinking can be found, according to this argument, in pollution of the air, seas and soil on a global scale; the unplanned expansion of cities to the detriment of quality of life; as well as the unfolding crisis associated with climatic instability and the growing encroachment on the habitats of other species, threatening their survival and denying them the dignity they deserve. The green critique of anthropocentrism (Dobson 2007) is not identical to but converges with the Jain belief in the connectedness of all forms of life and the need for us to remember these connections in both our individual and collective decision making.

Whereas in emerging economies environmental problems such as pollution and deforestation induce greater material hardship, in the 'developed' world a sense of spiritual crisis or alienation often accompanies growing environmental awareness. Jain philosophy recognises an intimate link between spiritual practice and consciousness of the natural world. It reminds human beings that they are part of nature and not separated from it by their intelligence and inventiveness. Such separation is an illusion with dangerous psychological consequences, closely related to the consequences of excessive material accumulation without social responsibility. Environmental awareness is part of a Jain conception of social responsibility which demands, often quite rigorously, the avoidance of actions that increase inequality, pollute the environment or threaten other species and their habitats. The implications of this philosophy are, for its adherents, radical in the literal sense, for they require an examination of every action – and intention – from the roots upwards. For the conduct of business and finance, the effect is profound and offers a potent challenge.

The financial crisis of 2007–2008 has thrown into sharp relief the unpredictability of the neo-liberal model of capitalism, which has enjoyed political and intellectual hegemony for the past three decades. This model has encountered widespread criticism for its inability to redress inequality and is increasingly cited as a cause of widening social and economic disparities. It is sometimes dubbed 'free market fundamentalism', because it shares with extremist or iconoclastic expressions of religious faith a doctrinaire certainty and disregard for accumulated wisdom and cultural history. At the same time, the neo-liberal model is still perceived as the main engine of global wealth creation and its ideological hegemony remains unchallenged by countervailing forces of any power or substance. Even protest movements such as Occupy tend to present lists of single issues instead of an overarching critique. More theoretical studies of neo-liberalism (e.g. Klein 2008 and 2015; Standing 2014; Piketty 2014; Graeber 2014) have, despite their trenchant oppositional arguments, produced mostly incremental proposals for change rather than a counter-ideology. Graeber (2014), for example, argues that throughout history, culture and values have been at the centre of finance, although in the late modern era, they have been effectively stripped out of the discipline, with the qualitative approach giving way to a more abstract emphasis on quantification. Our book aims to move this argument on by drawing from the wisdom and experience of a long-established, non-western culture that has developed ways of understanding and practising finance sustainably and successfully.

Neo-liberalism's 'strange non-death' (Crouch 2011) arises from the lack of a worldview such as that offered until recently by Marxism, which is no longer linked to an effective political movement spanning national frontiers, although its economic analysis remains pertinent and it is undergoing a process of intellectual renewal, not least in India (Bagchi and Chatterjee 2014). The future of Marxism as a political project is in flux. Meanwhile, social democratic parties and movements are undergoing a crisis of identity and purpose, scarcely able to navigate the economic turbulence unleashed by the neo-liberal ascendancy, the collapse of collective certainties and – in the west at least – the end of the industrial system as previously understood (Keating and McCrone 2015; Cramme and Diamond 2012). The terms 'right' and 'left' are increasingly anachronistic on a global level, and yet there remains in both the radical and conservative strands of political discourse an unspoken assumption that solutions are to be found within the familiar experience and intellectual traditions of the west. Our intention is to broaden the parameters of the discussion of global finance to examine a living non-western tradition that has proved durable and adaptable to the needs of a modern economy – and at least in theory is the polar opposite of fundamentalism. It has also had a vast record of sustained success in finance, dating back at least a thousand years. Jainism's much vaunted commitment to 'many-sidedness' will be one of the principal themes of the ensuing chapters because of its impact on the way business is perceived and conducted. In both theory and practice, Jain philosophy provides a compelling and comprehensive critique of the prevalent Eurocentric models. It offers an alternative way of thinking about the underlying purpose and social role of financial institutions, money and material possessions themselves. Moreover, Jain communities have a strong historical record of combining financial success with rigorous ethical standards.

An exercise in thinking

This book is at once an exercise in thinking and a cross-cultural encounter. It aims to shed light on an Indic tradition whose doctrines and practices remain little known and under-reported. The belief system in question, known as Jainism, moves freely across the boundaries between secular philosophy and religious faith, abstract thought and practical action, including the commercial activities in which Jains have been productively engaged for many centuries. Statements such as 'Jainism is an Indian religion', 'Jainism is a philosophy', 'Jainism is a practical guide to modern living' are all partial truths or aspects of the truth. As we shall see, the term 'Jainism' is not fully descriptive of what is simultaneously a worldview, a distinctive culture and a way of life, lived for the most part unobtrusively in India and the extensive Diaspora.

Multivalence is a key feature of Jain culture. Reality is said to have many facets, like a diamond. Objective knowledge can be attained by an infinite variety of methods and by following many paths. In practice, few if any of us get there. From a Jain perspective, the closer we believe we are to the truth, the further we are likely to be from it and the more likely we are to be deluded by 'one-sided' absolutism. For this reason, Jains attach great importance to ideas being constantly tested against each other and respect for the viewpoints of others. It is easy to confuse this way of thinking with a form of extreme relativism, whereby nothing is 'true' in an absolute sense, but all possibilities are open to investigation. Jains, however, adopt a more subtle position than this and regard extreme relativism as a form of human self-deception. For them, there is an underlying reality to the universe and our task as conscious beings is to understand it as far as possible, so that we can apply its principles to our lives.

Hence it is precisely because objective reality exists that we are obliged to explore as many competing ideas as possible in the hope of getting closer to it. The philosophical aspect of Jainism promotes scientific methods for understanding the environment, human psychology and social organisation. The religious aspect promotes meditation and detachment from worldly concerns so as to distinguish more clearly between what is real and what is illusory or superficial. Meanwhile the practical guidelines of Jain doctrine by which most adherents live from day to day are based on the pursuit of knowledge, educational attainment and professional success including, crucially, success in commercial activities and the material rewards this brings.

The aim of such accomplishments is twofold. First, the individual is encouraged to realise as much of his or her potential as possible. In one sense, Jainism is a highly individualistic system centred on spiritual liberation for each person, indeed for each being. However it is also highly focussed on the way each individual interacts with the community around him, the environment as well as the society of humankind. Therefore the second goal of the Jains' pursuit of academic and commercial achievement is that knowledge and material resources should be deployed for the benefit of the society as a whole. The definition of 'society' begins with the nuclear and extended family and then fans outwards to the whole human community, other species and the environment. The premise of wealth accumulation is that surplus wealth will be redistributed voluntarily. This form of social conscience underlies the practices of charitable giving and philanthropy that have become defining characteristics of Jain businesses and households. Wealth is defined inclusively to encompass knowledge, educational attainment or specialist skills, qualities held to be useless if not put to constructive use. Jains are enjoined to participate in educational programmes, both as participants and donors, and thus to challenge entrenched forms of ignorance and prejudice that hold back individuals and communities or damage environments. Scientific research is also highly prized, for there is no recognised dichotomy between religion and science, faith and reason.

This science of giving, or non-possessiveness, is known as *Aparigraha*. It is one of the vows made by lay men and women in Jain communities, and its relevance to business and finance is this book's unifying thread. Just as critical to an understanding of how practising Jains think and behave, in the context of business as much as other areas of life, is the awareness that each being has its own 'viewpoint' that is worthy of respect. This is the basis for one of the defining characteristics of this Indic philosophy: the practice of non-violence, or the avoidance as far as possible of any action that will injure others. The first of Jainism's vows, non-violence is predicated on the concept of interconnectedness of all life forms, which anticipates (although it is by no means identical to) the founding premises of ecological or green movements today. Non-violence, or more accurately the minimising of harm, is binding on commercial activities, as it is on the professions and crafts or the running of the household. Each business deal, each financial transaction, should be assessed in terms of its effects on others, including in some cases future generations. All life is interconnected, and so the concept of 'others' reaches beyond humanity to encompass animal and plant species and the environment as a whole. Although these injunctions are not always fully observed, they provide a rigorous backdrop against which commercial activities are played out.

For Jains, the speculative and philosophical, the faith-based and the practical or quotidian aspects of their tradition are part of a unified whole, the *Dharma*. The term Dharma means at once cosmic order, the structure and character of the universe and the codes of conduct or enlightened teachings that lead to spiritual liberation, equated by Jains with equanimity and objective knowledge.

Thus Dharma is both the goal and the path towards it. It is also the thread that connects all areas of life and thought. An essential feature of the Jain way of life is its emphasis on balance. The individual is sovereign and so ultimately in charge of and responsible for his or her own spiritual progress and personal destiny. Yet this perspective is extremely far from *laissez faire* individualism, as it imposes obligations on individuals that increase in relation to their education, wealth and experience of life. A creative tension exists between individual and society. Self-interest is identified, ultimately, with the collective interests, just as 'self-conquest', the overcoming of personal and attachments, is viewed as the realisation of the 'true' or original self: the return to a point of origin. A similar balance is identified between continuity and change, equally important principles which interact continuously in the universe and our individual lives:

> Reality does not admit of absolute predication, but is characterized by appearance and nonappearance in the midst of permanence. One can speak neither of an absolutely unchanging permanence [in Jainism] nor of absolute change without permanence. The reality, however, maintains its identity and permanence although it expresses itself in multiple forms. ... [as] unity in multiplicity
>
> (Prabhavananda 1979: p.167)

With considerable scientific foresight, Jains have for millennia understood the universe as cyclical in nature, alternating between long periods of expansion and contraction. This perception gives rise to a blueprint for the life of an individual as a cyclical pattern in which achievement and activity yield to renunciation and contemplation. A large part of the latter phase revolves around the divestment of possessions to the next generation or to charity and the retreat into simpler forms of living. Progress is also seen in cyclical terms, so that it includes regression to first principles or reinvention. This has an important bearing on commercial activity, for expansion is not automatically equated with advancement, as tends to be the case in the dominant business models. Instead, periods of consolidation and downsizing are often viewed as crucial to a firm's success and well-being. Downsizing, in this context, means returning to first principles rather than necessarily shedding employees. Often, these methods enable the firm to preserve its family and community ties and its values, as well as avoiding absorption in larger enterprises or the creation of impersonal bureaucracies that induce alienation and sclerosis. In this study, we shall see examples of Jain businesses that have chosen not to be listed on the stock market and have consciously avoided the corporate model, pre-ferring the extended family closely linked to the wider Jain community. Sometimes, because of the spread of Jain settlement, these family ties cross continents.

The 'many-sided' tolerance of Jains accompanies a way of life that is, in many respects, quite rigorous and demanding. Jains are asked to adhere to a worldview that puts them in a perpetual minority, whether in India or the many other parts of the world where they have settled. As such, they have survived through a process of simultaneous integration and retention of cultural practices and doctrines that differentiate them from surrounding populations. Far from segregating themselves, they play a full part in the economic, political and cultural lives of their surrounding communities. Historically, their bias has been towards skilled trades, accounting and finance and in the modern era medicine, law, pharmacy, dentistry, optometry as well as new areas of interest such as tourism and real estate. Commitment to non-injury means, for the most part, the avoidance of occupations directly involving armaments or anything that harms or destroys animal life. These restrictions, along with the high esteem accorded to education, have led Jains to concentrate their energies towards business, the professions and clerical work. There is also a tradition of activism for social justice and environmental protection, often carried out through practical projects rather than overtly political campaigns and often aided by the commercial sector.

At the same time as they maintain a unique and coherent philosophy and an often tightly knit community life, Jains often adopt – and adapt – aspects of the surrounding culture. Although non-theistic in the sense that they do not acknowledge a Supreme Being or First Cause, Jain communities frequently revere Hindu deities, which they view as representing aspects of the Dharma. Many Jains 'look upon themselves as quite within the Hindu fold, and are so regarded by the main body of ... orthodox [Hindus]' (Prabhavananda 1979: p.156). The diversity of beliefs conveniently classified as Hindu can include many of the tenets familiar to Jains. Non-injury or *Ahimsa*, the first Jain vow, is also deeply significant for most Hindus. It forms the core, for example, of Patanjali's *Yoga Sutras* (*c.*400 CE), a work studied increasingly in the west. Hence the statement 'I am a Jain, not a Hindu' at times becomes problematic. Despite this ambivalence, Jains are also keen to assert that theirs is a distinctive religion and culture. They regard their faith as having evolved from the earliest Indic spiritual practices, which venerated nature as well as being in awe of its power and strength. The connections that bind all life together were sensed intuitively, while humanity's dependence on and vulnerability to the rest of nature was reflected in a precarious everyday life. On these preliterate foundations an edifice of reason, creative inquiry and scholarship has accumulated. The balance between reason and intuition is carefully maintained, with both assigned equal value and each holding the other in check.

The holistic emphasis of Jain culture means that activities are rarely viewed in isolation and the widespread western process of 'compartmentalising' is largely absent. This means that it is hard to view the commercial and financial sectors as discrete segments of Jain life. The motives that guide transactions are rarely exclusively commercial in character. Where they are, they are by no means invariably concerned with profit and expansion. Nonetheless, enterprises run by Jains have proved to be successful, durable and innovative. To examine the ethics behind them, it is necessary to consider concepts and practices that at first glance do not appear to have much to do with business and finance. Or, to express this idea differently, we should be willing to engage with business plans that include the dispersal of wealth and (at some critical junctures) the avoidance of growth. Even when they become transnational, such businesses retain many of the features of small or medium-sized enterprises. In particular, they tend to give precedence to family ties and bonds of friendship over impersonal or (from a western point of view) objective processes.

Through their apparent preferences for family members, friends and immediate community, these enterprises challenge many of the assumptions of twenty-first century politics about equity and impartiality. Such practices also seem, at face value, to be incompatible with a wider social conscience. Defenders of Jain custom might point, with good cause to the strategies of survival adopted by minority populations. They might also cite, again convincingly, the discrepancies between the theory and practice of equal opportunity and meritocracy. Evidence from the actions and attitudes of Jain businesses points us towards a more complex conclusion. These businesses, it seems, make a direct link between valuing interpersonal relationships and their practical work for charities, including donations. The preservation of the 'human touch' in their business management, including their familial or informal relationships with the personnel, keeps the business grounded and provides a sense of perspective. Economic decisions remain affected by personal and long-term considerations rather than relying on short-term calculation. The character of the business is not considered separately from its commercial viability, but as integral to it. The concentration on personal relationships ensures that the enterprise remains a manageable size. Even when it expands or becomes transnational, it strives to maintain its founding characteristics and purposes. The needs of future generations are considered on a personal level, and these encompass the environment in which they live and the values they imbibe. For many of the businesspeople we, as authors, know well and have cited in our text, charitable giving is seen as an extension of provision for family and immediate community. The sense of connectedness spans outwards in a ripple effect.

Jain commercial methods and the principles behind them challenge the presumptions about family businesses that have now become conventional. The process of questioning underscores our exploration of the values applied to business management and financial transactions by this ancient but dispersed and highly 'globalised' community. A critical mirror is held up to the mentality that still generally prevails in the academic study of business and finance, especially but not exclusively in the west. For Jains, these areas of life are not isolated or discrete and do not follow quasi-scientific rules abstracted from lived experience. The study of Jain business and finance is an exercise in thinking because it involves discarding a great deal of intellectual 'baggage' and learning to think in a different way, one that involves multiple possibilities rather than binary opposition: both/and in place of either/or. Throughout our research for this book, we have found issues which at face value have 'nothing to do' with business and finance, but are at a deeper level closely related to them. Our exercise in thinking is itself part of a cross-cultural dialogue and encounter taking place at a personal level between the two authors and at an abstract level, as the thought processes of Jain culture become more fully understood.

A cross-cultural encounter

The two authors of this book, Aidan Rankin (AR) and Atul Shah (AS) are both interested in and influenced by Jainism. Rather than being identical, or even uniting to form a synthesis, our thoughts intertwine in an unending spiral. This is, we believe, true to the Jain intellectual tradition of questioning and comparison. It is also an example of the multifaceted approach preferred by Jains. Frequent references to that approach will be made in the chapters that follow because it has had such a profound influence on their business and financial activities.

The views of the two authors converge in a shared belief that the public discussion and academic study of economics has too strong a bias towards western paradigms. In this century, the convenient if often artificial distinctions between 'developed' and 'developing' worlds are breaking down. Societies once subordinate to political and economic colonialism are emerging as global economic powers. In this context, non-western voices are needed to create a balanced global conversation. Where necessary, such voices might provide alternative views of what 'development' and progress should mean. The prevailing view of progress as a straight line moving inexorably forward is challenged by a philosophy like Jainism, which thinks in terms of cycles of expansion and regression and values continuity as much as change. Other Indic traditions, including the many permutations of Hinduism and Buddhism, issue similar challenges, as do many areas of Chinese thought, including the nature-centred aspects of Daoism.

Furthermore, accumulating evidence of environmental crisis created by awareness of climate change, urban pollution and the depletion of animal and plant species has led to a sense, partly political and partly spiritual in the broadest sense, that the hegemonic model of industrial development at best has serious flaws and at worst has become dysfunctional and outmoded. This is not the same as the 'crisis of capitalism', for which orthodox Marxists constantly search. Their solutions have, after all, been as committed to continuous economic expansion – the pursuit of growth as an end in itself – as the many varieties of capitalism to emerge in the modern era. The object of Jain philosophy is not to provide a template for a new economic system. In a sense, its aim is more radical: to influence the way we think about business and finance so that the welfare of employees, clients and the wider community (including animals and the environment) becomes part of economic calculation, instead of disconnected from it. Jainism is characterised above all by concern for nature and the connections between all forms of life, along with its belief in the power of individuals to transform themselves and their surroundings. These qualities make it well adapted to twenty-first century concerns and arguably highly prescient.

Jainism's tradition of tolerance and ability to speak across cultural divisions make it a useful countervailing voice in an age when fundamentalisms, religious and secular, threaten (sometimes with deadly violence) freedom of thought, expression and action. These regressive ideologies arise from the sense of uncertainty brought by rapid economic change and the dissolution of many previously accepted patterns of behaviour or ways of life. Changes of this type simultaneously bring liberation and possibility for many, and anxiety or insecurity for others. Often, this includes economic insecurity of an extreme kind, including the emergence in advanced capitalist economies of a 'precariat', a new class dependent on short-term contracts despite, in many cases, high educational attainment (Standing 2011, 2014). Such phenomena provide evidence of a distorted view of economics whereby the abstract 'model' takes precedence over human needs in their most basic forms. That model also includes an education system in which, all too frequently, a narrow and over-academic 'mindset' takes precedence over social and cultural skills. In spite of impressive statistics for growth and a political climate in which the desirability of expansion is taken as a given, the precarious state is becoming increasingly the global norm. Technology liberates at one level and at another increases alienation and fanaticism. Against this background, a non-western worldview based on balance, freedom and social responsibility can provide the calm space required for questioning our present economic priorities, including their influence on business management and financial planning.

The terms 'western', 'the west' and 'non-western' are, we realise, unsatisfactory at many levels. There are other ways to present this concept, including Global North and Global South, but these expressions lack clarity and correspond even less to physical and political geography. We use these terms for convenience, and in the absence of any satisfactory and easily comprehensible alternative. In the case of 'the west' and 'non-western', they denote the prevalent view of business and finance as they are practised and, more especially, the way they are studied and analysed. We have in mind here the virtual cult of 'objectivity', whereby economic calculation is held to exist as if in a sealed container, isolated from the environment, communities, emotions, artistic creativity and (in the widest sense) the spiritual dimension. 'Non-western' denotes the voices that are, if not actively silenced, rarely heard in economic discourse, in academia perhaps more than anywhere else. Their marginalisation is cultural as much as geographical, but in the context of this study, 'non-western' describes worldviews that do not embrace an exclusively linear view of progress and do not separate economics from other areas of life, notably animal welfare and the environment.

This terminology is, as we are aware, open to challenge from many angles. The most potent charge is that it creates another binary opposition. In reality, European and Indic thought have converged and interacted for millennia and stem from the same cultural roots. Many policy-makers in India and other re-emerging global powers have enthusiastically embraced the linear view of progress and a mechanistic view of economics. There have also been trenchant critiques of mechanistic and linear thinking in Europe and North America since the beginning of the industrial era, of which the green movement is the most prominent heir. We acknowledge this in the pages that follow. AS, for example, cites the work of John Ruskin, the nineteenth century art critic whose views on the superiority of craftsmanship to mass production would now be described as holistic. AR refers to Mahatma Gandhi's vision of *swadeshi* or self-sufficient local communities engaged in production for their own needs. Gandhi was influenced by Ruskin, and by Jain philosophy, although he always remained a devout Hindu. These intersections or cross-cultural encounters show a far greater fluidity in the world of ideas than the terms 'western' and 'non-western' imply. That said, the dominant voices in the current economic discourse are geographically and culturally of the west. In a global economic order that is no longer unipolar, this creates a one-sided narrative and excludes alternative points of view. It also ignores the values by which large swathes of the world's population live and the way business is conducted outside the centres of corporate power. The Jain voice is one of many that have yet to come to the fore. The purpose of our book is to shed some light on this little-known culture and way of thinking, which exerts a quiet background influence over the lives of millions of men and women, whether or not they are practising Jains.

These goals we share as authors are enriched by our different experiences and the creative tension arising from them. AS is the scion of a Gujarati Jain family based in Kenya and the UK. Over several decades, he has emerged as a leading writer, innovator and thinker within the global community of Jain Dharma. His commitment to raising the profile of the Jain community has led him to become interested in the connections between the tenets of his faith and the achievement of a more equitable economy (e.g. Shah 2007a). He is a philosophical Jain but also, importantly, a religious Jain, whose beliefs and practice are woven into his daily life, founded on family history and reverence for the past balanced by positive engagement with the present. AR, by contrast, comes from a secular western background. His PhD is in Political Science and he is the author of four books on non-western philosophical and spiritual systems: Jainism and Shinto. The religious rituals and dietary prohibitions of tradi-tional Jain society mean nothing to him at a visceral or emotional level. Nonetheless, he respects and strongly values them on a personal level and as a friend to many Jains. He does not follow the Jain diet, but it has influenced him in eating more ethically and avoiding the products of intensive farming. Religious communities, including some Jains, tend to adhere to exclusionary and conservative definitions of the family. AR adheres instead to a pluralist and secular definition of family life. Marriage and family life are not in his view defined or restricted on grounds of gender or sexual orientation. In an era where families are often geographically and culturally dispersed, friendship and shared interests or values can sometimes mean more than biological kinship. This is not a rejection of traditional family models, but an extension of possibilities. By the same reasoning, AR is opposed to any attempts to impose religious-based precepts on those who do not wish to live by them. At the same time, he listens to, learns from and is in favour of contributions to public policy debate from individuals and communities of faith, whether he shares their conclusions or not. Such considerations have led him to work closely with AS and other practising Jains on projects such as the international magazine *Jain Spirit* and a privately funded report on Jainism and community cohesion in the UK.

There is no contradiction, in AR's view, between those two positions. He is interested by the pluralistic elements in Jain philosophy and the possibilities they offer for resolving the misunderstandings and conflicts that arise within increasingly culturally diverse societies. He is impressed by the commitment of Jains to environmental conservation and their practical work for human and animal welfare. In the context of this study, he is especially interested to explore ways in which Jain doctrines might contribute to a more rounded and inclusive way of appraising financial considerations and business practices. His own experience of property management has made him aware that qualities such as empathy and compassion make good business practice. In 'pure' commercial terms, their results are more effective than the box-ticking and process-driven mentality that he has found to be prevalent in this area of business activity.

The difference in our backgrounds is reflected less in the conclusions we draw as in the way we process and present them. AS works from within the Jain community, but looks outwards. He makes frequent use of religious terminology and drawing upon his experiences of spiritual practice. AR looks at Jain Dharma from outside its direct influence. He does not address religious themes with which he has no direct connection, focussing instead on philosophical concepts and the ways they are implemented (or omitted) in practice. These differences in our perceptions are reflected in differences of literary style, choice of words and, at times, the areas of Jain life and culture on which we concentrate. AS, as a community leader and a campaigner for social justice, is influenced by a Jain tradition of stern injunction to human beings to fulfil their potential, resembling in some ways the western prophetic tradition. AR, by contrast, is drawn in particular to the parallel and equally influential tradition of latitudinarian tolerance in Jain culture. However both of us draw upon our direct experience of the community we are studying, combining anecdotes with interviews and case studies. In this sense, our method is openly subjective, but its principal aim is to ask questions rather than to provide set answers. These questions move beyond the realms of enterprise and finance towards the way the economy is organised and, most important of all, the values that guide us in the conduct of business.

Our book is divided into nine chapters, including this introduction. In Chapter 2, AR describes the process of learning how to 'think like a Jain'. As a researcher, he has undertaken this task although he sees it as an ongoing project to which new insights are continuously added. Learning to think like a

Jain is important to understanding how information and ideas acquired from this ancient philosophy might be applied on a wider context. The process of immersion in an alternative worldview involves challenging and sometimes 'un-learning' the received wisdoms associated with the dominant culture. Learning about Jainism is presented in the context of giving a greater voice to 'non-western' modes of thought and the ways in which they can enlarge the present discourse on business and finance. The chapter also addresses the question of Jain identity by exploring the community's origins, beliefs and role within Indian society and subsequently the Diaspora, highlighting the Jains' current and historical relationship with business.

As in many other sections of this book, the contradictions between a philosophy and faith tradition based on renunciation and the lived experience of widespread commercial success are scrutinised in this chapter through the prism of Aparigraha. This religious vow of non-possessiveness is translated into a secular practice of simplicity, charitable giving and philanthropy. In Chapter 3, AS takes the exploration of Aparigraha further by examining its connections, surprising at times, to financial practice and the ways in which it leads Jain businesspeople to acknowledge the limits as much as the possibilities of financial activity. The overarching concepts of renunciation and non-possessiveness make financial and all other material 'successes' appear relative and transient. Rather than leading to apathy and indifference, this attitude gives rise to a judicious programme of financial planning coupled with a strong tradition of community and environmental service by businesspeople. Chapter 4, also written by AS, examines the financial concepts of risk and return from the standpoint of Jain enterprises. Family and community based businesses are key features of Jain economic activity. They not only offer defence against unnecessary risk, but also provide practical ways to ensure the continuing collective nature of the enterprise and its returns. Excess profits and wealth must be 'digestible', which means that they should be put to a positive use, including charitable activities, education, health care and community building. This form of financial planning involves the careful assessment of long-term as opposed to immediate or short-term outcomes.

In Chapter 5, AR explores the concept of interdependency, the 'binding together' of all of humanity and all forms of life. This concept is central to the beliefs and practices of Jains today, including the principle of Careful Action, which is examined in Chapter 2. Another theme from the second chapter that is expanded upon here is the concept of 'society' as extending beyond the human realm to other species (animal and plant) and the environment that sustains life. The notion of 'binding together' arises from an ecological sensibility familiar to the environmental movement today, although it should not be naively equated with green politics. On the spiritual plane, it is based on the belief that each life form contains *jiva*, the animating principle or soul. At a philosophical level, all individuals (*homo sapiens* or otherwise) are bound together in a shared search for greater understanding or enlightenment. Such beliefs are likely to seem esoteric to many students of business and finance. For most Jains, by contrast, they influence the way in which commercial activities – indeed all activities – are carried out. The concept of interdependence gives rise to an equally strong emphasis on personal responsibility. Thus the entrepreneur or business leader is obliged to govern his or her actions in order to minimise harm to others: self-governance in the world of work as much as in spiritual practice is viewed as the highest form of responsibility and accountability. This section of our book works towards defining a Jain theory of organic growth. Consciously or otherwise, the life cycle of a business reflects the view of the universe as following a series of progressive and regressive cycles. Jain enterprises tend to go through periods of expansion and contraction. The latter are closely linked to Aparigraha and the release of surplus income in community projects. Business owners also impose limits to the size of their enterprises to preserve its founding principles, ethics and family or community links, even in cases where the business has become transnational.

There are, we explain, many areas of life, including philosophical speculation, that are central to Jain entrepreneurs but which are more generally held to have little to do with business practice or which are seen as benign optional extras. This theme is pursued further by AS in Chapter 6, which looks in more detail at the socially transformative aspects of Jain financial planning. Business is held to be a component of nature and society rather than separate from or above it. It is an essential engine for providing necessary products or services, and for creating jobs or sustaining families and communities. As Jain entrepreneurs are already members of living and closely connected communities, this helps them to stay grounded and to invest ethically and for the long term. Bankruptcy or fraud are not viewed as 'options', and investments are undertaken with a process of careful evaluation, a form of meditation applied to commercial practice. The social capital that is a core part of the community becomes a useful tool for making positive and ethical (as well as profitable) investments and using the accumulated knowledge of the community to make judicious evaluations. The fruits of investments are used for the benefit of nature and society, for example medical care, education and training. In India, Jains were the first community to establish *Panjrapoor* (animal hospitals and sanctuaries) to care for sick and dying animals: these animals in Jain ethics are, like humans, part of a wider conception of community. Many Jain entrepreneurs directly engage in social action and charitable organisations, acting as trustees or active volunteers.

Closely related to the principles of Aparigraha (non-materialism) and Ahimsa (non-violence or non-injury) is the concept of *Anekantavada* (known as *Anekant*), or 'many-sidedness', which AR examines in Chapter 7. In Jain philosophy, Anekant is known as the doctrine of multiple viewpoints. It is based on the assumption that each viewpoint is important because absolute knowledge is unattainable by humankind, at least at our present evolutionary stage. Even a seemingly negative viewpoint can sometimes yield unexpected insights and non-human viewpoints matter at least as much as our own. This is different from, for example, the 'postmodernist' assertion that there is no objective truth, only subjective experiences. Universal truths *do* exist but for the most part they are only partially discernible. The quest for understanding, whether personal, social or spiritual, resembles the scientific quest, where new frontiers of knowledge are continuously breached, but in the process new questions arise. Knowledge is viewed with humility and can also be arrived at from many angles. As mentioned above, Jains use the analogy of a diamond with many facets: this comparison has a double significance given the prominent role that Jain families have played in the jewellery trade, examples of which are frequently cited in our text. Another analogy often used is that of the summit of a mountain that can be reached via many paths.

Translated into the political sphere, Anekant has the potential to be a potent inoculation against fundamentalism and doctrinaire certainty. In the spheres of business and finance, the idea of multiple viewpoints reinforces the commitment to ecologically based, sustainable practices and the principle of careful action. The resulting spirit of open-mindedness can help businesses to welcome creative insights and work with individuals from any background and work with them on a lasting basis. The sense that each living being or living system has its own viewpoint or *naya* is the basis of Careful Action, which involves the ability (or at least attempt) to envisage the long-term effects of each commercial decision. It points towards an ecological view of business practices, setting them in the context of the rest of nature, with its many 'nayas'. Anekant also resonates with the current global economy, which is increasingly 'many-sided', as well as with businesses that need to be increasingly open to diverse cultural influences. The many-sided perspective also addresses in potentially radical ways current concerns about transparency and corporate responsibility. It ensures that businesses – and their leaders – are engaged in a process of self-questioning, and that they see themselves as responsible to society rather than themselves alone. Observers of Jain culture (including AR) should also adopt a many-sided outlook and attempt to delve below that which is most clearly visible or obvious. For example, to develop an under-standing of how Jain businesses work requires abandoning many preconceptions about family-owned enterprises.

A recurring theme of this study is that finance is a means to an end, not an end in itself. Understanding this, and acknowledging the 'limits of finance', helps investors and entrepreneurs to maintain a sense of 'active detachment' from the fruits of their actions, argues AS in Chapter 8. Active detachment means an ability to step back and look on achievements with humility and objectivity. Regular practice of reflection and meditation reduces stress by enabling practitioners to discriminate between what is important and what is ultimately trivial. Such practice keeps many Jain business leaders spiritually detached from the fruits of their success and wealth. This frame of reference gives them an understanding that material possessions are not the 'be all and end all'. Instead, they are advantages that confer obligations including social and environmental responsibility.

The attitude of humility required by Jain ethics enjoins business leaders to respect people from all social classes. There is a clear understanding that although success arises from one's own intelligence, creativity, actions and efforts, it is also the product of 'good karma' and more general good fortune. In Chapter 9, AS concludes by making the case for Jain culture as offering an alternative perspective on the study and practice of business and finance. It is at once an intellectual resource and a focus for ethical guidance. The study of Jain financial ethics redresses a profound imbalance within the current academic disciplines of accounting, finance and business studies, which amounts at worst to an institutionalised form of cultural bias, even racism, and at best to a lazy and outdated equation of western practices and modes of thought with inevitable 'progress'.

The Jain concept of karma differs substantively from those of other Indic traditions and has been explored by AR in Chapters 2 and 5. One of its attributes is that each individual assumes a strong sense of personal responsibility, assessing every decision – including commercial decisions – against a larger ethical framework. This process has enabled Jains to combine commercial success with a sustainable approach to business and investment over a period of centuries and amid changing economic and political conditions. In today's global economy, their experience, principles and practices can shine an important light on the philosophical and practical dilemmas affecting business and finance. In Chapter 9, the concluding chapter, AS relates Jain practice of financial and business management to recent academic literature and offers criticisms of an academic approach that seems to divorce business and finance from its cultural surroundings and does not listen enough to non-western voices.

Whereas AR's background in Political Science enables him to explore the wider social implications of business ethics, AS brings to this study his specialist knowledge of 'pure finance' and accountancy as an academic discipline and business activity. Both authors aim throughout the book to avoid unnecessary academic jargon, whether sociological and financial. By so doing, we aim to communicate across the boundaries of subject or discipline. We also hope to place our thoughts and conclusions at the disposal of the general reader as much as the student or specialist. Our work is given a personal dimension by our examples and case studies. These come from a range of entrepreneurs and enterprises, and examine attitudes to financial management and how these are shaped by faith or philosophy of life. Our examples are drawn from both India and the Diaspora. AS has wide personal knowledge of Jainism and its relationship to finance in East Africa, the United Kingdom and India. There, communities of Gujarati Jains have played a prominent role in the development of a commercial culture with a global reach. AR is especially interested in the Jain communities of the UK, with which he has worked for more than a decade. To an extent, our chapters reflect these experiences and interests.

Jain philosophy is not presented in these pages as the hidden answer to the problems and opportunities thrown up by globalisation. Its greatest value is, perhaps, in the questions it raises about the purpose of finance and what the goals of a business should be. Nor do we seek unrealistically to portray Jain communities as mini-utopias devoid of contradictions and conflicts. Yet our study shows that a belief system that can seem abstruse and complex to outsiders has a practical dimension guiding many successful commercial enterprises across a wide range of cultures, political systems and working environments. As such, it is surely worthy of consideration.

2 Learning to think like a Jain

Aidan Rankin

The omniscient Jina states that purity of business activity is the basis of dharma. Purity of money in worldly existence comes about from pure business activity; through pure money there comes pure food; through pure food comes purity of body in worldly existence; with a pure body one becomes suitable for dharma. Whatever action he performs, yields fruit in worldly existence.

Ratnaśekhara Sūri, 'Light on Purity of Business Activity',
Jain text, first half of fifteenth century CE

The Jains are a community of between five and ten million people, concentrated in India but with Diaspora communities in eastern and southern Africa, North America, Europe and Oceania. In India, where they number just below five million, they are noted for their high literacy rate, 94.1 per cent against a national average of 65.38 per cent. Significantly, they have the country's highest female literacy rate, 90.1 per cent, in comparison with a national average of 54.16 per cent (Chakrawertti 2004). These statistics, drawn from the Indian national census of 2001, arise from the Jains' traditionally high regard for education and the pursuit of knowledge. India's Jains are a powerful presence in professions such as law and medicine. They are also one of the country's most successful business communities and by some measurements have the nation's highest per capita income and pay a proportionally high percentage of income tax in India. This pattern is repeated in the Diaspora, where the Jain story is one of high achievement in business, finance and the professions along with a judicious blend of integrating and preserving their cultural values. Were it not for Jainism's strong commitment to non-violence, it would be easy to say that Jains in India and elsewhere are 'punching above their weight'.

Jains regard their system of beliefs and values as directly descended from the most ancient forms of Indian thought (Jaini 2001). Their philosophy is at one level nature-centred, holistic and intuitive, based on the connectedness of all forms of life and a sense of wonder at the beauty and subtlety of nature. At another level, it is rational and scientific in its methodology, and therefore open to continuous experiment and new ideas. In the search for objective truth, multiple possibilities are acknowledged and celebrated in a spirit of open-mindedness. The Jain community is highly traditional in its ethos, centred on family and community and also profoundly focussed on the inner life. Simultaneously, it has positioned itself at the cutting edge of the new India, in the vanguard of its re-emergence as a global economic and cultural powerhouse in the twenty-first century. These are not the only paradoxes associated with the Jains. Business and commerce have always been central to their way of life. At the same time, they follow an ascetic ideal, at the centre of which is renunciation of material possessions and worldly preoccupations. The manner in which these apparently opposite principles are creatively reconciled is the principal theme of this book, as are the ways in which Jain ethics and practice present a valid alternative to the prevailing commercial models. In subsequent chapters, the problems and pitfalls of the Jain approach will be analysed and discussed along with the positive aspects. The focus of this chapter, by contrast, is on learning how to 'think like a Jain'. For in the same way that Jainism challenges the prevalent western perceptions of 'religion', the Jain approach to economic activity reverses many of the assumptions behind the hegemonic financial model.

Such challenges are based predominantly on quiet practice rather than the conscious articulation of an alternative view. Jain thought, in this sense, is a hidden gem. As such, it deserves a gentle light shone upon it as a non-western belief system that has endured for millennia and translates successfully into modern commercial activities. Increasingly, the global economy is no longer dominated by western assumptions and yet the language of business and finance, both at the theoretical and practical levels, is still couched overwhelmingly in western terms. The inclusion of non-western perspectives and voices is critical to resolving some of the contradictions of globalisation, not least environmental problems and disparities of wealth, about which Jainism has many things to say.

For some readers, this might sound suspiciously like campaigning rather than academic objectivity. There could be said to be an element of truth in this charge, not least because in exploring the relationship between Jainism and the commercial sector, we call some of the tenets of such 'objectivity' into question. That said, we do not attempt to offer a fixed programme for 'Jain Economics' or 'Jain Finance' along the lines of the many highly illuminating studies of the Islamic banking system published in the early twenty-first century (e.g. Alrifai 2015; Kettell 2011; Wilson 2012). To do so would be contrary to the nature of Jain practice, which is often more about suggestions than rules, despite the well-known ascetic and highly disciplined aspects of Jainism. We share with E.F. Schumacher (1993) the sense that economics should operate 'as if people mattered' – but in the spirit of Jain philosophy we would extend his remit beyond human beings. We believe that economics should return to something closer to its original meaning derived from classical Greek: the law (*nomos*) of the household (*oikos*) and by implication wise stewardship of the environment, the resources of the global 'household'. How this happens will vary according to local circumstances. Recent history shows that the attempt to impose identical solutions on different regions and cultures is doomed to failure or worse. Nevertheless, we intend to make the case for Jain philosophy as intimately connected with business and finance. The principles embodied in this philosophy can serve as an ethical guide for business practitioners of all backgrounds. They form the basis for the way of life pursued by Jain communities and specific to their historical experience, but from which others can draw inspiration or at least study with interest. We believe that, contrary to immediate appearance, Jain principles have a natural affinity with the commercial and financial sectors. This is demonstrated in part by the lived experience of generations of Jains who have made successful careers in these sectors. From their foundations, Jain communities have been engaged in trade. These business endeavours are an expression of their principles rather than a contradiction, as a more cursory examination might suggest.

The term Jainism, although used for convenience at many points in this and later chapters, is arguably insufficient or even misleading. Jain doctrines are more than an '-ism' or narrowly defined ideological programme. They are the components of Dharma, which is at once a cosmology, an ethical system aiming for spiritual liberation (*Moksha*) and a practical code for living in the world. Dharma, which may be translated approximately as 'cosmic order' is a term frequently used in this text because the words 'philosophy', 'religion' and 'ethos', like '-ism', convey only isolated aspects of Jain thought. Jain Dharma is a culture and an aesthetic sensibility, a sense of perspective on the individual, society and the world based on long-term thinking and an understanding of the universe as vast, eternal and cyclical. This disposition is described by the mathematician Kanti Mardia as 'Jain-ness', a concept that captures the intuitive and ecocentric as much as the rational and humanistic aspect of Jain Dharma:

> Jainness is concerned with reconciling continuity and change, possibility and limitation. It offers the possibility for spiritual liberation through self-knowledge, while accepting the mental and physical limits of the human form. ... Rather than asserting or seeking to impose its own truths, [Jain Dharma] asks is to look inside ourselves, find our own truth and continuously question it. Jainness is the disposition or frame of mind that enables us to begin this process.
>
> (Mardia and Rankin 2013: p.26)

In the spheres of business and finance, this disposition has exercised a profound influence. This chapter therefore presents an overview of Jain culture and the concepts behind it, with an emphasis on the creative tension between the ideal of reducing consumption and the system of values conventionally associated with business practice. In some instances, the connections with business will not seem immediately obvious, especially for those accustomed to a rigid division between the commercial and the philosophical or speculative realms. This is because the concept of Dharma does not acknowledge such distinctions, which means that boundaries are often unexpectedly abolished or obscured. We begin with a brief explanation of the most important and enduring Jain beliefs and then progress to the ideal of Careful Action. This principle exerts strict control over the behaviour of ascetic men and women, but also influences the thinking and decision-making of the lay population and underlies all of Jain thought, including the foremost – and best known – commitment to non-injury to life. The summary of beliefs held by most Jains, including the 'non-religious', is followed by two examples of businesses with ethical systems reflecting Jain philosophy, with particular reference to material possessions and the accumulation of wealth. These cases are intended to set the tone for the remainder of this study.

Jain Dharma: the way of the conquerors

The traditional Jain greeting *Jai Jinendra* literally means 'Hail to the Conquerors'. At first sight, this has connotations of militarism and dominance, but in fact it means exactly the reverse. For the Jain, conquest is an internal process of self-discipline to overcome negative aspects of the self. These are principally associated with attachment, desire and 'passions' (*Kasaya*) ranging from acquisitiveness to fanaticism and doctrinaire certainty. From this point of view, it is too simplistic to regard material possessions earned through commercial activity as the central 'problem' for spiritual development. Instead, it is the attachment to those possessions and the desire for further material gains that becomes an obstacle to self-knowledge. An instructive parallel here comes from the Christian tradition and is exemplified by the Latin biblical verse *radix malorum est cupiditas*. This verse originates in St Jerome's Vulgate Latin translation of the Bible in the late fourth century CE. It is used by the fourteenth century English poet Geoffrey Chaucer as the moral for his 'Pardoner's Tale' (Chaucer 2008: pp.393–411). Often mistranslated as 'money is the root of all evil', its true meaning is more subtle: 'the love of money is the root of all evil' (1Timothy 6:10, King James Version). The term 'cupiditas' can also mean 'strong desire' in the material sense, which is close to the Jain idea of 'attachment'. Concepts of evil and 'sin' are not part of Jain Dharma, at least in its original form. As a rational faith, Jainism prefers to emphasise positive and negative developments, that is to say behaviours or thoughts conducive to self-knowledge and behaviours or thoughts that perpetuate ignorance. Aparigraha – non-possessiveness – is primarily about attitudes to possessions and the uses to what they are put. Liberation, for Jains, involves becoming a *Jina*: one who has overcome inner passions and to whom material or temporal considerations no longer have any import.

Individual conscience and individual consciousness are central to Jain philosophy. The aim is self-realisation, which means peeling away fabricated layers of personality to understand the true self and hence the true nature of reality. This is quite different from the type of 'self-realisation' promoted in New Age or 'inspirational' books and seminars, which tend to focus on the satisfaction of immediate emotional needs or wishes. Knowledge of the self involves seeing beyond such superficial or apparent 'needs' and viewing them as no more than transient satisfactions. The individual continues to exist as an independent entity after 'liberation' from karma. This belief in the importance of the individual markedly differentiates Jain philosophy from mainstream Hinduism and most of the Buddhist schools. It is closely connected to the strong Jain commitment to equality, pluralism (including freedom to disagree) and the importance of the individual making fullest use of his or her abilities. The pursuit of knowledge is valued over uncritical adherence to doctrine, which is seen as an aid or a guideline rather than a series of set texts that have to be obeyed uncritically. Thus 'the individual must find the truth for himself as no priest or scripture is believed to have all the answers. The principles are intended to be self-verifying so that the follower "discovers truths for himself rather like a research worker in a laboratory"' (Mardia 2007: pp.4–5).

Jainism is a nontheistic doctrine, in which the workings of the universe are not attributed to any Supreme Being, Creator or First Cause. It follows that each man or woman is effectively his or her own guru. Personal enterprise, individual initiative and education are all highly prized in Jain culture. Crucially, this individualism is balanced with an ethos of co-operation, whether with fellow human beings, other creatures or the natural environment that sustains life. The guiding precept is a Sanskrit verse from the *Tattvartha Sutra* of Umasvati composed between the second and fifth centuries CE: *Parasparopagraho Jivanam*. There are two translations for this verse: the secular and philosophical, 'All life is bound together by mutual support and interdependence' and the more exclusively religious, 'Souls render service to each other'. Both translations are of equal value but with differing emphasis. Parasparopagraho Jivanam has become a popular aphorism, signifying the belief in non-violence and pluralistic approaches to problem-solving. It is the central tenet of the *Jain Declaration of Nature* drawn up by the prominent Indian jurist L.M. (Laxmi Mall) Singhvi in 2006. Written in Devanagari script, it is found at the base of the emblem adopted by all schools of Jainism in 1994 to mark the twenty-five hundredth anniversary of the Nirvana (Enlightenment) of Mahavira. The most significant historical figure in modern Jainism, Mahavira is the twenty-fourth *Tirthankara* (ford-maker, path-finder or source of inspiration) and the final one for this cycle of the universe. The principle of interdependence operates at the level of friendship and family ties, community, business and the way Jains aim to interact with the natural world. Vegetarianism is considered important because it minimises harm to life: although plants contain *jiva* (life essence) and have some consciousness, it differs in degree and quality from that of mammals, reptiles or birds. Similarly, Jains are enjoined to avoid unnecessary disturbance to living organisms when constructing homes, offices, temples and gardens, or merely walking across grass.

The concept of jiva is better translated as life monad, life essence or individual unit of life rather than soul, which conveys only one aspect of its meaning, usually associated with ritual and religious practice. Jiva, by contrast, also has a secular and quasi-scientific context. Like the soul in most Christian traditions, jiva is the part of the individual that survives outside the physical incarnation, and which animates that physical body or sustains life within it. However, jiva is also different from the mainstream Christian concept of the soul (or most other concepts familiar to western thought) in two critical respects. First, it is the originating essence of the individual, passing through many incarnations in physical form before returning to its original state of pure consciousness when enlightenment is achieved. In this way, the individuality of each physical incarnation is transient and secondary to the jiva which transfers from one being to another. Secondly, every being contains jiva, which is why all beings, or from the religious standpoint all 'souls' are irrevocably bound together. Human beings have high levels of intelligence and creativity, but are not inherently more important than other animals, or indeed plants and other features of the natural world that contain life essence. Human intelligence, in particular, brings with it immense potential for destructive behaviour as well as equal potential for spiritual development, creativity and reason. The conscious actions of each incarnation inform future incarnations and the journey towards Moksha. It follows that the more conscious the incarnation, the greater the responsibilities that befall it. Human beings are viewed as having special responsibilities, collectively and as individuals. This perspective affects the decisions they make in a wide range of areas, not least the commercial sphere and financial transactions. For it is in these areas of economic life where decisions most often arise relating to the treatment of fellow humans, other species and the environment, as well as the use and disposal of material possessions. The universe is filled with jiva, many of which are microorganisms or beings that barely exist in terms that are comprehensible to humankind.

Thus the belief in jiva has four important results for Jains. First, it underscores the importance of individual consciousness and individual sovereignty. Secondly, it reinforces the principles of *Ahimsa* (non-violence or non-injury) and Careful Action because even seemingly elementary organisms have individual consciousness worthy of respect. Thirdly, it is the basis for a doctrine of pluralism or multiple viewpoints, because each living being has its own *naya* or point of view that needs to be taken into account. Fourthly, each jiva is held to reincarnate continuously until it attains enough knowledge and understanding to break free from the cycle of *samsara*: birth, death and rebirth, which arises from the influence of karma. These reincarnations can alternate from human to plant, animal, microorganism or even extraterrestrial forms of life. The sense of individuality at the heart of Jain Dharma is balanced by a parallel sense of obligation that extends beyond exclusively human society to a community of beings, taking account of the long-term impact of every action on the environment and future generations.

In this way, all life is bound together literally by karma, the glue that holds all living beings in samsara. This facet of Jain doctrine is the hardest to grasp for non-Jains, whether they are approaching it from a secular-rationalist position or the viewpoint of another faith. The closest analogy is, perhaps, with the evolutionary process that connects all forms of life at varying stages of development. Jain philosophy is humanist in that it regards human beings as most receptive to knowledge and understanding of the universe. Yet as we have already seen, it does not regard human intelligence as a justification for human dominance, but the reverse. Because of their intelligence, human beings have special responsibilities to control their desires and refrain from harm to others or damage to the natural world. The same precept works at the level of social organisation. The affluent or successful man or woman has a moral obligation to ensure that others benefit from that wealth or success.

Karma is an increasingly familiar concept for those outside Indic traditions, although the term is often used loosely and half-understood. In essence, it is the cosmic law of cause and effect, with every action (karma) creating a reaction. It underlies the series of connections or 'web of life' of which everything in the material universe is a part. In Jainism, there is a distinctive interpretation of karma not merely as process but as substance. The universe is eternal and, like energy itself, can neither be created nor destroyed. Within it, there is both continuity (the overall character and functioning) and continuous, pulsing change. This latter process brings forth new life and in turn causes each new jiva to respond and vibrate, beginning the process of involvement with karma. Karma, in this context, is portrayed as invisible particles of subtle matter that adhere to the jiva. The karmic particles together form a film of darkness that obscures true consciousness, making the jiva lose touch with its original essence. They are also viewed, through the prism of recent scientific understanding, as subatomic particles or 'karmons' (Mardia 2007: p.10). This 'inflow' of karma, known as *asrava*, is the beginning of 'karmic bondage' or *bandha*. The natural tendency of karmic particles is to attract more of their number, much as ignorance deepens when it is unchecked and leads to destructive actions. Karmic influence is the root of the attachments that prevent knowledge of the self. Enlightenment is the shedding of karma, a process that corresponds with the dispersal of needless possessions.

Whether this depiction of karma is interpreted as an elaborate metaphor or an aspect of objective truth is a matter for personal conscience. The importance of karmic theory is that it reminds the practising Jain of how individual actions impact on others, even actions that might seem insignificant. It underscores the belief in interconnectedness of all life and the value placed on all forms of life as unique and endowed with their own naya or viewpoint. As such it influences ethics and social behaviour, balancing a form of radical individualism, in which each of us is self-reliant (our own guru), with a concept of co-operation so wide-ranging that it goes beyond commitment to fellow humans. While this world view might appear to have little to do with economics, it can have a strong effect on attitudes towards commercial activity. It requires of the adherent a continual process of balancing private gain, or the benefit of the commercial enterprise, with the welfare of the surrounding community and the ecological implications. The five vows (*Vratas*) undertaken by Jains are rooted in this ethos of personal and social responsibility:

- *Ahimsa:* Non-violence, non-injury, respect for all life
- *Satya:* Truthfulness, honesty, personal integrity
- *Asteya*: 'Non-stealing', avoidance of theft, taking what is not given, exploitation of human beings, animals, natural resources
- *Aparigraha*: Non-possessiveness, avoidance of wasteful consumption or unnecessary accumulation of possessions, or viewing possessions as ends in themselves
- *Brahmacharya*: Chastity, avoidance of promiscuity or exploitative relationships

Ascetics, who can be male or female, undertake the *Mahavratas* (Greater Vows) whereas lay men and women practise the *Anuvratas* (Lesser Vows). A good example of the distinction is Brahmacharya, which for male and female ascetics is practised as a vow of celibacy, whereas for lay men and women it means fidelity in relationships and mutual respect. The wider significance of this vow is its stress on responsible behaviour and respect for the integrity of others. Far from serving as discrete injunctions, the Vratas intersect like circles in a Venn diagram. The overarching theme is reduction of activities that lead to harm (*himsa*), whether social, environmental or personal. At the same time, they promote social engagement and responsible choices. For individuals, the level of responsibility and social obligation increases along with their levels of knowledge and material success. Possessions are not seen in simple terms as a burden, but as an opportunity for both personal development and positive social activities.

Jain Dharma combines the rational pursuit of knowledge, the scientific and literate approach, with an intuitive mentality derived from a sense of 'enchantment' and strong identification with the natural world. There is no opposition or conflict between these two approaches, but they are seen as points on a continuum. The intuitive faculty recognises that all life is interconnected, whereas the rational and scientific faculty recognises the role and importance of subatomic particles as building blocks of life. This balance of the two principles accords well with the twenty-first century sensibility. Atmospheric pollution, climate change and species loss have increased the sense that an exclusively growth-based economics is distorted and potentially dangerous because it lacks sufficient reference to the conservation of resources and interprets human need in terms of quantity above quality. A measure of 're-enchantment' with nature is viewed by many as a welcome corrective, hence the renewal of interest in 'indigenous' spirituality and alternative, nature-based approaches to health care. Also increasingly acknowledged is the importance of the intuitive leap to scientific advance or creative inspiration: the so-called 'Eureka moment'.

The doctrines of Jainism have been passed down from pre-literate antiquity to the present through a series of 24 Tirthankaras, or 'ford-makers', who have transcended the cycle of samsara or 'normal' existence. A Tirthankara is a type of Jina whose purpose becomes the guidance of others by explicit or implicit example. Samsara is presented in Jain teachings as a *tirtha* or ford to be crossed and the Tirthankaras act as pathfinders or points of inspiration. Many Jains direct meditation and prayer at the Tirthankaras. This is not worshipping them as deities, but viewing them as inspirations or role models. Most of the 'ford-makers' are prehistoric figures whose life stories are barely remembered except through fragments of hagiography. The mythical lawmaker Rishava (also known as Rishabha) is the first Tirthankara and he is recognised by some Hindus as an aspect of Shiva, an example of a complex interaction between the Jain minority and the Hindu majority within Indian civilisation. Parshva, the twenty-third Tirthankara, is the first whose historical existence as a human being can be verified with reasonable reliability. He is held to have lived at some time between 872 and 772 BCE. The discernible 'modern' philosophy of Jainism emerged in a systematised form at the time of the twenty-fourth Tirthankara, Vardhamana Mahavira, who was born in 559 BCE and whose *Nirvana* (full enlightenment) took place in 527 BCE. Mahavira means 'Great Hero', a name symbolic of spiritual victory or conquest of the inner self through non-violence and the refusal of conventional power or wealth. A contemporary of Gautama Buddha, Mahavira's path was one of more radical austerities. He is the model for the Jain ascetics of today, although he is equally responsible for the pragmatic, socially engaged philosophy of life practised by lay Jains. Mahavira plays a supremely important role in popular Jain culture, again not as a divine figure but as a source of philosophical inspiration. Many Jain households and businesses have statues or images of Mahavira and Parshva, although others view them in their more abstract form as fully realised beings, in other words pure jiva or pure consciousness.

For Jain Dharma, the starting point is an alternative view of power based on a sense of proportion and a perception that each act or thought has long-term consequences. Applied to business, this leads to an emphasis on planning for the long term, with detachment as the eventual aim. From a western perspective, this position appears contradictory and possibly counterproductive. Business, after all, is surely about profit in the short term and continuous growth, and is based very much on attachment to the present. The Jain approach has the same aim and in many cases the same practical results as the western paradigm, namely prosperity. However the commercial operation is necessarily viewed from a variety of angles: the economic welfare of the employees, the relationship of the business to the surrounding communities (Jain and non-Jain alike) and the environment, and last but not least the spiritual development of the business owner and his or her family. These considerations, even the last one, are not by any means confined to Jain enterprises. However in Jainism they are brought together as part of a holistic 'package': a world view based on the principle and practice of Careful Action. This imposes a series of obligations that override considerations of short term growth or require a form of payback of that growth to the community. Limitations on long-term growth can also be based on environmental factors, or on preserving the traditional ethos of the company (the two are often related). Above all, they derive from the Vrata of Aparigraha, which means that the proceeds of commercial success (or at least a significant portion of these) should be ploughed back into society, which is inclusive of humans and non-humans. This conception of business is cyclical, with the possibility of contracting or returning to first principles after an initial period of expansion. Another possibility is the achievement of a 'steady state', which is not associated with passive stasis, 'ticking over' or gradual decay, but continuing with creative activity and innovation while working within consciously set limits, many of which are social and environmental. In the context of the increasing importance of green issues in the public policies of corporations, Jain businesses may be viewed as pioneers.

To understand more fully this cyclical approach to business and its philosophical roots, it is useful to consider in more detail the concept of Careful Action. Although it is interpreted literally by those who choose the ascetic path, it is a crucial component of the thinking of lay Jains, including those engaged in commercial activities.

The principle of Careful Action

For many, the word 'Jainism' conjures up the image of a monk clad in white, mouth concealed by a small band of white cloth, advancing with slow deliberation as he clears the ground in front of him with a wooden broom. This is, perhaps, the 'purest' image of the Jain community among non-Jains in both India and the west. It captures one of the most extreme expressions of what for most is still a mysterious faith, rarely mentioned and little known. The ascetic's actions are those of a man who has renounced conventional worldly concerns, especially those involving the accumulation of material possessions. His ideal is to own nothing and, eventually, to be able to refrain from any action that interferes with the natural world. The brush and the covered mouth are designed to protect against injuring the most minuscule forms of life, including those that can only be viewed through the lens of a microscope.

The ideal of renunciation and quietism seems, at first glance, to be a surprising component of a discussion about Jainism, business and finance. As with many aspects of this cultural and spiritual tradition, it is important to attempt to delve deeper, and the results of such a quest will often be unexpected. That is not necessarily a simple task, for one of the distinguishing features of Jain culture is its modesty and frequent reticence about communicating its principles to outsiders. As a faith tradition, Jainism does not proselytise or seek converts. As a philosophy, it does not assert its primacy or 'rightness'. This apparent reserve is rooted in a theory of knowledge that accepts the value of multiple viewpoints. Paradoxically, however, it can create the impression of an inward-looking and almost closed-off community. Another problem for the student of Jain philosophy arises from this embrace of 'many-sided' logic. Viewpoints and ways of life that might seem incompatible or even contradictory are reconciled with relative ease, a stance that challenges the western bias towards theoretical consistency, whether or not it corresponds to consistency of practice.

The ascetic or *Muni* who avoids injury to minute organisms gives us a useful example of Jainism's multilayered nature. He enacts, in a literal form, the principle of Ahimsa: non-violence or more precisely translated as 'non-injury' and 'the absence of harm'. The centrality of Ahimsa is one of the distinguishing features of Jain doctrine. It is a yardstick, against which all activities including thoughts are measured. The Muni is practising the vow of *irya-samiti* (Careful Action or more literally 'care in walking'). Derived from Ahimsa, because care in movement minimises harm to small life forms, irya-samiti is one of five *samiti* (rules of conduct) undertaken by ascetic men and women. These are combined with three *gupti* or restraints, which involve 'a progressive curbing of the activities of mind, body and speech' (Jaini 2001: p.247). The process of stilling the mind, body and tongue is intended to induce the state of calm and equanimity that is associated with self-knowledge. It is also linked to the Jain view of karma, which is the product of all activity, especially acquisitive activity. Hence the reduction of activity leads to reduction of karma and reduced desire for possessions leads to greater wisdom. Both forms of reduction should be conscious choices, undertaken at varying levels by ascetic and lay people, who take different versions of the same vows.

Thus the behaviour of the ascetic serves a dual role. First, it is part of a series of vows undertaken in accordance with ancient customs as a means of spiritual development and pursuit of knowledge. The eventual aim is *Moksha*, the liberation of the true self and its return to pure consciousness. In the *Svetambar* (White Clad) monastic tradition, the white robes worn by male and female ascetics are associated with purity and clarity of vision. (The other prominent Jain tradition is the *Digambar* or 'Sky-Clad', where the most advanced male ascetics are naked.) Secondly, the ascetic's way of life is a continuous reminder to the 'civilian' Jain population of its ultimate priorities. Lay men and women are reminded of the value of all forms of life, however small or elementary these might appear to be. They are also reminded that accumulation of material wealth can lead easily to a form of egoism that is the opposite of self-awareness. Materialism produces a form of 'false pride' (to adapt a similar Judaeo-Christian concept), instilling illusory notions of success and invulnerability. Such illusions are based on a concept of the atomised individual competing with others to 'win' at all costs. This in turn gives rise to a sense that humankind is separate from or superior to all other aspects of nature, which become resources to be exploited. The activity that goes with the desire to keep and increase material possessions obscures any clear perception of reality and is likely to induce forms of himsa (harm), whether through interference with nature, exploitative relationships with other human beings and negative passions (Kasaya) such as greed, fanaticism and anger. The ascetic holds up a critical mirror to the lay person, inviting constant reflection on his or her life and the priorities that govern it.

From this description of the ascetic, it would be easy to conclude that Jainism is a viscerally anti-business philosophy. Explicitly and implicitly, the attitudes and practices associated with commercial activity are portrayed as transient and ultimately signifying nothing. Furthermore, Jain doctrines appear to favour co-operation over competition, poverty over wealth, the individual conscience over organised power structures and steady-state economics over growth. Jain values, it would seem, regard human intelligence as an illusion and technological advances as, in the memorable words of the eighteenth-century Franco-Swiss philosopher Jean-Jacques Rousseau, 'garlands of flowers over the iron chains with which [men and women] are burdened' (Rousseau 1987: p.3). All of this is true of Jain doctrine. It is also true that the ideal human being is one who has nothing, or next to nothing, in material terms, but 'everything' in terms of understanding the universe. Omniscience is equated with spiritual liberation, which is the same as freedom from karmic bondage (bandha). Viewed from the western perspective, these principles might translate into a socialist system of common ownership or an anarchistic system akin to those of isolated, mainly hunter-gatherer 'people without government' (Barclay 1982). Yet this analysis represents only a partial, one-sided truth about Jainism. A doctrine that preaches simplicity and renunciation has also produced ornate and elaborate temple art and architecture. It has nurtured a community enjoying exceptional success in trade, finance, craftsmanship and the professions, where the entrepreneurial spirit is valued as much as the spirit of scholastic inquiry, and where the model unit is usually the enterprise owned and run by an extended family group.

A useful starting point for resolving this seeming contradiction is the other popular image of the Jains, the sanctuaries in which abandoned or injured animals of all species are sheltered and helped. Ahmedabad, Gujarat, is one of the notable centres for the Panjrapoor animal sanctuaries, and is also a stronghold of Jainism in western India. Like the careful actions of the Muni, the existence of the Panjrapoor reflects the commitment to life in all forms and the abhorrence of injury to or destruction of life. But their importance lies in the fact that although they are supported by the Jain community as a whole, their main source of funding comes from businesses, or from individuals and families who are engaged in commerce. The creation and funding of animal hospitals – as with human hospitals, schools and universities – is part of a process of wise use of wealth and the dispersal of material benefits to the wider society. The business man or woman who funds such projects does so out of altruism. At the same time, he or she is practising one of the most important of the vows undertaken by lay people as well as Munis: Aparigraha, or non-possessiveness, which in practice means the absence of possessive impulses and the renunciation of unnecessary wealth and its accoutrements. Aparigraha contributes to the process of reducing karmic influence and breaking free of the cycle of *Avidya* (ignorance, lack of knowledge) perpetuated by karma. Yet the shedding of wealth can easily turn into an empty gesture unless that wealth is put towards a positive social use.

The ascetic's dramatically expressed commitment to Ahimsa and the protection of life is widely – and understandably – portrayed as otherworldly or absolutist in its demands. Viewed from a different standpoint or naya, it can be viewed as part of a highly pragmatic world view. The belief in working with rather than against the natural world has been popularised by the environmental movement and confirmed by the science of ecology. As one of the foundations of Jain thought it is a practical guide to human life as much as an ideal of 'right conduct'. Guided by the doctrine of Ahimsa, practising Jains aim to integrate the principle of Careful Action into their lives. It influences choice of occupation and affects the way business is conducted. It is, for example, characteristic of Jain businesses that they prioritise long-term survival for future generations over risky expansion that might yield only fleeting rewards. With regard to the environment and natural resources, there is a bias towards conservation and the minimising of demands placed on the Earth, as opposed to unstructured and limitless 'use' or short-term exploitation.

Many Jain business decisions are based on the belief in living within limits, because all natural resources are finite and cannot be indefinitely consumed. It would be simplistic to classify Jainism as a 'green religion', especially if we define green in terms of the western-led political movement. Nevertheless, the concepts of 'sustainability' and 'living lightly' adopted by green politics and increasingly aspired towards by businesses of all size are ingrained in Jain culture. A cyclical view of the universe is one of the key tenets of Jain Dharma, influencing the attitude of the whole culture. Jain doctrines interpret the universe as eternal and indestructible, but passing through a continuous series of progressive and regressive cycles (*utsarpini* and *avasarpini*) that last for aeons. It is also teeming with life in an infinite variety, including microorganisms and subatomic particles or *Anu* (Mardia and Rankin 2013: pp.106–7). This awareness of cosmic cycles encourages a perspective of equanimity. Humankind, however intelligent, powerful and successful, is just a small part of the cosmos. Part of the process of becoming enlightened is to be aware of limits as well as possibilities. While human advances have been immense and human potential remains great, it does not represent the totality of knowledge and at a cosmic level can only be fragmentary.

All living organisms are seen to play an important role in the coherent functioning of the universe. The smaller the unit of life, the more powerful and subtle its role is likely to be. This position, arrived at intuitively, is also underscored by particle physics (Mardia 2007) and other physical sciences. Oceanographers, for example, are increasingly aware of the role of plankton in regulating the temperature of the sea and thus affecting the global climate (Fortey 1998: pp.122–157). The conscious human being has a responsibility to guard as far as possible against interference with or damage to other beings, especially when it is tempting to do so for short-term profit or gain. This is for ethical reasons, as commitment to Ahimsa is part of spiritual practice, but it is also rational self-interest. Arbitrary interference with nature can injure or even eliminate ecosystems, species and organisms on which we depend for our survival. The increasing crisis created by deforestation in Amazonia is a case in point that would readily be recognised by Jain ethics. In the interests of (in both human and cosmic terms) short-term considerations of economic growth, unchecked human activity is destroying trees that influence the Earth's atmosphere and climate, as well as plant species that have been valuable sources of medicine and nutrition for indigenous peoples, whose knowledge is being lost with the forest that sustains it (Beyer 2009; Dobkin de Rios 1992).

Translated to the sphere of business, these emphases on equanimity, long-term planning and the importance of all life forms have profound implications. Chief amongst these is that there is no automatic presumption in favour of growth as a worthwhile end in itself. Other priorities assume greater prominence, including the preservation of the company's culture and values, and its roots in the community, locality and extended family. This can easily be mistaken for a turning inwards or contraction, as opposed to a creative engagement with the outer world. Instead, the Jain position is more accurately explained as one of engagement with the outer world as if the outer world mattered, rather than viewing it as something merely to be controlled or overcome. Thus the environmental impact of business expansion, or other commercial decisions, becomes important, because it can affect the survival of the business several generations from the original point of decision-making, as well as affecting the community the business serves – a community wider than humans and their concerns. Secondly, the act of expansion can mean that the values and familial or communal ties that nurture them can be lost, either in the immediate or indefinite future.

The principle of Aparigraha derives from the Jain view of a universe filled with life forms, each one individual and unique but all of them ultimately reliant on each other. Applied to business, Aparigraha is at once centripetal and centrifugal in character. By emphasising the limits of commercial expansion, the practice of Aparigraha involves looking inwards. It calls for a move from commercial activity as an end in itself to a more contemplative, even introspective approach to the future of the business. Simultaneously, it looks outwards as wealth is divested through community projects and charitable foundations. This is how the ideal of asceticism or renunciation becomes compatible with the strongly 'pro-business' ethos of the Ratnaśekhara Sūri quoted in the epigraph to this chapter, reflecting an aspect of Jain culture and belief as enduring as that of the Muni. It is not commercial activity itself that presents a spiritual 'problem'. What become more important are the forms of commercial activity, the ways in which they are undertaken and the attitude of mind that governs decision-making.

Furthermore, the ascetic way of life, which for most is only a distant ideal, is openly sustained by commerce and the material success of the business community. The business person, in turn, might take ascetic vows at a midpoint in life or in old age, as might other family members and friends. For many, asceticism is also a possible future arrived at through reincarnation. The importance of the cycle of birth, death and rebirth cannot be overstated in a philosophy that sees enlightenment as a journey through many cycles of existence. The continuity of the individual consciousness through a multiplicity of forms, human and non-human, is part of the Jain belief that all life is 'joined together' and the viewpoint of each being is significant. Both the business person and the Muni are on the same cyclical journey towards self-knowledge. The connections, direct and indirect, between the material and ascetic realms provide the foundations for a business ethos that promotes outward success, but which sees that success as a means rather than an end:

> The benefits of acquisition of wealth by legitimate means on the part of the lay community have long been recognised within Jainism. In the eighth century [CE] *Dharmabindu* of Haribadrasuri, there is a description of the qualities of an ideal layman (*sravaka-gunas*). The first and foremost of those qualities is that of being endowed with honestly earned wealth (*nyaya-sampanna-vibhava*), for wealth acquired by honest means not only brings freedom from anxiety in this world, it also leads to a happy [i.e. auspicious or positive] reincarnation.
>
> (Jaini, in Chapple 2002: p.145)

In this way, a philosophy that initially appears to be rigid or even puritanical turns out to be flexible and remarkably free of judgemental orthodoxies. Honestly conducted business is perceived as a force for good both for self-development and for the society served by that business. The business person who acts as an 'ideal layman' becomes a community leader, assuming responsibilities which increase with the size and scope of the business and include, ultimately, the responsibility to downsize and disperse wealth and power. From this standpoint, the practice of Aparigraha is given added dynamism when there is 'honestly acquired wealth' to divest and put to a practical use. For a tradition of renunciation, this might once again appear surprising, but an equally important feature of Jain Dharma is its inclusiveness, its belief in 'both/and' rather than 'either/or'. To gain an impression of how this sense of multiple possibilities works in practice, guided by the precept of Careful Action, we shall consider a highly traditional area of Jain commercial activity, the jewellery industry of western India. Jewellery is one of the areas of the Indian and increasingly the global economy where Jain individuals and family businesses have deep roots. The jeweller in question, Jyoti Kothari, works within a long-established community in Jaipur, Rajasthan, but he and his fellow professionals are part of a global network spanning continents, successfully practising a form of globalisation before the term became common currency. In a cyclical pattern typical of Jain-led enterprises, the process of expansion acts as an instrument of Aparigraha. Expansion takes place only within boundaries set by the company to preserve the values on which it has successfully based its operations.

Business ethics in practice: Vardhaman Gems and the culture of Jain jewellers

In an unusually direct account of the Jain jewellery business, its history and culture, the Jaipur entrepreneur Jyoti Kothari, owner of Vardhaman Gems, described to *Jain Spirit* magazine the way in which the industry is still based on workshop-centred craftsmanship. Skills are transmitted between generations of extended families and the apprentice is trained in the ethos and values of the industry as part of their wider training. At the same time as maintaining this traditionalist stance, Vardhaman Gems and other firms in the sector have become an integral part of the outward-looking India of the twenty-first century. Kothari also makes explicit connections between the jewellery trade and Jain ethics, which are important to an understanding of the priorities and goals of the business community as a whole:

> Many modern Jains face a quandary when attempting to combine their personal values with their career aspirations. Yet, the jewellery trade is, arguably, a business that has the power to corrupt its professionals due to the pressures that come with dealing with high-value items. An honest jeweller is a rarity, yet many Jains have found prosperity through the trade precisely because of their religious beliefs and strong reputations. As Jainism advises that achieving purity is determined through facing and overcoming life's temptations, I would argue that the core religious values fit well with the honour code of the jeweller.
>
> (Kothari 2004: pp.48–50)

The gemstone and jewellery trade is also regarded by practising Jains as *alparambhi*, or 'requiring minimum violence' (Kothari 2004: pp.48–50). Therefore, it is attractive to members of a culture that seeks to avoid inflicting himsa on the living Earth. In this context, the jewellery industry refers to the jeweller's craft and the skills of gem identification and grading, rather than the process of gemstone extraction, which is unlikely be undertaken by devout Jains. That said, the jeweller or gemstone grader's lack of violence against people or ecosystems has made these occupations 'ideal for Jains wishing to adhere to the principle of ahimsa':

> Motivation for wealth earned with morality (*nyaya sampanna vaibhava*) was exactly the solid background for ethics and morality that fit in with Jain values. The high character and moral conduct of the Jains enabled them to be trusted by kings and aristocrats. The love for one's religious community (*sadharmi-vatsalya*) also played its role, and the established jewellers contributed to this growth by training generations of Jains with the secrets of the trade, which led to many Jains prospering in the trade.
>
> (Kothari 2004; pp.48–50)

The skill of the jeweller, including the identification, grading and valuation of gemstones, is transmitted from teacher to pupil in a relationship that transcends apprenticeship and resembles in many ways the relationship between guru and disciple:

The teacher nurture(s) his students with the qualities required of a true jeweller, whilst equipping them with the necessary practical skills and theoretical knowledge of the trade. They were taught to be patient, calm, vigilant, creative and diplomatic, fitting the sort of values Jains were traditionally taught. Jain jewellers functioned according to the following basic rules in particular: imitations were never to be sold as real; substituting of goods was treated as a major offence; a certain percentage was deducted in every transaction for charitable purposes.

(Kothari 2004: pp.48–50)

These attitudes and practices confer on the jewellery trade the status of 'vocation' or 'most honoured profession', requiring careful thought and action from its practitioners. Careful thought includes avoiding the greed or lust for possessions that can be easily associated with gemstones, but valuing their beauty and intricacy instead. The tradition of scholarship associated with Jains is also brought into play. During the fourteenth century CE, Thakur Theru, a court jeweller in Delhi, published the *Ratnapariksha* (*Gem Inspection Manual*) and in the introduction 'clearly highlights the importance of [the Jain] religion to him and his trade' (Kothari 2004: pp.48–50). The link between jewellery and spiritual practice is made explicit in major texts such as the *Kalpasutra* (first century CE), where gem identification is listed as one of 72 principal skills to be acquired by men. Trishala, the mother of Mahavira, is also quoted as describing heaps of gemstones appearing in the thirteenth of 14 auspicious dreams before her son's birth. Significantly in this context, Jains aim to live according to the Three Jewels or 'Triple Gems' (*Ratnatraya* or sometimes *Triratna*): *Samyak Darshana* (Right Vision or Viewpoint); *Samyak Gyana* (Right Knowledge) and *Samyak Charitra* (Right Conduct). The image of the jewel is also applied to the concept of *Anekantavada* (many-sidedness): each naya or viewpoint is likened to one of the facets of a cut diamond so that the same multiple viewpoints clear light is viewed from many angles. It is also worth noting that Vardhaman Gems is named in honour of Mahavira.

Through the jewellery trade, Jains have expressed their adaptability and internationalism. In India, they have served as court jewellers for Hindu and Muslim rulers alike, their influence surviving and growing under British colonial rule. During the twentieth century, Jain families involved in the jewellery trade moved to areas as distant as Thailand and Japan. In Kobe, Japan, they formed a community associated with the pearl industry. Today, Jains continue to work as jewellers, gemmologists and diamond cutters in the principal markets of New York, Antwerp, Geneva and London. East Africa attracted Jain jewellers from Gujarat in the late nineteenth and early twentieth centuries, because of the opportunities afforded by the discovery of gold and diamond deposits. They continue to play an important role in the Diaspora communities of the region, as well as in the gold and diamond industries of southern Africa. Charitable giving is important to the lives of Jain families in the jewellery trade:

A large number of educational institutes, hospitals, rehabilitation centres, *dharamshalas* [religious guest houses; lodges for pilgrims] and animal welfare centres are run by Jains in various parts of India. Many prominent charitable trusts were established by the Jain jewellers for social and religious services, and it is the jewellers' contributions that have maintained some of the Jain temples and *upashrayas* [lodging houses for ascetics] built outside of India … [and] the conservation of old temples in India.

(Kothari 2004: pp.48–50)

This long-established industry serves as a template for other Jain businesses. At one level, Vardhaman and similar companies in the trade (often more like colleagues than rivals) are expansive, internationally minded and receptive to change. At another, they remain largely family-centred and focussed predominantly on the surrounding Jain population. Vardhaman is culturally conservative, in that it perpetuates practices that have been successful over many generations and retains an extensive network of social obligations and responsibilities. Much of Jain commercial activity remains community based and cleaves to its local or familial roots during the process of expansion. Indeed, as the enterprise expands, those roots usually become longer and deeper. Yet, for a company like Vardhaman, the limits of expansion are set when it becomes incompatible with its core values and practices and loses touch with its communal base. The firm's economic activity is a continual balancing act between its outward-looking cosmopolitan approach to trade and retaining its cultural anchor in the Jain business networks of Jaipur. Centrifugal and centripetal principles complement each other, with charitable donations and traditional systems of apprenticeship being at least as important as international recognition.

In other words, it is accepted that there are natural limits to growth for corporations much as there are for living organisms. Expansion gives way to contraction in a process that mirrors the belief in progressive and regressive cosmic cycles. This mirroring effect arises from the concept of Dharma. Jain doctrine, as we have already observed, is not compartmentalised as a 'religion' and confined to the area of worship, or as a 'philosophy' to be confined to theoretical discussion. On the contrary, Jain Dharma is a system for daily living and a continual point of reference from which even those who have if any conventional religious commitments can draw, including those who have abandoned most of the tenets and prohibitions associated with religious orthodoxy. The internal logic of an enterprise like Vardhaman Gems should be viewed in the context of Jain social and cultural priorities, which combine protection of the extended family's interests with the better use of material resources for those who need them more urgently or where there are possibilities for social progress. The company has attracted a global clientele and at the same time remained 'rooted' in terms of place, values and social interactions.

The conscious choice to stop expanding at certain points in its cycle enables this type of Jain business to retain its founding ethos and the network of personal connections that gave it the initial lift off. This commercial enactment of the vow of Aparigraha is also a tool for economic and cultural survival. Communal projects and charitable works cement the relationship between the business and the wider Jain community. They help that community to remain self-reliant and able to survive as a minority culture at the same time as it adapts to local conditions. Equally, the practice of Aparigraha is a way of achieving business success, since that success is measured not by endless expansion but by the survival of the business in its distinctive form. The company's character as an extended family firm is maintained, even when its remit extends across continents. By setting limits to growth, such enterprises avoid being absorbed or swallowed by corporations which might have very different agendas and values.

Companies like Vardhaman operate successfully within a competitive economic framework but work from precepts that might challenge the assumptions of most business studies students. Their central characteristics are a preference for the long view over immediate or even medium term, coupled with a concern for the ethos and values of the company, the preservation of which becomes part of the overall business plan. From this vantage point, expansion can be perceived as a threat as much as a promise. Uncontrolled, it can erode the system of values which sustained the business since its foundations. With equally serious implications, it weakens the influence of the family group that gives the business its identity and the standards of behaviour which are perceived as a 'unique selling point'. For those observing Jain communities from outside, the idea of an extended family network in apparently exclusive control of a business runs counter to ideas of meritocracy and equality of opportunity. To an extent, this is undoubtedly the case, although the degree to which the corporate model is genuinely meritocratic remains contentious and fortunately lies outside the scope of this study. And although valid at one level, such criticism of Jain business practice misses an essential point. Within this distinctive culture, the central role of the extended family is part of a wider concept of commercial activity. It is part of the organic development of the business within the community and with an overview that includes the environment and the remote future. From a Jain perspective, the super-ideology of industrialism and growth (Adams 2001: p.248) is partial viewpoint or 'naya', valuing only one aspect of the business and so simplifying and reducing the commercial experience, which is as much social and cultural as it is economic in nature. The process of learning from the Jains begins with un-learning many of the assumptions of 'textbook' business studies. In a process not unlike some forms of meditation, it involves clearing the mind of preconceptions.

The problems and pitfalls associated with the Jain business model will also be scrutinised. The Jain approach is not 'perfect' for all situations and in all circumstances, and nor is it entirely remote from other business cultures as to be unrecognisable. Jains engaged in business frequently draw upon other traditions and models. However, a distinctively Jain approach to business seems to resonate strongly with the dilemmas and opportunities afforded by the global economy of the twenty-first century. The balance between global and local, for example, has been addressed by Jain communities for centuries, both as a cultural minority within India and in the many countries where Jains have settled and established commercial enterprises. Many Jain businesses also continuously strive to reconcile commercial imperatives with ecological limits. They have done so well before the rise of the green movement in the western world, and hence offer a valuable non-western contribution to the debate over 'sustainable' economics that has been largely articulated by the Global North. The next chapter will explore the relationship between Aparigraha as a practice of voluntary renunciation and wise use of resources, and the workings of the financial sector, which is frequently portrayed as the apogee of acquisitiveness and materialism. It presents a system of finance with radical implications because renunciation rather than accumulation is the ultimate goal.

3 Aparigraha

Understanding the nature and limits of finance

Atul Shah

The principal ethic of business today is the maximisation of profit and wealth. This is enshrined in the texts on economic and finance theory (Brealey *et al.* 2014; Ross *et al.* 2012), and also commonly espoused in the language and actions of modern business enterprises across the globe. In fact, many argue that this has to be the only ethic of business – no business can survive without profit at its very heart. This materialistic ethic has been supported and encouraged by modern views about individualism, freedom, the perceived dogmatism of religion, liberalism and the mass media, which help glamorise wealth and its accumulation. Success is often equated with wealth and profit, and rich lists abound all over the world and rich people are worshipped and idolised. There are also more fundamental unstated assumptions behind the importance attached to materialism – that animals, nature and the environment are not relevant to personal happiness and fulfilment, and the natural world is a free commodity to be used and exploited. Also excluded in this utopia is the potential effect the pursuit of money has on physical and mental health and well-being. Another fundamental assumption is the denial of community, social capital and social cohesion – at an extreme level, it is felt that there is 'no such thing as society'. No limit to greed is needed or recognised. This 'religion' of greed has been authenticated by eminent economists like Friedman (Friedman 1970) as the 'right' and even the 'only' way to run a business – an ideology has been given a scientific justification. Little mention is made of the fact that such thinking was strongly influenced by the novelist Ayn Rand (see e.g. Rand 1957) who wrote novels from a *laissez faire* perspective she called Objectivism, the theme of which, in essence, was the achievement of personal freedom through the pursuit of self-interest, and a denial of the significance of community, social well-being and state welfare (Finel-Honigman 2010).

What is often missing is a discussion about the consequences of profit and wealth to people, environment and societies, and the real link between wealth and happiness or personal fulfilment. This chapter explores the following questions:

- How sustainable is the logic of profit maximisation, and are there limits to profits, growth and finance?

- What does Jain wisdom and experience say about the role of finance in social, cultural and ecological life?
- How important are people and relationships to success in finance and its sustainability?
- In what ways can we remake finance as personal and cultural as opposed to impersonal and transactional?

One effect of such a 'religion' of profit maximisation has been the ignorance of wider stakeholders in business and the political economy that supports business and enterprise (Hertz 2001; Korten 1995; Bakan 2004; Peston 2008). For example, the state plays a very important role in providing the infrastructure and resources needed for business to function (Murphy 2015; Palan, Murphy and Chavagneux 2010) – such as roads, energy, policing, security, communications and regulated financial institutions and markets. Yet when it comes to paying taxes, it is somehow theoretically legitimate for businesses to minimise these in order to maximise profits. In his unique essay on political economy 'Unto This Last', first published in 1862, Ruskin (1985) has concluded that 'There is no wealth but life'. He grounds economics as the pursuit of human welfare, spiritual health and personal and social well-being.

Sadly today, the preservation of natural and social capital are at best peripheral to business (Hawken 1994; Elkington 1999) and only important in relation to compliance with laws or regulation. As profit and wealth creation have permeated social life, they have in the process damaged cultures, animals and the environment all over the world. Imperialism has also played a strong destructive influence on culture and faith traditions all over the world (Said 1994). The growth of the multinational corporation has helped globalise this destruction (Korten 1995; Bakan 2004), and spread the ethic of materialism and profit all over the world (Hertz 2001). In the process, cultures which have had different ideals and value systems, have found themselves battling against a tsunami whose short-term attractions are appealing, but the wider social and ecological damage is not measured or accounted for. It is more subtle, lasting and often irreparable.

We shall now examine the principle of Aparigraha as it relates to the apparently contrasting principles of profit and the generation of wealth.

Defining Aparigraha

The Jain ethic of Aparigraha is radically different from profit or wealth maximisation. Aparigraha means 'not engaging in possessiveness'. There are many layers to the meaning of this phrase:

- Any form of possessiveness is wrong – 'when you possess, you become possessed'.
- Money, wealth and profit are human constructs, and possessing these without limits would constrain personal growth and happiness.

- Individuals need to be detached from their possessions – they should not become obsessive about their assets or wealth. Possessiveness leads to attachment, and this creates bondage rather than freedom.
- Often one person's possession is another's sacrifice. Aparigraha recognises the interdependence of all living beings.
- Personal happiness and fulfilment cannot come solely from material objects and their ownership and accumulation.
- When organisations become possessive, they are likely to lose their 'inner' happiness and well-being. This may lead to collective damage to all the people associated with the business enterprise.

The principle of Aparigraha expresses a very different world view from mainstream business and capitalism. It recognises the dangers and limits of possessiveness, and explicitly links this to the human soul and its well-being. Aparigraha cannot be understood in isolation from wider Jain ethics and wisdom as it is an integral part of it. As explained in Chapter 2, Jain Dharma is a 'science of sustainable living', where individuals act in ways which promote compassion, cohesion and harmony and preserve society, culture and nature (Tobias 1991). Aparigraha is a practical manifestation of this Dharma, explaining clearly the nature and limits of possessiveness. Because of this fundamental difference, Aparigraha offers us radical new ways of looking at finance and developing its knowledge in ways which are more ethical, responsible and sustainable.

(Jain 1998: pp.63–4) has identified four fundamental postulates of Aparigraha:

1   The source of happiness and peace lies within the human individual and not outside him/her.
2   External possessions are only meant to be used and not to be owned. The ownership of everything in the world lies with nature, which is the true caretaker of everything.
3   The human being has tremendous energies and potential which is not based on external possessions. Possessions therefore limit the personal growth and development of an individual.
4   All human passions such as anger, conceit, crookedness, attachment, ego, have their root in external objects or possessions.

The above postulates have fascinating implications for business and financial ethics. The first postulate shows that lasting happiness comes from within. This is totally antithetical to conventional thinking about wealth and happiness. In contemporary finance teaching, there is little discussion about the source of happiness of the owner/entrepreneur, and whether or not money and wealth are sufficient proxies for this happiness. The second postulate directly challenges the principle of ownership of assets like property, plant and equipment, and land. Nature is the ultimate owner of these assets, so the business should not try to take ownership or even trade these assets. At the very least, businesses need to explore the meaning and limits of ownership, and the humility and responsibility that comes with it. This is a very radical observation, with highly controversial implications. In the case of oil for example, we know that it has been made by nature and is dug from the ground, and instead of bringing wealth and happiness, its discovery has often been a curse on societies, leading to inequality, corruption and pollution (Shaxson 2007). Ownership can breed inequality and exploitation.

The third postulate discusses something completely new to finance – the potential of the human being or entrepreneur that lies beyond ownership and control. It suggests that *Parigraha*, or acquisitive thinking and behaviour, significantly limits the entrepreneur or leader in realising their own true potential. When books celebrate business leaders and their achievements, they overlook the real potential of such people beyond the ability to profit and create wealth. In fact, for Jains, the potential for human growth and spiritual development is unlimited and infinite, but the potential for business and economic growth is limited and finite. Care needs to be taken to ensure that growth is sustainable and not at the expense of society or the environment. Somehow, we seem to have focussed a huge amount of public energy on material growth, and not understood the limits and destruction this has caused. Our lived culture and habits seem to have been swamped by competition, materialism and the hunger for so-called economic progress, without meaning and purpose.

Finally, the fourth postulate shows that greed is an open slide, and can easily lead to anger, conceit, crookedness, attachment, ego – all vices we commonly see among business leaders and managers. Thus business premised upon acquisition and profit maximisation could become a key source of moral decline of a community and society. Far from being a force for good, it actually can ignite a collapse of the moral fabric. This is also a radical suggestion, as most books on business try to defend business endeavour and do not see business as a potential engine of wider ethical decline.

Greed and mental health

The *Acharanga Sutra* (Amar Muni 1999: p.130) explains the essential problem in these terms:

> A man having greed for wealth cannot sleep at bed-time. He can neither bathe nor eat at the proper time. Day and night he is plagued by the ghost of wealth. He becomes a lost man. So much so that he even fails to recognise an inevitable consequence like death.

Extreme greed can lead people to the denial of death – something that I have personally observed amongst some entrepreneurs. This denial can help them justify their accumulation and possessiveness, but when death comes knocking on their door, they become very scared and frightened. Often they are profoundly insecure, but try to hide it.

This text is also clear about the connection between greed and mental health and well-being. It notes (Amar Muni 1999: p.179):

> A man motivated by mundane pleasure is said to be with many minds. This is because driven by greed, he indulges in numerous business activities like agriculture, trading, industry, etc. Day and night his mind is obsessed with thoughts and worries of such business activities.

The text also compares this experience to water being poured through a sieve. The sieve of mundane desire keeps getting poured with money and possessions, but the water keeps seeping away – the pleasure is ephemeral and transient, never steady or containable.

It is therefore possible that organisations driven by greed have an adverse influence on the mental health of their founders, managers and employees. This can have negative implications for the quality of decision-making and the sustainability of business actions and strategies.

Aparigraha brings the entrepreneur to the heart and soul of finance – the organisational actions cannot be detached and separated in a dualistic way (Shah 1996b). They are foremost the actions of individuals or collections of individuals, and their conduct and behaviour is paramount to the sustainable success of the business enterprise. A public limited company quoted in a stock market may have many different stakeholders, but it would be managed by an executive board that sets the tone, culture and personality of the organisation. Aparigraha means that leaders need to take their organisations and actions personally, and understand that their personal happiness will not come from maximising their fortunes and exploiting their various stakeholders. It requires entrepreneurs to be thoughtful and reflexive, to monitor levels of greed and possessiveness in the culture and ethos, and acts as a self-control mechanism. Contemporary economics and finance theory tries to depersonalise finance and thereby make it universal, but Aparigraha implies that finance has to be personal and therefore it is very dangerous to make it generic and universal. Mechanisms and institutions created for the practice and promotion of finance should never fail to remember and implement their primary purpose – to implement humane and environmentally sustainable ethical standards. The more finance is depersonalised, the more reckless and irresponsible it becomes. We somehow need to take back ownership and control of financial institutions and markets, and connect them to more fundamental and sustainable purpose.

Grounded enterprise

Satish Kanabar, a UK banker with 40 years of commercial banking experience with the South Asian business community in London explains that for most family businesses, relationships and sharing are very important, and their orientation is for the long term. They view business as a means to an end, to preserve and sustain the family, and do not like operating in a transactional manner – stakeholders must be known and respected – be they customers, lenders or suppliers. Even their community membership grounds the merchants and enables them to meet people from all walks of life, and also restrain themselves from committing a fraud or crime and damaging their reputation and status in the community. In his experience, he has seen tremendous humility among many Asian entrepreneurs – who often do not see themselves as selfmade. They acknowledge the help of others in getting where they are, and do not forget this. In a fascinating example he says: 'When it comes to business, they will try and get the best deal from suppliers or lenders, but when it comes to charity, they will open their generosity without restraint.'

If happiness cannot be attained through more and more wealth and possessions, and to the contrary, happiness is actually limited by greed, then we have the potential to transform the science and understanding of economics and finance. The role of finance becomes that of enabling an equitable distribution of resources and assets, and of understanding the differences between human needs, wants and luxuries. Business organisations should explore innovative ways of fulfilling human needs and ensuring the equality of access to these needs, and forbear from fuelling desires and luxuries which are fundamentally ephemeral and wasteful. This means that their products and services should be geared so as not to fuel consumerism and the desire to acquire or obtain temporary pleasures or fulfilments, but instead to meet basic needs and enable social cohesion and personal respect and enjoyment of nature. Profit, and its pursuit, should be lasting and meaningful, and not encourage excess, greed or wastefulness, nor destroy societies' mental health and well-being.

For Jains, service is and has always been more important than profit. One of the first words of their central prayer is '*Namo*' which means to bow down and respect. This attitude of mind, gives them a sense of limit and humility, and a connection with people and wider society. It helps them stay grounded in their pursuit of business activity, and in their relationships with all the various stakeholders which support and influence the business – from customers, to government and suppliers, lenders and employees. Most Jains do not engage in business which has a directly adverse impact on animals and the environment – like the meat trade or forestry and oil extraction. Even the choice of employment, profession, business products and services is influenced by these considerations – not anything and everything should be done for the pursuit of profits and wealth.

Agency as accentuator of greed

Agency theory is a whole branch of finance which attempts to align managers' actions and decisions to the interests of shareholders in order that they may not act irresponsibly and shirk or exploit the firm. Jensen and Meckling

(1976) pioneered this approach. It focuses on public corporations where the managers of a business are separate from the owners or shareholders. Its fundamental assumption is that efficient contracts can be constructed to monitor managerial performance and reduce greed. It deals with and exacerbates the division and depersonalisation of finance (Erturk *et al.* 2007; Kay 2015), and suggests contracts and schemes which encourage managers to act in such a way as to increase the wealth of the shareholders. Ethics like morality, professionalism, honesty and faithfulness are not discussed or elaborated – it is assumed at the outset that managers will be greedy and selfish, and need to be incentivised to behave otherwise.

Paradoxically, in recognising the tendency towards managerial exploitation, agency theory in effect promotes it and depersonalises finance even more (Erturk *et al.* 2007). In practice, it is often CEO's who control corporations today, not shareholders (Boyer 2005), so the contractual restraints are a chimera. If a manager is a responsible human being, then he/she will act in order to protect and support all stakeholders. By and large, Jain businesses are family owned, so this divorce between owners and managers does not arise in such an obvious way. In fact, family ownership is itself an act of personalising finance, and recognises the shared nature of money and wealth. The Jains' reluctance to list their businesses in stock markets, in spite of their entrepreneurial prowess, may itself be an acknowledgment of the limits of finance and an adherence to principles of personal responsibility and accountability. Jains are reluctant to 'marketise' their business, in spite of the opportunities for growth provided from external finance, because they recognise that expansion is not costless, and do not wish to lose control of their enterprises. How they handle this control would also test their true practice of Aparigraha.

Everyday practice of Aparigraha

The ways in which Jains practice Aparigraha are themselves diverse. The daily discipline of prayer and meditation encourages them to engage with their inner spirit and soul, and to reflect on their daily actions, and the extent to which they have hurt others. In fact, self-discipline is central to Jain culture, and a disciplined life is also likely to contain indulgence and gratification through the pursuit of greed and excess. Discipline itself helps them understand that true happiness and freedom cannot come from limitless profit maximisation and accumulation. A Jain entrepreneur and financier I know from Uganda (Abhay Shah) whose business has enormous growth potential would rather grow his philanthropic and charitable activities and spend less time on accumulation for its own sake. Around him, he sees local people suffering from joblessness, crime and alcoholism, and cannot understand how his own success and happiness can be isolated from their experience of inequality and hopelessness.

Community festivals and activities help Jains stay grounded and rooted, and often business relationships and knowledge are cultivated and sustained through such gatherings. The funding of community centres, temples and worship centres, including their building and maintenance is often directly from businesses (Rankin and Shah 2008; Shah 2007a). So charity and social cohesion are active expressions of Aparigraha for Jain entrepreneurs. There is no clear boundary between private and social enterprise. Both are seen as interdependent and interconnected. In an indirect way, greed and excess is checked through the participation in these communities – if wealthy Jains do not contribute their fair share, the community could influence their standing and reputation. We need to reflect more deeply on what separates business from society and how and why this separation is created and sustained. If we can understand and break down this edge or boundary, we can truly have businesses where social responsibility is a duty not a choice or public relations initiative.

Satish Kanabar explains that not everyone is able to 'digest' their wealth and success. Having culture and values, and a desire to protect the family can be very helpful in enabling entrepreneurs to understand the limits of wealth and to contain its extremes and excesses. Many Asians see their business as a trust held for the benefit of the wider family, and as a result, have developed a skill in maintaining purpose and equanimity in both good times and bad times. They do not get overexcited by wealth, nor do they allow their egos to be overblown. There is an understanding and satiation, and when windfalls are earned, often business leaders restrain from raising their standard of living or expenditure, and live simply and modestly.

Groundedness in living communities for business and finance executives is priceless. When people are born and raised in a selfish, individualist culture, they may fail to see the value of being part of a collective, and also may find it difficult to challenge their own greed and selfishness. They do not trust others easily and have not been trusted much themselves. In fact, such people may even conclude that everyone is greedy and selfish, so there is nothing wrong in being personally greedy and selfish. Their individualistic lifestyle and upbringing may nurture ambition and hard work, but for the pursuit of very personal goals, where business and industry is a vehicle for wealth and excess, without any conscience or restraint. Bharat Shah, CEO of Sigma Pharmaceuticals, one of Britain's most successful Jain entrepreneurs, regularly attends community events, supports them financially, and also joins in community prayers. He is very well respected in the community and in wider business circles, and yet has not lost his humility and respect for people. He understands the importance of preserving and nurturing community and the ways in which entrepreneurs can limit their possessiveness through such active engagement.

Diversity and community

Living communities comprise people from a cross-section of society – young and elderly, women and men, children and teenagers, rich and poor, people with disabilities, and so on. Membership of such communities provides one with a real experience of diversity, of the value of trust and mutuality, and equality and respect for one and all (Shah 2007a). The practice of Aparigraha is supported in such non-hierarchical communities, where no special respect or status is accorded to wealth or business success. In fact, at many Jain community events, entrepreneurs act as volunteers, helping to serve the food, wash the utensils or clean the tables or floor. Such actions help them to nurture humility and see richness in others – be they teachers, social workers, nurses, employees or professionals. They also help nourish their social and ethical values, and see the limits to wealth and excess.

For many entrepreneurs, having ownership and control are key to financial management. Ownership entails responsibility and accountability which is very different from the responsibility and accountability created by laws and regulations for stock market quoted companies. Just because this cannot be measured easily does not mean that its influence on practical finance should be ignored as it is, all too often, in contemporary finance teaching and research. We will also observe that most family-owned businesses are small or medium in size – it is possible that even scale and scope are maintained so that owners do not lose control and limit the growth – as they are not interested in expansion for its own sake. In their actions lies a very important statement about the limits of finance, and about their own very high sense of responsibility and accountability which is much beyond any regulatory or legal control mechanisms. Conscience and personal ethics seem to be a strong 'self'-regulator of business actions and conduct, where there are such leaders and cultured communities.

Once we acknowledge that finance has a central role to play in business, and that its practice necessarily binds the owners and managers to money and financial transactions, Aparigraha can seem very challenging to implement. The Jains have proactive practices of detachment which help individuals regularly understand and support them in avoiding Parigraha – preventing themselves from becoming 'possessed' by their possessions. One method is simply to limit one's own possessions through living simply with few properties and assets, and non-ostentatious lifestyle and clothes. A billionaire Jain entrepreneur, the late Mr Deepchand Gardi of Mumbai, wore the same kind of suit every day – his wardrobe was very simple and limited. His wealth and success came from the ownership of land. He was also one of the most renowned philanthropists of India, and his charitable foundation continues to this day. Another method of cultivating detachment is to value people and relationships, and be patient at profit and wealth creation. Many Jain businesses have survived for generations, something which is a rarity for modern corporations which change hands several times in a generation, if they survive. Their approach to business is not merely transactional and contractual, but fundamentally based on trust and a desire for long-term success, rather than a quick profit. Having a longer time horizon in their goals and actions helps Jains to operate in a sustainable way, and thereby see the larger connection of their success with wider society and nature.

Giving and receiving

Regular and active charity and philanthropy is another dimension of Aparigraha. In the *Tattvartha Sutra* it is noted that:

> Charity consists in offering alms to the qualified person for one's own benefit. The giver gives for his own benefit with a sense of gratitude to the recipient.
>
> (Tatia 1994: p.183)

This is a very unique definition of charity – the donor must be thankful to the recipient, for giving her/him the opportunity to share his profits and wealth. When businesses act in this way, it is an acknowledgement of the wider stakeholders that support their progress, and the desire to build a sustainable society and planet. It also helps entrepreneurs detach themselves from the fruits of their actions, and not get entwined in greed and its evil tendencies. Such charity can take a variety of forms, from active involvement in grassroots organisations, to donations and gifts in kind which help charities pursue their goals of just and equitable living. In mainstream finance theory, there is no role for charity at all – it is seen as an expense which reduces the profits and therefore the value of the firm. It is antithetical to the capitalist enterprise. Corporate social responsibility (CSR) is a recent attempt to encourage businesses to act and give responsibly, but research shows that most enterprises see it as a burden, and are more interested in the 'commercial' benefits of such activities through spin and marketing, then really seeing this as a duty and responsibility. Fundamentally, CSR is tinkering at the edges of greed (Fleming and Jones 2012), rather than questioning the very logic of enterprise, and its relationship with human vices and inequality.

Kay (2015) and Graeber (2014) show how modern finance has become increasingly transactional and 'a-cultural', in spite of the fact that money is a human social creation, an instrument created for enhancing human welfare and community. It seems that as money has penetrated everyday life more and more, society has become increasingly transactional, and relationships, social capital, and whole cultures and communities have been wiped out by the tsunami of financialisation. Large global businesses have also played a strong part in this (to use an inelegant buzzword) 'transactionalisation' of business and its destruction of human character, culture and social and ecological capital (Elkington 1999; Hawken 1994). What economists see as the growth and success of finance, has actually become a curse on society rather than a boon (Shaxson 2012; Shaxson and Christensen 2013). Paradoxically, such a level of penetration of finance in everyday life makes it very difficult to discuss the subject of ethics, as often the theories, financial institutions and experts have themselves become financialised and dehumanised.

The Jains see Parigraha or possessiveness as a form of violence. This is rarely discussed in contemporary business practice – that the pursuit of greed is a form of violence and harmful to people, society and the planet. The violence may not be easily observable – as in war – but its pain may be deliberate and lasting – a simple example being the use of child labour for mass production. In the *Acharanga Sutra*, it is noted (Amar Muni 1999: p.102):

'A man having greed, while seeking pleasure, does not care for pleasure or pain of others. Consequently he also becomes tormentor and exploiter. Therefore it is believed that violence is connected to possessions. Thus it is necessary even for a person obsessed with attachment to understand that as he likes pleasure others too like pleasure. Therefore he should not seek pleasure by depriving others.'

Greed is also harmful to the owners and employees of the business (Shefrin 2000) – even though they may think otherwise. Jain ascetics are not allowed to have any assets or possessions, and definitely do not touch or carry any money. It is explained in our stories that our Munis are the highest philanthropists because *'they leave nature's wealth to itself'*. The need to acquire, to own and control, may appear to give security and comfort, but in truth can breed insecurity and pain. As a simple practical example, the more assets and wealth one owns, the greater the effort and energy required to maintain them, invest them, and monitor their performance. This reduces the time and energy one has to enjoy the assets, spend time with family and friends, and to meditate and reflect on a regular basis. Acquiring and preserving assets saps a lot of energy, and often one person's acquisition is another person's loss. Greed thrives on and perpetuates inequality.

At root, Aparigraha is antithetical to inequality. By limiting one's possessions, one practices sharing and caring, and also controls any excesses. The practice of Aparigraha need not require external regulations and controls on inequality. It is a self-regulating mechanism, done through wisdom, understanding and virtuous conduct. If a person decides that they do not want to have private happiness at the expense of someone else's – then their actions will promote greater equality and social cohesion. And this lived example, may have wider ripple effects among the other people who come into contact with such a person. Jains have and continue to be very important role models for many people all over the world. Their conduct and behaviour has motivated thousands to live simply and respect people and relationships, as action speaks much louder than words.

Engaging with conscience

Conscience is the key to Aparigraha in practice. For Jains, conscience is the inner voice, the collective memory of love, pain and suffering, accumulated over previous experiences and lifetimes, something which becomes an inner warning system against harmful acts. Conscience is an intuitive signal, which feels like a conversation between the body doing the action and the soul driving the conduct. For conscience to manifest itself, an inner dialogue and respect needs to be established, and there needs to be an active desire not to harm the soul and its transmigration. Parigraha can be checked by conscience, often spontaneously, without any warning an inner voice may say: 'please reflect on this plan as it may not be desirable or sustainable'. In contemporary economics and finance, there is no place for conscience (Shah 1996) – only reason and science are meant to be the guide and guru. The fact that people are not always rational, and the science may not be that 'objective' or 'evidence based' or even internally consistent, is often ignored or forgotten. In fact, some have argued that to novice students who are brought up in secular households, economics becomes the religion and belief system they get converted to whilst at university, and they then end up practicing this religion of greed and selfishness (Mackenzie 2006; Daly and Cobb 1994). In such circumstances, conscience disappears from personal acknowledgement and experience.

Yet the fact of the matter is that leadership in finance can give a person huge power and influence as we saw from the experience of the 2008 financial crash (Angelides 2011; Tyrie *et al.* 2013). Hubris, greed, the silencing of critics and a lack of challenge were critical to the downfall of giant and prestigious financial institutions (see e.g. Fraser 2015; Cohan 2011; McDonald and Robinson 2009). Paranoia, distrust and psychosis are often the result of such extreme behaviour.

The essence of Aparigraha is holistic – it integrates the person to wider community, society and the planet. Its practice is an expression of respect for the triple bottom line – business, society and the ecosystem. When businesses truly practice Aparigraha, the outcomes we would observe are:

- An active interest in simple living, with a minimum of waste and a scaled business operation which is manageable
- An operating culture which values people and relationships, and is not driven by financial goals at any cost
- An investment in protecting society and the planet and not depleting them
- A deeper understanding of the role and limits of finance, and an active desire to be in control of finance rather than to allow finance to dictate business actions and conduct
- A sense of responsibility and accountability which is self-determined and not reliant purely on external rules and regulations. The business itself should want to do the right thing in the right way without greed or debauchery.
- An acknowledgement of various stakeholders and their rights
- Respect for government, laws and political economy
- Growth is pursued sustainably and patiently
- Internal systems and processes are created to provide a measure of the impact of the business on the triple bottom line and guide business strategy and actions – a systematised conscience
- Borrowing and wealth creation are not pursued for their own sake but instead to support the business strategy

Just as the Jains understand fully that money is a means to an end, and not an end in itself, business is also seen in this light. The entrepreneur may conduct business as a means to providing for his/her needs, but should not allow the business to overwhelm him, and should always be mindful of the higher goals in life. A personal friend, Dr Shugan Jain, recited a true story of multi-millionaire Jain industrialist in Delhi who in the 1970s moved out of his mansion into a single bedroom near a Jain temple, where he could concentrate on prayer, study and meditation. Even for food, he had his own stove where he cooked very basic food so that he was not dependent on anyone else, and could focus on his goal of liberation. To manage his various businesses, he would call the factory managers for a total of 30 minutes in a day – he had become detached from his businesses, and focussed on the goal of self-realisation.

Reflexive entrepreneurship

There is a popular and beautiful story about Shrimad Rajchandra, an eminent Jain philosopher-merchant who became a key mentor and friend of Mahatma Gandhi and guided him on the meaning and interpretation of non-violence. He was highly successful in the pearls and gemstones business, and respected for his honesty and integrity. During the day, he would be fully immersed in his business, but as soon as the office was closed, he would straight away go to his philosophical studies and writings, and he was also a highly accomplished poet. Today there are many temples and centres all over the world dedicated to this life and teachings – Shrimad Rajchandra was a businessman who became enlightened. He was reflective, and whilst engaging in business, found a way to stay detached from the fruits of his success.

There are significant implications from the above for the qualities required for sustainable business and entrepreneurial leadership. Such a leader would need to be unselfish, egalitarian, and non-possessive. They would need to be interested in their own personal growth and development beyond wealth creation and business expansion. There should be evidence of a rootedness in their conduct and behaviour to living communities – their actions and thinking should be grounded and not aloof and irresponsible. Their behaviour should not be driven by status and ego, but by a sense of humility, responsibility and accountability. A deep respect for nature would lead to conduct which would be compassionate and non-exploitative or non-acquisitive. Their growth ambitions would be hampered by the limits of nature and finance, and an understanding of the limits of managerialism and control. The approach to leadership would be democratic and empowering, giving space to various stakeholders and encouraging the personal and ethical development of employees. Relationships would be key to business success, and these would be nurtured and built over time, and care taken not to diminish or destroy them without reason or cause.

From the above, we can see that the concept of Aparigraha offers an alternative ethic for business and finance, with many fascinating dimensions. As a concept, it is integrative, not separating the business from the owner or manager.

Rather than treating nature as an externality, or something to be considered after the profits are made, it puts the relationship with nature at the heart of the business and personal enterprise. Aparigraha emphasises self-discipline, and a wider understanding of the impact of personal values and actions on the organisation and its social and natural environment. At heart it is a reflective principle, encouraging businesses to be very careful in their conduct and transactions, and also measuring and evaluating their impact. It recognises explicitly the interdependence of all living beings, and encourages the pursuit of organic growth and profit, through causing a minimum of harm to other life forms. Stakeholders like the state and government are given their due respect, and taxation is not seen as something to be avoided or minimised but as a respectful way of helping the state provide its services.

Humility and character

Aparigraha cannot be seen in isolation from a wider set of values. These include Ahimsa (non-violence and compassion), Satya (truthfulness and integrity), Asteya (non-stealing), Anekant (pluralism and respect for alternative viewpoints), *Kshama* (forgiveness) and *Dana* (charity, giving). These values provide a comprehensive basis for implementing non-possessiveness, and also a barometer for business strategy and ethical leadership. There is a deeper understanding of the limits of greed, acquisitiveness, ownership and profit. An active detachment is cultivated from wealth and possessiveness. Emphasis is placed instead on the growth and progress of people, society and the planet, with business as a means to attain these wider goals.

When one of India's largest bankers and financiers, Mr Motilal Oswal, was recently interviewed, the interviewee was very surprised by his humility and simplicity (Vadukut 2008). His diet was simple, his manner was gentle, and there was no arrogance about his huge success, in spite of his fame and fortune. His founding business partner (Mr Raamdeo Agrawal) is treated as a member of the family, so there is no case for any dispute, he explained. Even in this day and age of extreme wealth and fortune, such values are lived and treasured by the community, which takes pride in its roots and culture, and fully understands the limits of wealth and material success.

There is of late a groundswell of concern about financial exploitation and financial literacy. The above discussion suggests that just as we need to educate the poor about basic financial management, it is equally and perhaps even more important to educate the rich and greedy about the impact of their behaviour on themselves and others. All over the world, a huge amount of energy and resources are being devoted to the teaching of corporate finance, business success and profit and wealth maximisation. What is crucially needed is an equally important emphasis on educating people about ethical business and finance, and in particular the links between greed and social and environmental devastation. We need to show the benefits of simplicity and contentment, of creating markets and institutions which are a force for good, and promote social and environmental respect and cohesion. Values not value should be at the heart of finance, and not at its margins or fringe. The entire edifice and construction of contemporary finance theory is such that it prevents any discussion of ethics – probably because such a discussion would seriously challenge its very premise and foundation.

Relationship finance – understanding means and ends

A training course or initiative which helps people to understand their relationship with finance, to see the wider impact on their personal health and relationships could make important breakthroughs and transformations. A practical starting point for such a course would be to encourage the rich to write their own obituary – this would force them to reflect on their death and legacy, and sustainability of their actions and character. Businesses and financial institutions could chart an honest and empathic impact analysis of their enterprises on different stakeholders including animals and the environment. Helping the super-rich understand their footprint on society and the environment and learn from different cultures and traditions about the values and limits of finance is urgently needed today. Instead far too many universities and business schools focus primarily on wealth creation and profit maximisation and ethics, if taught at all, are marginal to the mainstream education rather than integrated or integral. Wealth and financial success may be important to a degree, but their limits and excesses also need to be widely discussed and debated. Also the personal and psychological dimensions of wealth are important for budding MBAs and executives to understand. The inequality of modern society also opens up a huge opportunity for reform and transformation. Making finance leaders aware of the cultural and social impact of their actions and transactions may help transform behaviour. Business schools could play a very important role in encouraging greater personal reflexivity for business leaders and executives. It is possible that many rich people are unaware of their insecurities and loss of freedoms through excess, and if scientists were able to demonstrate these, they could be convinced to change their behaviours and reduce their exploitation and instead help improve equality and sustainability.

When means become ends, society faces serious consequences, and there are many voices today who say that finance has become uncontrollable, delusional and ungovernable (Das 2011; Kay 2015; Graeber 2014; Luyendijk 2015). Some even argue that it has become a *curse* on society (Shaxson and Christensen 2013). We are living in a period which is at the height of financialisation – where the combinations of neo-liberalism, globalisation and capitalism have given rise to a hugely powerful and influential ideology and institutions which are now a menace to society. Unlike the slavery of the past, where the master was human and visible, with financialisation we have created a 'willing slavery' where people have become slaves to their mortgages, employers and other credit institutions. The master of ideology and institutions is no longer human or visible, and we are increasingly blaming ourselves for a lack of success or financial independence – we must work harder, be more competitive and entrepreneurial, and then all will be resolved. Such a mindset helps the rich and powerful, and it is no surprise that inequality has grown significantly in recent decades.

When the world is financialised, everything – including culture and ethics – is measured with or against money and material objects. Quantification becomes the norm and quality and aesthetics are submerged. Even governments lose control against financial markets and institutions, and find themselves in a situation where they constantly have to bail out reckless finance. States do not benefit from high finance – often they become slaves to banking and the industry actively practices and promotes tax avoidance, so the revenue base for governments is depleted rather than replenished. There is an increasingly reliance on law and regulations as a means to control the ends, but often the people and systems continue to fail as culture and social transformation are bankrupted by the finance industry. Morality was required to create free and fair financial markets, but their very growth and expansion has eroded the moral fabric.

For Jains, the human body is a means of pursuing the end of true liberation and enlightenment – the immortality of the soul. The industry of finance is obsessive about the body and its physical needs and comforts, at the expense of inner happiness and contentment. It has detached itself from the human soul, and a deeper sense of meditation and reflexivity about its actions and wider planetary impact. In fact, we can safely say that finance today is in denial of the soul, and the reality of physical death. Money has become a source of fear and mistrust, rather than a means of human exchange, development and social cohesion and transformation. Its currency and physicality has reduced the need for human contact and community, and as a result has destroyed human bonds and social fabrics. The power of finance today is such that even states cannot control it, as it often plays one state off against another. What is urgently needed is an active re-engagement of finance with the human spirit, as instead of a servant to society, it has become its master.

Recognition of imperfection

The above principles may cast Jains as a perfect people and role models for business conduct. This is not always true, nor the intention of these writings. Jains would be the first people to admit this. There are examples of Jains who are greedy, acquisitive and selfish, and domineering and egotistical. Jain businesses tend to be male dominated and not egalitarian. And yes, there are Jains who are very rich, and many would see this as a contradiction with their faith. They may have the principle of Aparigraha, but do not appear to practise it. We acknowledge these weaknesses and contradictions, and doubt if any human society would be 'perfect' in its ethical conduct and behaviour. In fact, if we look closely at life there is a fundamental contradiction – it is called death. Contradiction lies at the very heart of human life – in Indian languages there is no single word for contradiction. That should not mean that we stop learning from timeless wisdom or theories and human and environmental experience.

Another major issue in ethical finance and business today relates to taxation, and the extent to which businesses minimise their taxes. I have spoken to a range of Jain businesses and accounting professionals about this, to get an understanding of Jain ethics in relation to taxation. Among the major drivers of aggressive tax avoidance are professional accountants who develop and market schemes which help businesses to minimise taxes. I spoke to many Jain accountants who would be prepared to lose and have lost clients who wanted to practice such aggressive avoidance. There are also some Jain accountants who do support clients in this way and help them minimise tax liabilities through their expert advice and fees. Business attitudes to taxation vary – there is a feeling that in places like East Africa, there is less trust in government as a manager of public funds, so Jains do not feel too badly about minimising taxes there. In the UK, due to transparency and public accountability, Jains do not feel badly about paying taxes, and of course those who are in jobs and rely on salaried income have no choice to avoid their taxes. As India's *The Hindu* newspaper reported (20 August 2007), Jains constitute less than one per cent of the Indian population, but pay 24 per cent of all the taxes collected. Some of the highest taxpayers in the country have been Jains.

One common feedback is that Jains do like to have control over their assets and income, and in taxation, they see a loss of that control, with money going into a big pot where they have little say in how it is spent. I would think this feeling would be generally true of most owner-managed businesses – the advantage of ownership is freedom and control, which can then get into the DNA of the owner. If not checked, control can become an obsession, and breach the principle of Aparigraha. Another reason given is that community activities and institutions require a lot of capital and ongoing funding, and businesses would like to give first priority to giving money to such institutions, where they can also see where and how it is spent. The general feeling is that where certain businesses and owners have become greedy and selfish as a result of their success, they also tend to be aggressive tax avoiders. Where entrepreneurs participate in community life, and have understood the roots and limits of their wealth and success, they tend to be more generous and less aggressive about their philanthropy and tax avoidance.

The fact that Jains have been and continue to have enduring success in business and finance, suggests that they practice many elements of their faith, and have a sustainable orientation. There is evidence of excellent relationships and social capital, and a very active community life wherever in the world they may live. For example, they have only migrated to the US in the last 50 years, but have built over 50 temples and community centres all over the country – costing millions of dollars. The idealism that is expressed in this chapter can also act as a barometer for righteous action, and life would be empty if we did not have ideals.

4 Risk and return

Careful action and relationships of trust

Atul Shah

Contemporary finance research and education are booming. Their rise and growth has been synonymous with the growth of business education all over the world and the rise and spread of business ideology and method as the keys to social and economic success and progress. The origins of finance as a separate discipline from economics dates back to the mid-1970s in America – it is a relatively young subject (Mackenzie 2006). The profession of accounting has an older history, although its research and teaching has recently grown significantly alongside the discipline of finance, partly fuelled by the growth of business schools and the need to teach and train accounting professionals (West 2003). Fundamentally though, most of accounting teaching and research can be viewed from a Jain perspective as 'a-cultural', amoral and apolitical – focus has been on the technical craft and the desire to apply the tools and techniques of economics to 'defend' these fields as scientific and worthy of university study (Shah 2016). The fact that the 'science' and tools of economics are themselves flawed and profoundly questionable is by and large ignored. Research and education in these fields has become an industry (Daly and Cobb 1994), motivated by the desire to defend jobs and tenure, rather than to address contemporary business and global problems and transform the world. An MBA at Harvard can cost nearly US $200,000 so this investment has to be justified by a higher return for the students. Even in the field of business education, risk and return are deeply embedded in its culture.

Given that money itself is a social creation, financial risk has to be primarily a cultural phenomenon (Das 2011; Douglas and Wildavsky 1982). Sadly, this is not how risk is taught in finance (McGoun 1995). It is stripped from culture, and explained as something that can be measured, calculated and hedged or mitigated using financial instruments (Ross et al. 2012; Hopkin 2012; Eales 1994; Roggi and Altman 2013). This explains why when global society experiences major risk events like the 2008 Global Markets Crash, there is confusion and chaos, and a wide range of explanations and justifications are given by scholars often from very narrow perspectives (McSweeney 2009; Admati and Hellwig 2013). Most of these are fenced around their particular technical expertise, and it took outsiders like Charles Ferguson and the other makers of the Academy Award winning film *Inside Job* (C. Ferguson 2010), to reveal the depth and breadth of the crisis, and the frauds committed by both bankers and regulators. A whole section of the film is devoted to the role of conflicted expert academics peddling the ideology of free and unfettered markets as the surest way of regulating finance and its weapons of mass destruction like derivatives. At heart, the film reveals a total breakdown in culture and values, and responsible leadership from top professionals in various industries, who were selfish, greedy and reckless in their risk-taking and very short-term in their orientation. Powerful networks of bankers, academics and regulators ensured that ordinary people and governments were duped into inaction (C. Ferguson 2010 and 2014), until it was too little too late. In fact, even the rescue of the banking industry has been proven to be fraudulent, with bankers and professionals benefiting both from the collapse and the subsequent recovery (Fraser 2015).

In his book *Other People's Money*, John Kay (Kay 2015) identifies fundamental flaws with the science and industry of modern finance, the key ones being irresponsibility, greed, corruption and abuse of power. He argues that there is an obsession with the historical measurement of risk, without understanding the fundamental causes and consequences of risk-taking. There is a herd mentality, where the masses rely on a few 'experts' or 'branded institutions or products' and then invest in them as others are doing it so they must be safe and vetted – a herd mentality. Intermediation, far from reducing risk, can actually increase risk as fewer understand the whole picture about the nature of a risk product and its possible outcomes. 'Tail risks', which are the small chances of a significant adverse events, are often ignored by the herd through ignorance or sheer greed and short-termism. The correlation of adverse events is also not included in the risk analysis through myopia and lack of experience and understanding of risk.

The technical science of risk is often used to mask its underlying reality (Beck 1992), impacting on people's lives and the wider economy and society. The bonuses and incentives of bankers and financial traders are skewed towards the upside of risk, and rarely adjusted for levels of risk-taking. When people take significant risks, there are chances of high rewards but also large losses. Banks often are casinos, where traders are allowed to gamble with other people's money (Strange 1986; Luyendijk 2015). This would never happen in a real casino – where chips have to be bought and paid for at the entrance. The huge growth of intermediation in finance has meant that risks have often been sliced and diced far too much, so that very few understand the big picture or are incentivised to do so.

Fundamentally, John Kay and others (McGoun 1997; Das 2011) argue that the modern industry, science and practice of finance has become self-referential – we know very little about the fundamental values, risks or returns of anything. All we know is how these values change in relation to other assets or prices or fluctuations in indices like interest or exchange rates. We have also seen that after the crash, evidence emerged of the manipulation of these very indices for asset pricing – like Libor and FX. Bankers will stop at nothing to make significant returns very quickly (Luyendijk 2015), and get away unnoticed. Their culture is riddled with extreme selfishness – it is one of few industries where employees set their own salaries and bonuses without an official trade union. And given that bankers are at the top end of finance, this is the culture which then trickles down throughout the system.

Protecting one's own wealth, family and community: the Jain experience

The history of Jain conduct and experience is very different. It is true that they have been consistently successful in business, banking and finance, but it is also a fact that their success has been primarily through family-based ownership and management. Often this success has been intergenerational, so that business and finance skills have lasted hundreds of years in the family name. Such conditions and values ensure that risks are taken in a careful and considered way, and there is responsibility and accountability at all times. Although it is rare, when Jain businesses have gone bankrupt, the owners have used personal and family resources to pay back creditors and lenders rather than run away with any loot or ignore their debts and responsibilities as moral citizens of the town or city. The science and practice of Aparigraha has given them a sense of restraint and reflexivity in Jain business conduct, and helped them to ensure that risk-taking is understood, experienced and controlled directly instead of through intermediaries.

Singh (2015) researched and wrote about the 'Sheherwalis' – a group of Jain merchants who migrated from Rajasthan to Bengal in search of business opportunity. An established Jain merchant, Manikchand encouraged the Nawab of Bengal to leave Dhaka and establish a city bearing his own name – Murshidabad. Manikchand was subsequently appointed the king's banker and given the title 'Jagat Sheth' – banker of the world. There is a long history in India of Jains advising kings and princes and even taking up roles such as chief minister or treasurer, because of their integrity, astuteness, leadership and diplomatic skills – the current president of the ruling Bharatiya Janata Party (BJP) in India is a Jain, Amit Shah. These are all behaviours central to long-term success in finance – a high degree of self-discipline and trustworthiness being critical.

As his business grew, Manikchand invited a number of Jain merchant families from Rajasthan to migrate to the area and they started adopting local ways of living, eating, attire, customs and language. The family were prudent investors and made a lot of money – they introduced a system of doing transactions with 'hundis' or promissory notes, instead of actual money (Doogar *et al.* 2014). These are short-term loans or bills of trade, which are discounted by the bankers to provide funding and liquidity, but must be repaid on time and in full. It was a business entirely dependent on relationships, honour and trust.

The principal risk was credit or default risk, and through active participation in the merchant community, the Jain bankers must have become very good at evaluating this risk and ensuring timely repayment. In fact, they also financed many foreign companies trading with India, including the British East India Company, as they were not far from Calcutta which was a major global trading hub. The Sheherwali Jains became very successful and built huge mansions, often designed by architects from England and France, which still exist today (Doogar *et al.* 2014; Singh 2015). With their accumulated wealth, they also built public hospitals, schools and colleges in Murshidabad – indeed they helped establish the whole town and its infrastructure. The sharing of profits with the wider society helped them to cultivate inner control of their greed and risk-taking, and also connected them with local people and their needs and aspirations – they were not happy just to accumulate riches for themselves. It is possible that as modern finance has become more transactional and instrumental, it is forced to be technocratic in the evaluation of risk, and in the process distances itself more and more from human experience, relationships and even holistic knowledge and intelligence. The science is used to dehumanise society and justify a lack of trust.

Financial governance and regulation become very critical when there is a significant concentration of risk and power, and when institutions have grown large and service a variety of stakeholders. Fundamental to any effective system of governance is the integrity of the leadership team and their honesty, sense of duty and responsibility, and accountability. Such systems, processes and regulations are very costly to create, monitor and enforce. The evidence of recent decades in finance shows that one of the primary activities and sources of income of the industry is 'regulatory arbitrage' (Shah 1996a and 1996b; Shah 1997) – the deliberate and active attempt to exploit regulatory loopholes for private profit. The cultural impact of such activities is very profound, and often ignored or legitimated by the religion of 'profit-maximisation' in economics.

In the above example of the Sheherwalis, there appears to have been significant concentration of power and very little explicit law or regulation of the financiers. Instead, there was a trusted relationship with the King who authorised Manikchand to have the Royal Mint and issue state money. In spite of this, the industry survived and grew, and it was sustained over a long period. The costs of governance and regulation were saved, and risk and behaviour were mitigated by the ethics and self-regulation of the Jain culture and community. Social capital and personal reputation within a community are likely to have played a major role in checking greed and excess, coupled with the desire to protect the family business for several generations. Long-term relationships, reputations and networks were highly valued. The creation in the West of the limited liability company and state 'protected' banks (Bakan 2004; Kay, 2015) have led to ineffective regulation and governance, and direct encouragement and subsidy of risk-taking and impersonal behaviour and recklessness.

One of the major shifts of modernity is the profound institutionalisation and corruption of finance, legitimised by the infiltration of state machinery and political capture (Mitchell and Sikka 2011; Shaxson 2012; Shaxson and Christensen 2013; McKenna 2011). Its professionals, institutions and markets have exaggerated the impersonality of finance, whilst at the same time lurching from crises to crises as the personal impact gets widely experienced. The traditional history of partnerships, solid reputations and prudent banking has been replaced by a selfish and transactional culture (N. Ferguson 2012), sheltered by limited liability and deregulation (Admati and Hellwig 2013; Sikka 2008; Mitchell and Sikka 2011). It is widely accepted that the industry plays a major role in the capture of governments, and uses its political influence to minimise regulatory control or any personal sanctions from reckless risk-taking. There is a growing argument of a 'Finance Curse' (Shaxson and Christensen 2013) where instead of the industry being a positive presence in a country, the larger its size and reach, the more it promotes inequality, corruption and social and economic breakdown. It is perhaps no coincidence that it took a finance scholar of Indian heritage, Professor Raghuram Rajan (Rajan 2005), to warn of the huge risks in the global financial system many years before the crash – although sadly his warnings were ignored by top central bankers and economists. He has also written an important book on the limits and excesses of capitalism (Rajan and Zingales 2003).

In the above example of the Sheherwalis, we see a very different form of finance which knows its place in society, is happy to serve industry and growth, and is humble enough to know its limits and support local institutions and community. Rather than trust, sustainability and ethics being at the margins or in official codes of conduct, they are at the very heart of conduct and practice. Far from capturing government or royalty, it supports it and works closely with it for the good of the citizenry. There is a deep respect for the 'banking licence' which has been given to Manikchand by the Nawab of Bengal – it is not a privilege to be exploited, but one to be honoured and fulfilled by the highest integrity and character. Such qualities and values cannot be manufactured or institutionalised, but are also critical to good leadership and prudent risk-taking in finance. At the very least, students and scholars of finance should be aware of the existence of such ethical methods and success stories.

In the UK, the regulators required prior approval and licensing of all banking leaders and senior risk officers, but unfortunately this rule was interpreted very loosely and the skills, experience and ethics of the applicants were not properly vetted or monitored and strictly enforced (Tyrie *et al.* 2013). Furthermore, the laws and systems of financial fraud prosecution are so weak that there has for a long time prevailed a climate of fearlessness, with many arguing that British finance is deeply hypocritical. In fact, Parker (2016) has shown that the origins of the Bank of England, one of the most famous central banks in the world, were based on theft and looting – rather than trust and honesty. There may be a regulatory framework, but it is only applied in the protection of the strong and the powerful at any cost – it is a charade of lax regulation and strong networks of white-collar crime and corruption

(Shaxson 2012; Das 2011; Kay, 2015). The Big 4 global accounting firms are also viewed as a key part of this fabrication and regulatory arbitrage (Mitchell and Sikka, 2011).

Expectations and returns

The concept of return and expected return are deeply embedded in contemporary finance theory (Ross *et al.* 2012; Brealey *et al.* 2014), without any acknowledgment of the materialistic cultural assumptions made in this modelling. In the world of western-led business, where focus, measurement and 'goals' are the key, return is seen as the sure way of monitoring business performance and the management and employees who run it. It is used to measure success and reward senior employees. It is also an important benchmark for capital allocation, performance measurement and investment choice – the higher the expected return, the greater the attraction for capital investment. Returns also have a direct influence on asset and firm valuation – profit and dividend announcements often have a big impact on share prices, as they not only report current performance but also influence future return expectations. In a very subtle way, this kind of thinking and science helped detach finance more and more from everyday culture and livelihood (Ekins *et al.* 1992; Elkington 1999). It became a technical craft taught by experts and used to prioritise measurement over people.

Growing up as a young Jain in the business hub of Mombasa, Kenya, I do not recall hearing about an obsession with return and performance. Whilst these factors were important, there seemed to be a tacit understanding that profits can fluctuate, and it was important to be careful and prudent in decision-making and not take big uncalculated or unknown risks. The focus was always on prudent effort and action, rather than measurement, reward or surplus. There was an active sharing of knowledge and information within the community through family and business networks – this probably helped the risk evaluation and monitoring. There seemed no obsession with competition as there was a feeling that there were enough rewards and opportunities for everyone. One story that kept on being repeated was how any new business from a community member was supported by advance credit in the form of stock or even loans from other members of the family or community, with no explicit contract or written terms and conditions. There was a strong sense of a collective – we were 'all in this together'.

A true story is appropriate here. Kenya was a British colony, and in the early days, the hinterland was not very developed. When Jains went 'up-country' to obtain new orders and customers, there was a question about where to stay. Hotels were never a strong part of the culture, so accommodation would be put up at short notice by other Jains living in the town, even if they were not friends or relatives. The vegetarian diet also meant that food could only be obtained from other Jain homes, so this was understood and visitors were always welcome for meals. Sometimes, they would turn up at 11pm at night after a long journey from Nairobi, and immediately the women would wake up and cook dinner for the visitors and clear a room for them – usually a stack of chapattis with some curry and rice. In this way, the local networks in the town were also shared, and references for credit or custom were given without any fee. Trust and camaraderie were enhanced through the practice of hospitality and generosity. We could now look back and say that this too was a way in which the community learned to manage and diversify its risk, although there was no calculation or expectation of return. Local information and networks are very helpful in risk management, but largely ignored in the literature of finance. It is possible that this results from cultural arrogance and ignorance, and the difficulty in developing a generic model or formula to reflect this.

The Jain perspective on risk seems to always be more qualitative than quantitative. It is more about knowledge, opportunity, awareness and monitoring. It is by nature holistic and restrained by a lack of greed or obsession with return or profit maximisation, and more in tune with ideas about organic growth and sustainability. The management of risk and its mitigation is often done through shared knowledge, experience and prudence. Trust and relationships are key to the understanding and management of risk – there is a reluctance to go into large transactions with unknown people or businesses. Working within known family and community networks is also an important way of sharing risk. There is a significant saving of legal and transactions costs when business is done through trusted relationships.

The Jain understanding of profits and returns is therefore more as a reward for good effort and sacrifice, rather than a score of personal success and accomplishment. It is not something which is deserved and detached from the wider society and earned through its uncaring exploitation and a ruthless drive for growth at any cost. There is no sense of a just or expected and calculated return, but instead a prayer is offered in thankfulness for any rewards. There is little celebration after a major growth year, and a regular mingling with people from all backgrounds, rich and poor, employees and professionals, entrepreneurs and family. Often, there is little change in the house or the car in spite of a good year, as there is little desire to show off one's wealth and success. If there is any visibility about good performance, it would appear through the donations given for a new charitable initiative. Success is recognized through acts of charity and philanthropy, rather than through the reported profits of the business or the wealth status of the business owner.

One key business gathering I vividly remember from my early childhood in Mombasa is the *Chopda Pujan* which takes place every Diwali (or Deepavali), the ancient 'festival of lights' celebrated by Indian communities in the autumn, including Hindus, Jains, Sikhs and Buddhists. This is an early morning ritual conducted by a spiritual mentor when new books of account are opened to mark the Jain (and Hindu) New Year. Prayers are recited for success and prosperity, and for greater empowerment to serve the community in every which way. Most entrepreneurs from our community would make it a point to attend this event and conduct the Pujan: the sense of collective business was very real. The goddess of wealth, Laxmi, was invoked, and people were reminded of her 'fickle and whimsical character', just like the real character of money and wealth. The goddess of wisdom and the arts, Saraswati, was also worshipped as business success is not devoid of knowledge and creativity. Ganesha, the elephant headed god, is seen as the protector of family and community, and prayers are also offered to him in this Pujan. Most importantly, the whole spirit of the event was a reminder of the role of the entrepreneur to serve the needs of society in the best way possible. The importance of social capital in achieving this was directly experienced by all those who attended – in fact, it gave a distinct feeling that risk and return were not private characteristics, but public acts undertaken for the well-being of one and all.

In contemporary finance theory and education, there are calculations about the cost of capital and expected returns which may or may not be risk-adjusted. Business performance and monitoring is demonstrated as a calculation and justified as such. Over time, the financialisation of society has led to this language becoming a religion, an obsession even. For Jain family-owned businesses, the calculations are likely to be more modest, starting initially from a desire for food, employment and shelter for the family, and then later transforming to savings and philanthropy. My father, Keshavji Rupshi Shah, migrated from India to Kisumu in Kenya at the tender age of 14, invited by his uncle to help him in his shop. Accommodation was often on the shop floor at night. In this era, calculations of return were a far cry from reality and expectations. In fact the main stock of trade was not financial but physical and moral capital – a desire to work hard and conduct honest business. Today, these fledgling businesses have grown substantially, but when and if windfalls are earned, they are understood and respected as such, and generally not used to inflate personal egos or greed. Faithful entrepreneurs would take windfalls as good fortune and not a result of personal risk-taking, skill, efforts and sacrifice. The culture and values help them to make success more palatable.

To understand how Jains apply risk and return in a global setting, it is helpful to look at the global diamond industry, where the mainly *Gujarati* and *Marvadi* Jains, are now acknowledged as world leaders and a quiet but dominant force (Lum 2014; Meena Peters 2014; Hofmeester 2013). One of the key risks in this business is of fraud – diamonds may be stolen or fake and only experts can certify – the average buyer is ignorant about the quality and value of diamonds. As they are portable, valuable and untraceable, it is impossible to enforce their quality and reliability through legal contracts. As a result, if one needs to succeed and grow in the industry, trust is crucial, as is demonstrated by a detailed case study of the role of Jewish communities in the diamond trade (Richman 2006). Jains have, in the same way, drawn upon values associated with communal endeavour and reciprocity. In this way, they have become a powerful, indeed arguably the dominant force in the current diamond industry.

The Belgian city of Antwerp is home to the global trade in polished diamonds. One of the hubs of this trade is the Antwerp World Diamond Centre. In 2012, five out of the six board members were Gujaratis (Lum 2014). When we examine the methods used in the success and growth of Jain influence in this business, it seems that there was no initial target of global dominance, merely a desire to compete fairly and provide quality and generate profits. One of the critical ingredients of this early success was the provision of short-term credit to the buyers of diamonds, who effectively became partners in the trade and both sellers and buyers grew together and their success was deeply intertwined. Family and community networks played an important role in this process, and most of the early pioneers originated from one municipality in India, *Palanpur*, and Jain *Palanpuri* families play a dominant role even today in the industry. In the early years, they concentrated on small rough diamonds, and getting them polished in India with cheap skilled labour, and thereby creating jobs and adding value.

For newly arriving Jains in Antwerp, the early years were a deep uphill struggle, but they worked hard at assimilation and provided very good and reliable service at a fair price. Families were happy to migrate to all corners of the world to build the trade and grow, and as English was a common language, they assimilated very quickly. As Lum (2014) explains, the business grew because they were polishing in rupees and selling in dollars. And the Jains managed this value chain by developing relationships (many of which were pre-existing, based on kinship ties) and keeping them, rather than taking short cuts or making excessive profits.

Migration and movement in the pursuit of business objectives also involves risk. One of the biggest risks is the lack of local knowledge, the feeling of being an outsider and the dependence on the host community for business custom and acceptance. It is often very difficult to break the barriers, and the act of doing so brings new strengths and resilience. Once again, contemporary finance theory is relatively silent on this question, and ignores the importance of cultural intelligence and assimilation altogether, despite the dual phenomena of globalisation and cultural diversity. Its focus is very operational and transactional, and so long as an investment is financially viable, it can work in any culture or country. This ignores the role of culturally specific customs, skills, people and networks in the practice of finance. In the above case, the Jains were initially seen as non-Europeans who were trying to break into a closed market and community. However, instead of threatening the local merchants, the Jains worked closely with the existing buyers of polished diamonds, starting from the bottom with small diamonds, which were not seen as a major threat. Also, the Jains have a strong win-win philosophy and approach to business, recognising that even the trade buyer needs to make a profit from the transaction. This helped them assimilate and become accepted in their chosen businesses and in wider society.

Risk, finance and trust are deeply entwined (Douglas and Wildavsky 1982; Beck 1992; Kay 2015). In the last 40 years, contemporary finance has grown in power and influence, but also been brought down by mismanagement, fraud and abuse of power through political and regulatory capture (Tett 2010;

Germain 2010; Angelides 2011; Das 2011). Research has shown that the finance academy and its research and teachings have had a direct influence on financial markets and innovation and in perpetuating the myth of free markets as the best way of regulating the industry (Mackenzie 2006). Values such as trust cannot be measured in the academic context and so instead, the focus has been on the design of efficient agency contracts and incentives which can be used to enforce outcomes without a need for trust or loyalty. In fact, agency theory often appears to start with the assumption of managerial greed and selfishness as given (Kay 2015) and tries to develop models through which these can be checked or they can be incentivised to build a profit-making enterprise in the interests of absent and irresponsible share-holder-owners. At root is a culture of greed and selfishness, backed by powerful financial markets and institutions (Luyendijk 2015; Santoro and Strauss 2013), rather than an understanding of diversity in finance cultures and ethics, and different approaches to risk, agency and returns (Graeber, 2014). Furthermore, the positivist approach of agency theory and most current academic approaches to finance seem to assume that there is no primary need for finance to be caring, responsible and accountable (Admati and Hellwig 2013). More fundamentally, the desire to create and protect a disciplinary boundary and perpetuate a notion of complexity and expertise has overwhelmed the importance of truth and objectivity (Frankfurter and McGoun 2002).

In spite of having turnover in the billions of dollars, Jain businesses in the diamond industry follow a pattern of owner-management and hence are not listed in the global stock markets. The diamond trade is primarily a self-regulated industry (Richman 2006), but one where self-regulation has worked, which is very unlike the global finance industry prior to the 2008 crash, where there was a collapse of self-regulation. Richman (2006) has demonstrated the remarkable success and effectiveness of this self-regulation in a global arena, as a case study from which there is much to learn. For self-regulation to work in an industry, each player has to have a sense of the whole, and an active desire to maintain high ethics and standards. Historical and ethical communities can do this as there is a legacy to protect, and keeping honour and saving face is highly valued – so there are few temptations to defraud or exploit. Instead what we have seen in modern banking in the absence of a trusted community is that each player has tried their level best to exploit and undermine the system to their advantage, without any concern for systemic risk or failure (Lewis 2008; 2011; Tett 2010). They are not ashamed to rely on government bailouts and to continue to exploit governments through the rigging of interest and exchange rates in their control. Through a direct focus on financial performance management and employee bonuses based on measured results, greed and selfishness have become profoundly institutionalised. Even after the crash, this fact has remained, and governments have had no luck in curbing these excesses due to their political and regulatory capture.

Risk and leverage

One of the biggest trends in modern finance has been about growth financed by debt and borrowing – the more debt the merrier, is the logic and proof (Coggan 2011). This is explained as the surest way to generate wealth and value for shareholders or equity providers, partly through the fixed nature of debt repayments, partly through the tax benefits of borrowing, and justified by the huge returns generated for owners through leverage (Ross *et al.* 2012). In actual fact, risk is often increased as a result of leverage, deliberately. The fiction of modern finance is such that debt equals wealth (Daly and Cobb 1994). The logic of this is that debt represents a fixed repayment, with surpluses going to risk-takers or equity holders, so the greater the proportion of debt in a trans-action, the higher the return on equity. The downside of course is that if the risk turns sour, then equity holders would lose their capital, but this is protected by limited liability. If risk can be managed or manipulated, there is huge opportunity for private gain at no personal cost, sacrifice or even effort.

The debt bubble of modernity combined with limited liability legislation has actually played a prominent role in the increase in risk-taking, and encouraged reckless business behaviour and growth. Whilst globalisation has opened bigger markets for products and services, it has also been accompanied by *intercultural recklessness*, where investments are made on purely financial and transactional motives, without recognising important cultural differences between countries, communities, employees and markets. Contemporary finance has been entirely culturally ignorant and illiterate, indirectly suggesting that for business and finance to grow, culture is irrelevant to the formulae of success. One of the preoccupations of large areas of finance research has been in trying to discover the magic formulae around risk, efficient markets and return which are then exported.

Jain culture and values have tended to counsel against excessive debt and borrowing. This has been for thousands of years the accepted practice and the norm, with prudence at the heart of the culture. The modern ease of access to global finance was not there in the past, and such access had to be negotiated based on relationships and reputation, rather than brand, financial markets, bribery, corruption, or size. For businesses to grow, finance often needed to be cultivated organically, thereby limiting growth, but also limiting risk and leverage, and keeping scale manageable. This is an important ingredient of sustainable enterprise. Personal credibility was a highly prized and valued asset, and in the event of failure, there was no place to hide. Bankruptcy was not seen as an option, let alone a tool of wealth creation.

The difficulty of access to finance may have also played an important role in tempering the scale of risk-taking in the past. In traditional Indian commu-nities, for example, India, there were no big financial markets for debt or equity, and no active trading of these instruments for their own sake. Debt and equity were not portable commodities, free from human relationships and accountability. The core fact remains – credibility in the past was primarily built on reputation, social networks and capital. There were no secretive hideouts such as limited liability companies which gave protection to risk-takers and their losses through corporate structures. Also there were solid culture and community structures where honour and name regulated risk-taking and hubris.

We have already seen how relationships and reputation have been very important for Jains and many other faith-based cultures throughout history, and restraints have been exercised – often, it has to be said quite harshly – through social norms and desires to protect family names and status. For to lose one's name in a community is to become an outcast, a feeling which can strip a whole family of its identity, connectivity and self-worth. This was often a price too high to pay – better not to take excessive bets and risks in the first place. Instead of a fear of default, there seemed to be a deeper fear of excessive or reckless risk, so conduct was often prudent and conservative. Communities acted as 'self-regulators' of risk and its management. In the past, such restraints were much more powerful than any form of external law or regulation. Risk management was through self-discipline and a deeper social and public conscience. For Jains, 'Trust Capital' mattered as much as Debt or Equity Capital. Sadly in today's finance textbooks, there is no mention of trust capital at all. It is as if trust does not exist or has no value. There seems to be a denial of its very nature and existence or relevance to contemporary finance theory and practice.

One of the major weaknesses of contemporary finance practice is the distancing of risk-taking from risk experience through layers of securitisation and intermediation. There is also an ignorance of 'tail risks' (Tett 2010; Das 2011). These are adverse outcomes which may not be very likely, but nevertheless, when they do occur, they can strike a heavy blow to the whole investment or enterprise. The housing bubble in North America built a huge number of these tail risks, which were by and large ignored by the gung-ho banking and securitisation industry. Everyone was joining the ride without taking account of the possible consequences (McGoun 1997) or anticipating that a series of risk-based activities could burst the economic 'bubble', as indeed happened in 2007–2008. This crash led to a tsunami of financial collapse all across the globe, and was truly gigantic in its scope and depth. Debt and leverage were major fuels for the excessive risks in the system, and the house of cards collapsed swiftly.

As contemporary finance has put more and more effort into the technical measurement and management of risk, it has led to a failure of the understanding of the fundamental essence of risk (Power 2007). Uncertainty has been structured and organised, rather than understood, accepted or even managed. Its social and cultural origins have virtually been forgotten or ignored, driven by the expert need to colonise the science of risk and to demonstrate the value of their expertise (Beck 1992). What is rarely discussed is the hidden agenda and bias underlying this myth – through sophistication and complexity, the experts can control the risk measurement and management process, and profit from it. Business schools have profited hugely from this complexity, and so too have scholars and academics. In the process, they have developed barriers to critique and entry (Frankfurter and McGoun 2002) and due to the prestige and importance of the finance discipline, managed to keep it closed and protected from the real world of inequality, pain and suffering caused by an abject failure in risk measurement and management. To openly discuss the weaknesses of assumptions, or the unknown factors about risk and uncertainty would for these experts and scientists be an admission of their failure or ignorance. As a result, there has been an 'intellectual capture' of the risk industry, and little sanction or penalty for its abuse. In the boardrooms of these financial conglomerates which collapsed, there has been a reluctant admission (post-crash) of their lack of understanding of complex financial risks (Tyrie *et al.* 2013; Angelides *et al.* 2011), and a reliance on in-house experts to evaluate and report it. However, not much conduct, character and measurement has changed in spite of the crash. In fact the LIBOR and FX frauds were committed after the crash, so the culture prevails to this day (Luyendijk 2015).

Risk management and its politics

With the increase in size and reach of global corporations, there has been a well-documented parallel increase in systems and processes for the measurement of risks, including financial risks (Power 2007). Risk professions have emerged and in financial institutions, regulatory compliance and risk management have often got armies of experts working ostensibly to monitor risk-taking and manage the 'risk appetite'. This phrase is often used for organisations to define their risk preferences, and then ensure that boundaries are not violated through active monitoring processes. The existence of capital markets increases the availability of risk capital to businesses, but also creates the potential for abuse as there is a divorce between ownership and control. Traditionally, Jains have created their own risk capital rather than relying on external sources.

From previous chapters, we have seen the Jain concept of 'wealth appetite' – where money and wealth are treated by Jains with a deeper sense of respect – not something that can be consumed or digested easily. There is a cultural and philosophical understanding about the human relationship with money, its limits and consequences, and the importance of cultivating detachment. Risk appetite is deeply connected with this understanding and not removed from it. More profoundly, the Jains have always been reluctant to delegate risk taking to others, fearing the lack of control and the scope for manipulation and exuberance.

The global market crash of 2008 was a colossal failure of risk management (Das 2011). Although some aspect of the failure may be technical – a lack of understanding of risks or inaccurate or unreliable measurements – a major reason was actually political. The size and nature of these risks can create internal tensions inside organisations, and more power was given to the conflicted risk traders and gamblers then to the controllers, and in many cases senior internal 'whistle blowers' were fired or ignored (Shah 2015a and 2015b; Peston 2008; Tett 2010; McDonald and Robinson 2009). High risks can bring significant short-term rewards, and in many cases, those very valuations and measures were conducted by the risk-takers themselves, resulting in huge bonuses for them, and a denial of underlying risk and chance of loss. Where major risk events were forced to crystallise, the tendency had been for the management to blame a 'rogue trader' rather than to accept their control failure personally.

Contemporary finance theory is also virtually silent on the politics of risk, in spite of its reality (Kay 2015; Das 2011; Roggi and Altman 2013). In fact, it denies its very existence, and covers it up with this ideology of rational organisations and objective measurement and management systems. Also where firms were to regularly practice recklessness, the ideology was that markets would self-correct, and such management or firms would go out of business very quickly. So the problem is not with the theory or models, but with their practice and implementation. As finance experts, we know a lot about risk and its consequences, and major risk events are not our fault at all, they would argue. They are very political in managing the perception of their expertise and talent, and preserving it through self-referential logics and systems. Beck (1992) foresaw this in his analysis of the risk-based society.

As Jain businesses are primarily family-owned, the active management of risk is a top priority, and poor management would have directly adverse consequences for the family. As there is no 'agency' involved in the risk-taking, or government bailouts in the event of failure, such politics is unlikely to occur. The politics that would occur would be within family structures and relationships, and it may be that certain members of a family are more risk averse than others. One issue that is arising in modernity is that large valuations of property and business investments have resulted in family conflicts over wealth distribution. Different members of a family may want to cash in on their inherited equity rather than to continue to participate in the business or draw dividends. Modernity has meant that family structures and relationships are now less stable and excess wealth can also create rifts within families and disputes about ownership and control, which at times have gone to court. The community is not immune to the disruption created by modern technology, travel and media, which has ruptured some relationships and loyalties.

There is a Jain legend about a sixteenth-century entrepreneur and multi-millionaire in Rajasthan, Bhama Shah, who was asked by his king for financial help in fighting the Moguls in India. He gave the king all his wealth at that time, which comprised 20,000 gold coins and 2.5 million rupees – for which the Maharaja Pratap Singh was overwhelmed. Bhama Shah explained to the King that his wealth was of no use to him if it could not be used to help defend the state in its hour of need. This highly risky action demonstrated a profound understanding of the relationship between risk, the citizen and the state, and the limits of private wealth. It also showed that in spite of his wealth, he understood the spirit of Aparigraha and was able to live by it. To gather profits through exploitation and state corruption were not in the psyche of most Jains. Loyalty and relationships were highly valued, and political economy was understood and respected. Politics was understood then as public duty rather than private opportunity.

Accounting for risk and return

The Jains are the largest per capita community of accountants in the world – there is at least one accountant in most families, if not more (Clayton 2016). They are therefore deeply involved in the calculation of risk and return, the profession of business finance, audit and advisory work, and the interpretation and calculation of taxation. In many parts of the world, accountants play a critical role in the growth and support of family-owned businesses, as professional advisors and consultants. Governance and stewardship are at the heart of contemporary assurance and accountability. The skills needed for these roles are not just technical, but more importantly sound ethical character and conduct are critical to good and effective stewardship (West 2003). Given the values and cultural integrity of the Jains, it would be no surprise to the reader as to why they have such a strong and enduring success in this profession. In the UK, there are many Jains who have their own accounting practices, or work for various accounting firms, and a few are partners in larger firms, including the Big 4 global accounting firms: Deloitte, PWC, EY and KPMG. Many young Jains join the Big 4 to get the training and experience, but do not survive the aggressive western profit-oriented and selfish culture, ending up leaving the firms. (I speak from experience here, as I was trained at KPMG in London in the early 1980s but saw no long-term future for myself there.) We also have many accountants either working in senior roles in industry as finance directors, or running their own business and commercial enterprises in areas such as finance, insurance, property, wholesale and a wide variety of other businesses. Through this work, they have accumulated a variety of skills and experiences.

I have met clients of Jain accountants who have expressed deep satisfaction with the levels and quality of service, and their integrity and reliability. Many small/medium businesses cannot afford to hire their own finance directors, and a good accountant can play a key role in nurturing and supporting the growth of the business, provided they are not greedy and selfish, but instead happy to help, guide and advise. One critical issue is that an accountant will get to know the entire assets and performance of their clients and how they use this information can make a difference to their advice (a fiduciary role). If for example, they become greedy and use this knowledge to exploit and even mislead their client for private gain, it could potentially destroy the business. In contrast, if the accountant uses his/her intimate knowledge of the business to objectively guide and support, the outcome may be very different, and also generate sustainable income for the accountant.

In fact, Jains occupy a variety of professions besides accounting, like medicine, dentistry, optometry, pharmacy and teaching, demonstrating that their culture and values suit them very well in professional careers. In choosing such careers, Jains are also showing that they are happy to provide quality public service, and are not always looking for high or excess returns, content with earning enough to support the family. In the case of small accounting firms, their clients primarily are owner-managed businesses, where it is easier to provide holistic advice, and also where the accountant is himself/herself an owner/manager, so they can relate to one another very well. Steeped in the science of risk and performance measurement, the Jains have managed not to lose sight of the bigger picture, and understand the limits of such measurement and any obsession with profit and wealth creation.

Given the present global crisis in corporate governance, audit, tax avoidance and accounting, having accountants whose integrity and values are deeply embedded in their culture and upbringing is a huge asset. I have known accountants who have lost clients when they were unwilling to stretch the interpretation of tax laws and help them with tax avoidance/ evasion. Mr Ashok Shah is one such example. More importantly, Jain accountants intimately understand the relationships between risk, prudence and return, and help clients not only succeed in finance, but also understand the excesses and limits of finance. They become role models and exemplars where clients directly experience their simplicity and humility, and openness and willingness to share their skills and wisdom. Rarely do they wear their Jain badge loudly – I have met clients who never knew their accountant was a Jain.

The accounting profession, like banking, does not teach ethics very well – if at all (West 2003). Its approach is technical and instrumental, rather than cultural and behavioural. Far too much reliance is placed on statements and codes of conduct, and legal compliance, then on showcasing good character and behaviour, and proactively building ethical cultures inside large organisations like global accounting firms. I know for a fact that even in the international firms where Jains are partners, their colleagues have little clue about the culture, history, heritage and integrity they bring to their craft. They would also not understand the vast social capital that lies within these communities – e.g. in the UK, Big 4 firm recruitment happens primarily at university campuses or through employment agencies. They do not go into such talented communities to recruit in a targeted and holistic way.

A mindset of sustainable risk management

The above case studies and examples show what changes when we look at risk and return in a holistic way. By studying the Jains as a living culture and community, we are able to see how our understanding of risk is actually enriched by a holistic approach and science. The context of risk and return is critical to its understanding and measurement – and when we remove it, there will be serious consequences for peoples, societies, countries and even the world. This has been our harsh human experience in the last four decades. When we look closely at Jain business and enterprise, irrespective of size and scale, the values infused and practiced by the pioneers have a significant impact on how risk is perceived, evaluated, managed and transformed into opportunity and growth. There is no magic formula or technical solution – but a way of planning, doing and operating which offers different insights into the ethics, measurement, analysis and management of risk in business and finance.

From what we have learnt so far, here is a summary of how Jains perceive and manage risk:

- An active personal investment in the understanding and methodical evaluation of risk – when risks cannot be understood, they are not undertaken.
- A lack of greed or a desire for quick profits or returns.
- Information and networks are shared freely within the community, helping to better measure and evaluate risks.
- Ownership and control are paramount, so risk is not delegated or subcontracted. There is no process of disengaging with risk.
- Leaders and managers tend to be rooted in living communities, helping them to directly observe the effects of greed and excess or poverty and exploitation.
- Debt is seen as an obligation, not an opportunity. To not repay borrowed money is seen as a deep personal failure and betrayal of the personal and community name and reputation.
- Relationships are nurtured and valued so that when there is real volatility, business or finance suppliers and customers are supported rather than neglected or bankrupted.
- Growth ambitions are restrained by an understanding of natural limits and a culture of patience and restraint.
- Charity is not seen as something to be done at the end of surplus creation, but as an ongoing activity and responsibility, checking greed and contentment.
- There is a deeper understanding of the wider stakeholders of business, and this is translated into the manner in which business is conducted and risk is undertaken and managed.
- Law and government are respected and not exploited or undermined.
- Bankruptcy is to be avoided at any cost, and there is a desire for long-term growth rather than short-term risk and success.
- Belonging to a faith and community is very critical to business progress and the management of risk. Self-regulation can be effective in building a sustainable society.

From the above, we can see that sustainable business and adaptability is a core part of the mindset and behaviour of the Jain community. Risk is seen as part of a much wider picture of self, family and community management. It is not a tool or technology which one can play with for earning excess returns, but something that entrepreneurs understand, analyse, share and manage over time. The human experience of financial risk is critical to its analysis and management.

5 Obligation and interdependency

Towards a Jain theory of organic growth

Aidan Rankin

> Desire has no end. ... In [the] vow [of limiting one's possessions] there is an attempt to control it, to limit it. Possession of land, houses, silver, gold, diverse commodities, grains, livestock and furniture is called external possession. Of the things owned by him, if a man [*sic*] keeps some for the use and enjoyment of his own self, his family and his dependents, he is not regarded as having internal possession; on the contrary, he is looked upon as their trustee. It is so because he has no attachment or delusion for them and keeps them for the benefit of others; he is like an honest keeper or care taker.
>
> Munishri Nyayavijayi, *Jaina Philosophy and Religion,* translated from Gujarati by Nagin J. Shah (1999: p.53)

The words of a twentieth century ascetic philosopher highlight two aspects of the Jain approach to economics, finance and prosperity. First, as with much of Jain doctrine, the starting point is the individual. For Munishri Nyayavijayi, spiritual discipline involves the increasing renunciation of material concerns and attachments, both the possessions themselves and the states of mind that accompany them. By contrast, the lay Jain lives 'in the world' and is necessarily involved in daily economic choices. His or her decisions and the attitudes underlying them are less clear-cut and present more of a challenge to the observer or student. As with other spiritual pathways, there is the quotidian reality of engagement with the world and the need to compromise with contrasting or sometimes directly opposing values.

In the case of Jainism, the chasm between belief and practice can seem especially hard to bridge. This is because Jain philosophy and religious practice adopt such an uncompromising position against materialism as representing transient concerns and offering dangerous delusions of grandeur. The central question is the stance adopted by the individual in his or her engagement with 'ordinary' reality, an engagement which is viewed as being ultimately 'unreal'. Yet simultaneously, for the lay man or woman, engagement in 'unreal' activities can be an instrument for positive actions leading to a more compassionate and enlightened world view. In the examples cited by Munishri Nyayavijayi above, an idea of stewardship or trusteeship replaces accumulation for its own sake. By extension, ethical business practice involves the use of possessions for the benefit of a larger community or society. To a devout Jain, involvement with the material world can seem like walking a spiritual tightrope, but when balance is achieved, it opens up a range of creative possibilities. In this culture, unlike the prevailing tendency in the West, philosophy and practice are not placed in separate compartments but continually reinforce each other. Ideas that might seem abstruse or superfluous in the context of conventional western business studies, such as the theory of karma, resonate with everyday thinking for Jains and can affect the way they organise their commercial ventures.

Economic and, for that matter, any form of social activity requires of the lay Jain a form of continuous meditation quietly integrated into everyday life to preserve a sense of proportion. This process includes accepting that, from the ethical perspective of Dharma, possessions are powerful inducements to self-delusion, self-centredness, complacency and thoughtlessness. At the same time, acquiring possessions and earning money both confer responsibilities, personal and social, that increase with the extent of the wealth accumulated. The cultural backdrop for Jain attitudes towards material possessions and business activities is a sense of the vastness of the universe and a belief in the cyclical nature of time. These intuitions have three principal effects. First, they remind the individual that the material achievements and assets of a lifetime have no ultimate significance and the only way to give them value is to use them in ways that benefit the wider community of beings. Secondly, cycles are not only cosmic but personal. Businesses, for example, can rise, fall and reinvent themselves within only a few years, both through internal decisions and external forces such as inflation, financial crisis or unprecedented economic expansion. Thirdly, it is an important component of Jain thought that any decisions made in one lifetime can have an impact on future incarnations. From this aspect of samsara springs a further awareness that decisions and actions not only affect 'you' as an individual, or even 'you' and your dependents or community of interest. Instead they have potentially powerful and often unexpected consequences for the environment (local or global) in present and future, because all life is bound together.

This mentality influences, directly and indirectly, the ways in which the householder or business person makes use of his or her property. Such influence comes into play both for short-term decision-making and the formulation of long-term strategies. In the material arena, including business planning, it is likely to involve the search for stability and consolidation, the continuity of values rather than unplanned and uncontrollable expansion or growth for growth's sake. As noted in Chapter 2, the centripetal aspect of Jain economic thinking has proven results. It is the basis for successful enterprises often operating across continents, displaying remarkable consistency and capacity to survive economic or political turbulence. However, the centripetal vision of business planning is often diametrically opposed to the conventional (and predominantly western) paradigm that favours expansion, views instability, rapid change and loss of control as sources of opportunity and does not tend to value continuity, perceiving it as an obstacle to 'progress'. The contrasting

Jain approach is based in large part on the experience of a perpetual minority seeking to preserve their interests, culture and traditions in indifferent or occasionally hostile surroundings. However it also stems from the ethical system that underscores the Jain experience. This system can influence those who have abandoned the faith tradition and those who do not consciously 'think' about Jain cosmology or envisage it in literal terms, much as Judaeo-Christian ethics and world view are likely to influence non-practising or non-believing Jews and Christians. As with these western traditions, Jain Dharma is a cultural frame of reference at least as much as it is an expression of faith.

From the person-centred ethos of consolidation, wise use of resources (including earned or inherited income) and foresight about the future emerges a view of society in which these principles are applied on a greater canvas. The social dimension to Jain Dharma is rarely explicitly proclaimed as a basic tenet of faith, partly because the Jains do not act as missionaries, preferring indirect influence and respect for equally valid alternative routes towards universal truth. Another reason, more important perhaps, is that there is a preference for practical action over blueprints and ideological positioning, which can so easily turn into rigid dogma or the form of arrogant assertion strongly linked to negative forms of karma.

The social, as opposed to purely personal, aspect of Jain doctrine is linked to the second aspect of the Jain view of economic activity highlighted by Munishri Nyayavijaya in the epigraph to this chapter. The householder or business person does not regard possessions and earnings as his or hers 'by right' to dispose of freely and without reference to others. Jain ethics, by contrast, emphasise possessions in their wider social context. Thus the owner becomes the keeper, steward or 'care taker' of possessions, which subsequently become socially significant goods rather than disposable items or objects with personal value only. The relevance of these possessions to the immediate and extended family, other dependents (for example employees), the surrounding Jain community and society (including the environment) must, each in turn, be taken into account. Accumulation or disposal of possessions has direct relevance for all these categories, and is regarded as being just as relevant to future generations. This view is in keeping with modern ecological concepts (scientific and political) and some of the most ancient views of continuity between past, present and future. At the same time, the individual's decisions about the use and disposal of possessions have a powerful bearing on his or her spiritual development. For the conduct of business or financial transactions, such ideas have far-reaching implications. They point away from a model that has become associated with unlimited expansion, with values partly or sometimes wholly subordinated to short-term economic calculation. Instead, they point towards a more co-operative way of working, with business and financial institutions rooted in the communities and environments they serve.

This chapter examines the ways in which Jain thought can contribute to an alternative model for business and the conduct of economic life, including a principle of economic growth that differs from the conventional and currently prevalent definitions. Such a model aims as far as possible to be compatible with Ahimsa, the principle of non-injury, Asteya, the avoidance of theft (the definition of which is far more extensive than this legalistic term suggests) and even Aparigraha, the disposal or renunciation of unnecessary possessions. The latter injunction would seem on first impression to be the least compatible with commercial processes, but in practice has proved to be one of the most potent instruments of business success within Jain communities around the world. The chapter explores two working examples from the Jain communities of the United Kingdom, which point towards a Jain principle of organic development. First, however, we explore in more detail the doctrinal or theoretical framework from which such practices emerge.

The paradox: material possessions, financial 'success' and the Jain view of reality

The Jain perception of reality regards material objects and possessions as *ajiva*, that is to say they are without jiva or life essence: they are in a literal sense soulless. The many-sided world view, arrived at through meditation and lived experience alike, allows the practitioner to arrive at a position known to Jains as *Samyak Darshana*. That phrase can be translated as 'correct view of reality' or 'true spiritual insight' (Jaini 2001: p.151; p.351), or as 'Right Vision or Viewpoint as one of the Three Jewels (Ratnatraya or Triratna). Samyak Darshana is a state of mind, a disposition rather than a dogmatic stance. It is based on the acknowledgement of multiple possibilities and perceptions of reality and the attempt to fuse these into a unified whole. That quality is referred to as *astikya*, which is sometimes rendered in English as 'faith' or 'belief'. It is, however, more accurately interpreted as an implicit understanding of the nature of reality, at once intuitive (deriving from meditation and prayer) and rational (based on lived experience, knowledge and personal insight). One academic whose work crosses the scholastic boundaries of India and North America describes astikya as 'affirmation' of reality, a stance giving rise to *Shraddha* or 'educated faith' (Jaini 2001: p.151), in other words intuition reaffirmed by reason and knowledge.

Reality, for Jains, is multilayered and is more easily visualised in terms of intersecting circles or spiral patterns than straight lines or joined dots. It is perceived as a series of possibilities. The 'unified whole' is therefore elusive, and so it is assumed that not every aspect of it will be grasped in its entirety and the quest for knowledge will be unending. However, according to the *Tattvartha* ('That-Which-Is') *Sutra* of Umasvati, written between the 2nd and 5th centuries CE, there are nine aspects of reality or 'things' (*tattva*), which give the practitioner a clearer perception of what is real. The tattva (or tattvas) are sometimes known as the 'Nine Reals' and consist of the following:

1   *Jiva*: life unit, soul, that which is sentient
2   *Ajiva*: inert matter, material 'things', that which lacks sentience

3   *Asrava*: influx of karma, obscuring the jiva's consciousness of itself (and blocking the individual's spiritual development)
4   *Papa*: negative or destructive karmic influence (including negative actions and thoughts, violent fanaticism, false material attachments)
5   *Punya*: positive karma (including creative and altruistic actions, benevolent or loving attachments and thoughts): punya activities are still 'karmic', because all activity is karmic, but they point the way towards eventual freedom from karmic influence
6   *Bandha*: karmic bondage, or the experience of being encased in karma and involved with material concerns
7   *Samvara*: stoppage of karmic influx (awakening consciousness)
8   *Nirjara*: breakage, shedding, falling away of karmic influence (further development of consciousness)
9   *Moksha*: liberation, release from karma, omniscience or full understanding of reality, knowledge of the true self (achieved by Jinas and Tirthankaras)

The awakening of consciousness – or discrimination between real and unreal – takes place through distancing oneself from material possessions and the concerns associated with them. Karma is perceived as a physical or quasi-physical substance composed of particles of subtle matter (see Chapter 2). Some Jains interpret this description of karma in a literal way. Many others perceive the idea of karmic particles as an elaborate allegorical interpretation of material entanglement, a 'mortal coil' of burdensome and mundane responsibilities, which block off awareness of what is real and what is important. Spiritual development is equated with the arrest or reduction of karma. Understanding that material interests and possessions are transient is one of the keys to addressing and eventually overcoming the influence of karma, thereby halting its 'inflow' and eventually reversing its effects. At the mundane level, this change of consciousness affects the way in which lay men and women view and manage their possessions, including the rewards of work, which cease to be purely personal rewards and acquire a communal or social purpose.

Material objects, including possessions, money and property are classified as ajiva or inert, lacking the essence of life. That is not the same as non-existent. Ajiva is, after all, one of the tattvas. It follows that material concerns need not be ignored or treated as if they were wholly irrelevant illusions. Even those who take ascetic vows are not ignoring ajiva, but making a conscious decision to avoid it as far as possible. Where material possessions become unreal, or part of a deluded belief system, is when they are held to be ends in themselves and become the governing principle of life. Many Jains refer to this phenomenon as *Maya*, deceit or illusion that stands in the way of Samyak Darshana (*Samyaktva*). Maya in Jainism is closely related to *Mithyatva*, false belief or false consciousness, a precursor of passions (Kasaya) or *Ekantika* (*Ekant*), the one-sided viewpoint that induces fanaticism, intolerance and blindness to other points of view.

To become dominated by material concerns is often as dangerous as it is to be taken over by a form of ideological fanaticism that arouses violent thoughts and actions. The delusions that materialism inspires make the individual focus on his or her narrowly defined interests and sometimes those of his immediate family and friends, without connecting these interests to a larger sphere of activity. However this state of mind means that the individual is further than ever from self-knowledge, having abandoned the principle of interdependency (Parasparopagraho Jivanam) in favour of instant gratification. It is not possessions, objects or money in themselves that are unreal, therefore, but the exclusive focus on them, that produces a state of unreality. Those economic activities connected with the accumulation or conservation of possessions become part of a pattern of delusion or Mithyatva when they are directed towards immediate gain without evaluating the consequences or thinking ahead. Acquisitiveness for its own sake is held to be psychologically damaging to the individual and make him or her more likely to inflict harm (himsa) through short-term thinking.

From this vantage point, it follows that those societies where acquisitiveness and short-termism prevail are most likely to be beset by social problems such as extreme inequality, environmental despoliation and the alienation of large numbers of citizens from economic and political life. Mithyatva can be a collective as much as an individual phenomenon. In the human person (or any other sentient being), all parts are 'bound together', including physical and mental processes: each individual life form is thereby a microcosm of society (the community of all beings) and the universe itself. In Jain cosmology, the universe is often depicted in a human or at least approximately human form (Gombrich 1975: pp.130–32). All parts of the *lokakasa* or 'inhabited universe' work together, their interaction making the cosmos a unified whole. The same cosmic law – the Dharma – applies on a more local scale to the Earth, where every life form has a role and each individual life is valued as unique. The idea of interconnectedness is binding on human institutions, including commercial enterprises, communities and households. Whether consciously articulated or not, this perspective has a direct bearing on the commercial activities of many lay Jains, for whom effective business is an extension of balanced household management.

Jain Dharma presents a radical critique of materialistic entanglement, both from the point of view of individual psychology (Mehta 2002) and collective well-being. In certain respects, this critique operates at a moralistic level. All of the injunctions contained in the Five Vows (Vrata) have a strongly moral orientation, requiring of the practitioner inner resolve, meditation and prayer. Yet Dharma also operates at the level of rational analysis of what is important and 'real', through the tattvas and, whether one interprets it literally or metaphorically, the way in which karmic particles attach themselves and fall away. A Jain understanding of reality neither sacralises material possessions (and by extension material accumulation) nor breezily dismisses material concerns as illusory or unreal. What is most important in the area of economic activity is the intention, which in practice determines the outcome. When the intention is shaped by Jain perspectives on the nature of reality, the approach to business management, priorities and goals diverges markedly from the 'textbook' discourse of business or financial management.

Interconnectedness, ownership and an alternative definition of growth

The concept of ajiva as applied to possessions, earnings and commercial activity engenders a different conception of ownership and management from that associated exclusively with profit and expansion. While insentient objects are 'real', in that they are not mere illusions, they do not reflect the most significant aspect of reality. Nonetheless, most activities concerned with insentient objects are both real and necessary, for lay men and women especially. Indeed they can be part of the process of spiritual development, by (for example) instilling a sense of personal, social and corporate responsibility. At the esoteric level, this involves the generation of 'positive' karma or punya. What is important is the attitude towards possessions, and – arising from that attitude – the manner in which activities concerned with material possessions are conducted.

The Jain attitude towards ownership is one of partial detachment rather than the absolute control now associated with the prevailing western-derived model. Property, including businesses, commercial profits and earned or unearned income, is essentially 'borrowed' or held on trust. Borrowing might take place over several generations, as in the ownership of a family firm, but it is still not the same as ownership in an absolute or final sense. The concept of borrowing does not necessarily lead to any legal definition, although it can sometimes be expressed and given extra strength through formal legal contracts, usually between family members. As a globally dispersed community, Jains conform to and work within a range of legal frameworks governing property, land and business ownership. They have proved themselves highly adaptable to such variations perhaps because of the capacity, induced by their faith, to be detached and dispassionate. Yet the idea of borrowing is ethical rather than legalistic, and transcends concepts and legal expressions of ownership. It is about attitudes towards that ownership and the social obligations that property investment and business ownership impart. Therefore, it derives ultimately from an understanding of the 'Nine Reals', but more immediately from the vows of Jain practice, above all non-injury, avoiding exploitation (of people, animals or natural resources), the dispersal of unnecessary acquisitions, and transparency in commercial dealings. Along with non-exploitative relationships, the latter quality may be interpreted as an aspect of Asteya: integrity, honesty and absence of theft. Anekantavada (many-sidedness), the other key doctrine, reminds the lay person engaged in commerce that other points of view are worthy of consideration and that taking account of them can in practice bring good financial yields. The ascetic ideal of total renunciation remains in the background as a reminder that there is an alternative to material goals, to which excessive attachment generates delusion.

Far from repudiating the idea of economic growth, Jain culture embraces it and many businesses have made successful and lasting contributions towards their local economies. Yet a typically Jain form of business planning aims consistently to balance that growth with consideration of a wide range of social and ecological issues. The business does not expand without reference to external forces and the expansion is followed by a period of consolidation and, where necessary contraction. Responsibilities to community and environment are not regarded either as optional extras or necessary but subordinate additions, but as integral to the operation and success of the enterprise. Jain philosophy and its practical applications are by no means unique in this sense, either in the Indian or global contexts. They are, however, particularly stringent in their demand for detachment, a sense of perspective and a long-term view, and so are a useful point of comparison and contrast with the prevailing business model. For such comparative purposes, it is also useful briefly to list the predominant characteristics of each approach to the ownership and management of commercial enterprises. For convenience, we shall describe the 'alternative' model as Jain (although similar patterns, or aspects of them, occur in other cultural contexts), while the dominant or hegemonic model is referred to as western, although it is no longer exclusive to the west or Global North.

'Jain' model

- Ownership confers responsibilities towards community, society and the natural world
- Presumption of stewardship of the business and avoidance of practices which create harm, whether to people, animals or the environment
- Emphasis on self-governance: accepting personal responsibility as owner and/or manager, including responsibility for conserving resources
- Presumption in favour of consolidating rather than expanding. Expansion can take place for pragmatic reasons (e.g. protecting a specific part of the business or to serve Jain communities in other regions of the world)
- Balance between continuity and change. Excessive conservatism leads to stagnation, whereas continuous flux and change leads to instability and loss of values
- Focus on personal relationships and community projects

'Western' model

- Ownership confers innate and inalienable rights
- Presumption of control: environmental and community concerns might be important, but they are ultimately 'add-ons' or subordinate to 'pure' commercial interests
- Emphasis on autonomy and self-reliance

- Presumption in favour of expansion and growth as inherently worthwhile Consolidation only on pragmatic grounds and viewed as an indication of 'failure'
- Change and flux valued over stability and continuity
- Focus on systems, structures and bureaucracy before personal relationships

These two summaries are accompanied by an important caveat. Many commercial enterprises in Europe and North America have strong and lasting community roots. Needless to say, this is true of businesses run by people of all ethnic and cultural origins. In no way do Jains, or Jain businesses, have any kind of monopoly on community projects or philanthropy. Other faith communities, including Christians, Jews, Muslims and Sikhs, have similar traditions which have for centuries been reflected in their commercial practices and adapted to many cultural and economic settings. What differentiates Jain culture is the profound bias towards non-materialism at every level and the role of the ascetic ideal as a constant ethical backdrop and point of comparison. The man or woman who is 'successful' in material terms looks for inspiration towards those who have renounced the quest for possessions and are, in secular environmentalist terms, attempting to reduce their ecological footprints to the barest minimum. Ascetics remind the householder, the professional and the businessperson of what is ultimately important and 'real'.

In one sense, this mental attitude consists of belief in two seemingly incompatible propositions at the same time: withdrawal from material concerns on the one hand and the pursuit of commercial interests on the other. At another level, closely associated with the theory of karma, commercial activity becomes a means of personal and social transformation, the 'self-conquest' to which both spiritual and temporal activities are directed. The social aspect of this process involves philanthropy and charitable enterprises, spreading outwards from the extended family towards local, national or sometimes global concerns. We have also noted above, but it is worth restating in this context, that the scope of the definition of 'social' encompasses far more than merely 'human'. Animal sanctuaries founded or sponsored by businesses are viewed as social enterprises in exactly the same way as philanthropic agencies directed at humans. Such insistence on equal status can be disconcerting to outsiders, but it is based on Ahimsa (non-injury) as the positive alleviation of suffering in addition to avoidance of actions that can inflict injury. It also derives from the idea of jiva – possession of the life monad or unit of consciousness – as a common factor that binds all sentient beings together and the shared journey of all jiva-endowed creatures towards eventual liberation. This is where the social overlaps with and eventually yields to the personal, for Jainism is ultimately a philosophy of personal 'salvation' attained through knowledge and understanding. In its metaphysical form, that means self-knowledge: a movement beyond all material preoccupations and ties. At the mundane level, it imposes an obligation to disperse personal power, including personal wealth and the fruits of economic success. Wise use of such resources for the benefit of others, coupled with a sense of when to stop the process of accumulating wealth is seen as part of the personal journey towards liberation. These mental processes correspond with the choice of positive or creative forms of karma (punya) followed by the cessation of karmic accumulation. The shedding of karmic material corresponds with the practice of Aparigraha: the reduction of possessions to those required for personal use.

Jain philanthropy is offered without ideological strings attached, or at least without the assumption that the beneficiaries will turn into grateful 'converts'. A pertinent example is the Veerayatan movement organised by Jain ascetic women in a region of Bihar, northern India, 'where Tirthankara Mahavira spent fourteen rainy seasons' (Shilapi, in Chapple 2002: p.166). The emphasis of this grassroots environmental movement is on planting trees and on educating rural communities in this impoverished region on how best to work with rather than against the grain of nature. The local population, which is mainly village-based, is shown in practical ways that a more harmonious relationship with the environment has beneficial effects on their health along with their economic and cultural survival. The ecology of the region becomes gradually less precarious and more yielding. Meanwhile, local people are equipped with new skills to enable them to plan as far as possible for unexpected natural events for storms, floods or droughts. The devastating effects of such episodes are exacerbated by unsympathetic human activities at local level in addition to global patterns. Veerayatan's educational projects attempt to provide a countervailing force, in which non-injury is an active source of resilience and strength:

> People are being given incentives to plant more trees. Drinking water, food, shelter, and employment facilities are being provided for the local population so that their dependence on the remaining natural resources for their livelihood is reduced. ... Villagers are taught [about] the protection of animals ... and the importance of protecting natural resources. ... The activism at Veerayatan is based on the universal principle of Tirthankara Mahavira that the sun, the air, the water and nature as a whole give of themselves silently and selflessly all the time. It would be selfish on our part if we take and do not at least return a portion of what we have taken by the time we leave the world. The mission works on this motto, given by Mahavira in ... the *Uttaradyayana Sutra* [Svetambar text]: 'Let friendship be our religion, not only in our thoughts but in our actions as well'.
>
> (Shilapi, in Chapple 2002: p.166)

A side effect of Veerayatan's work is its influence on the religious rites of many Bihari villagers in the area where the organisation operates. A form of rural Hindu practice is prevalent in the region which includes animal sacrifices as a way of propitiating or honouring deities, in particular those with close connections to extended family groups and village communities. Under Veerayatan's influence, these sacrificial rites have been widely abandoned, because they are viewed as incompatible with the new approach of working with the rest of nature in place of adopting an adversarial stance towards it. The 'new' approach is, in reality, a reinterpretation in a modern context of more ancient attitudes towards the natural world. Indian village communities of this type have a traditionally harmonious relationship with the environment, reflected in both practice and philosophy. However, pressures of population, climatic changes and consequent overuse of resources has increased anxieties about nature, making it seem more like an external adversary to be subdued rather than a rhythm of which humans are part.

In the activities of Veerayatan, there is no pressure on villagers to 'become' Jain or cease to revere cherished deities. Instead, other aspects of Hindu spirituality are brought to the fore and used as tools for a humane and eco-logical vision of development. Prominent among these values is, of course, Ahimsa, which is regarded by Jains as being one of the earliest expressions of Indic thought, predating sacrificial rites or institutions such as caste. There are parallels between this form of influence and that exerted by the Gujarati Jain scholar Shrimad Rajchandra on Mahatma Gandhi, when the latter was formulating his policy of 'nonviolent non co-operation' with the British colonial authorities in the 1930s, along with his vision of swadeshi: autonomous, eco-nomically self-sufficient village communes, based on Small and Medium-Sized Enterprises (SMEs) and co-operative ventures. The emphasis of Veerayatan's work revives the spirit of swadeshi, because one of its main objectives is to help the rural communities of Bihar survive, rather than disintegrate as others have done in response to environmental problems, diminished opportunities and the lure of the cities. This means creating the conditions where local people can start and build up businesses, preferably in areas that enable them to maintain their traditional way of life but at the same time interact with an urbanised, technology-led economy. Veerayatan exemplifies the overlap between philanthropy and the commercial sphere. Its activities have expanded across India and include the establishment of colleges of pharmacy, engineering and business administration. The organisation is founded on three pillars: '*Seva* (service to humanity), *Shuksha* (education) and *Sadhana* (spiritual development for inner peace') (Veerayatan 2015). Although the movement has at times a moralistic tone and refers to itself as a mission (language reflecting its ascetic base), the conventional missionary techniques of attempting to impose a religion or doctrine are avoided in preference to the characteristically Jain method of exercising indirect influence.

This form of philanthropy reflects the core principle of respecting alternative philosophical or cultural viewpoints, but it is based equally on experience. In India, Jains have interacted peacefully with Hindus for millennia, absorbing aspects of Hindu doctrine and adopting local customs associated with deities, festivals and rituals. In many respects, the relationship between the Jain and Hindu traditions is symbiotic rather than separate. Ahimsa is an idea strongly familiar to Hindus as well, although it is often accentuated by contact with Jains such as the ascetics of Veerayatan. Accommodation was also made with

Muslim rulers and communities, from a standpoint of mutual respect for each other's intellectual traditions. As traders and immigrants, Jains have accommodated themselves to diverse environments, cultures and political systems. They have done this by working from the roots upwards rather than attempting to impose their ideals and values on host populations, an approach that seems better suited to an increasingly pluralist – and fractious – world – than clinging to doctrinaire certainties.

For the Jain model of business development, SMEs are both the starting point and the point of return. As the business expands, it aspires towards a process of consolidation and even contraction, which often means the retention and enhancement of specialist skills and client loyalties. At its largest capacity, its point of reference is less the 'faceless' corporation and more its origins as a locally-based, community-centred and family-run enterprise. Growth is not defined primarily by size or scale, but in terms of retention of core values and their increasingly effective application. Expansion enables those values to be implemented on a larger scale, but contraction permits a return to the firm's original base. In the creative tension between expansion and contraction, commercial survival and financial acumen are highly prized, but they are viewed as a reflection of underlying values and as conferring personal and communal obligations.

An organic, cyclical form of business model has worked for Jains in disparate circumstances. It is constrained only (but crucially) in the need to avoid activities that do direct or indirect harm, whether to humans, animals and plants, or the environment that enables all these closely connected ('bound together') forms of life to survive. All actions, however apparently small, have consequences in the same way as all life forms, however apparently insignificant (in human terms) have a significant role. Therefore it is clear that there should be as little division as is practically possible between the conduct of business and an ethical system that values all forms of life, promoting non-violence as both a personal and collective goal. With reference to the jewellery trade, we have noted that Jains are involved in gemmology, valuation, sale and design in preference to the extraction of gemstones, a practice that can disturb small organisms and pollute the areas around it. The obvious (but for this no less valid) criticism is that Jains sometimes let others do their 'dirty work'. This criticism cannot be answered easily, except with the observation that it can be applied with equal effect to many ethical choices made by non-Jains. It is also surely to a large extent counterbalanced by the energy and creativity displayed by Jains in pursuing non-violent commercial activities and the emphasis their communities place on voluntary work to alleviate unintentional harm.

Jain ethics include no prejudice against trade and commerce. Nor is there any sense that commercial activities are less worthy of respect than intellectual pursuits or manual work. Because every action is regarded as karma-inducing, the value of an activity is measured almost exclusively in terms of its results. There can be constructive and creative industries, as opposed to those which merely disrupt or pollute the landscape. In the same way, some intellectual activities enrich our scientific knowledge, artistic perceptions or human compassion, while others point us towards destructive attitudes and acts. The ideologies of racial supremacy or cultural superiority are good examples of the latter, as are forms of economics that reduce human beings to a mechanistic level and regard the environment as subordinate to immediate human concerns. The lack of caste-based restriction or prejudice in Jainism opens up choices and possibilities, circumscribed only by the Five Vows and, in particular, the need to avoid or minimise harm. This helps to explain why a small Jain population such as the United Kingdom's, numbering less than 40,000, has nurtured such a varied range of commercial enterprises. The two we shall consider below could be said to lie on opposite ends of the business spectrum: vegan food and pharmaceuticals. While the former aims as far as possible at return to nature's essence, the latter seeks to adapt or improve on nature for the benefit of humans and other species.

Shambhu's: Ahimsa as enterprise

Businesses run by Jains rarely proclaim their ecological commitments loudly after the fashion of western corporations announcing their conversion to the green cause – and the previously untapped consumer demands that go with it. To do so would seem like proselytising, which Jain communities for the most part avoid. It would also be viewed an ostentatious assertion of values that are usually internalised and quietly lived out. Some businesses seek to apply principles of non-violence and ecological restraint to conventional (but non-injurious) commercial activities, as in the case of Sigma Pharmaceuticals. Others make an explicit connection between the personal values of the founders and the nature of the enterprise, selecting activities that promote and reflect Ahimsa. This trend is especially marked among young and highly educated members of the Diaspora in Europe and North America. These men and women (the latter, significantly, often assuming leadership roles in such enterprises) are responding to the impact on their lives of secularism and consumerism at one level, and on another the tendency of the majority culture to define them by ethnicity as 'Asians' – or in the case of the United Kingdom 'British Asians' – with the their specific cultural identity overlooked or obscured. Since the 1980s, organisations like Young Jains in Britain and JAINA (Jain Association of North America) in the United States and Canada have provided a vehicle for members of the new Diaspora generations to rediscover areas of their cultural inheritance that they had in many cases known little about, and then apply them to their economic and social milieu. Many members of the younger generation in the west are two steps removed from their cultural roots, being the descendants of East African Jains who left Gujarat or Rajasthan in the late nineteenth and early twentieth century. Applied to business, the revitalised values of the Young Jains can be used to find alternatives to the corporate model. More co-operative ways of working are often favoured, as are occupations that actively promote environmental conservation or animal welfare, areas traditionally associated with the charity and campaigning sectors. Yet the structure of the business generally remains that of the traditional, family-centred SME.

A case in point is the vegan catering company Shambhu's, based in London, founded by a married couple, Nishma and Mahersh Shah, both of whom are members of Young Jains. The name itself is testimony to the many-sidedness of Jain culture, for Shambhu is an ascetic aspect of Shiva, the revered Hindu deity. Shambhu's provides and publicises healthy and tasty international cuisine which aims to leave as low as possible an ecological – and karmic – footprint. As Nishma explains in a profile of herself written for the VegfestUK website:

> I am a Kenyan-born Indian, from the Jain community, and settled in the United Kingdom twenty-five years ago. In 2005, I launched Shambhu's, an award-winning vegan food business based in London. Our mission at Shambhu's is to show how great vegan food can be, and to teach how simple great vegan food is to prepare.
>
> I was lucky enough to have had a diverse cultural upbringing in Kenya, where family meals were always prepared using fresh seasonal fruit and vegetables. As such, my style of vegan cuisine tends to be a fusion of various culinary cultures, made using fresh ingredients and spices.
>
> Over the years, Shambhu's has been serving hearty home-cooked international vegan cuisine at festivals, private functions, company events and at London Vegans monthly guest speaker evenings.
>
> This year, I'm excited to have launched my new programme of vegan cookery classes in north-west London, in which I teach a range of delicious, nutritious and simple-to-make dishes covering a variety of culinary styles. I also run classes for children during school holiday periods, including a series of summer-holiday classes. … Otherwise, I regularly deliver cookery demonstrations at events in the UK and abroad.
>
> (VegfestUK 2015)

The explanation above is delivered in straightforward and accessible language, cutting through philosophical complexities but strongly reflecting the Jain world view. For example, Nishma and Mahersh find common cause with the majority culture in which they live and work, rather than asserting the 'superiority' of their values such as strict vegetarianism. In a predominantly meat-eating society such as Britain, there is still a powerful ethical undercurrent that favours vegetarianism, or at least the reduction of dependence on meat. This minority tradition has been present in Europe for millennia: references to vegetarianism occur in Homer, and certain schools of Greek philosophy such as the Pythagoreans and the followers of Empedocles followed a vegetarian diet, the former abstaining from fish and eggs as well as red meat. In the modern west, that minority tradition has undergone a significant revival and popularisation, partly because of contact with non-western ethical systems, including Buddhist and Jain thought, that express compassion for all beings. It is also inspired by greater concern for the environment and opposition to the methods of commercial agriculture, as well as more general grounds of improving human diet and health. Jains share all these objections to meat eating and aim to live out Ahimsa rather than proclaim it with simplified slogans. Veganism is the most thoroughgoing form of vegetarianism because it involves abstinence from meat, fish and poultry products, with the most fully committed vegans avoiding animal byproducts such as fur and wool (the latter practices are adopted by ascetics but not usually by lay men and women in Jain communities). The vegan diet and especially the 'alternative lifestyle' popularly associated with it have lent themselves to satire and caricature. All too often, it is identified with a dreary neo-puritanism, along with shapeless synthetic clothing and unappetising food. Shambhu's has therefore taken the vegan ideal of opposition to animal cruelty and combined it with concerns about agribusiness and ecological imbalances, linking these issues explicitly with the concepts of Careful Action, Ahimsa and concern for the welfare of animals as sentient beings with rights. It has dispensed with the drabness and 'grunge' too often linked in the public mind with western veganism, thus proving that a diet based on non-violent ethics can be life-enhancing, stylish and enjoyable. The recipes promoted by the company draw from cultural traditions including Italian, Mexican and North American along with Gujarati and other forms of Indian cookery. Nishma and Mahersh have thereby adapted and transformed an existing aspect of the majority culture and in the process increased the popularity and appeal of their products to that majority culture. In effect, they have brought veganism in from the fringe to the mainstream. Their cultural inheritance has proved to be both a potent marketing tool and a point of ethical reference. The Jain influence on Shambhu's is expressed with subtlety and discretion, but still permeates every aspect of the company. In this way, Nishma and Mahersh have made vegan cuisine attractive and raised its social profile, not least amongst other British Asian communities with vegetarian traditions, including Hindus and Sikhs. Shambhu's won recognition in 2015 through the Viva Best Vegan Catering Award and the Green Apple Award for ethical produce and production.

Another feature of Shambhu's is characteristic of many Jain-led businesses. It is a 'competitive' enterprise in the sense that it works within market-imposed disciplines, aiming for financial success and long-term continuity. Yet its aim is less to compete with similar companies and 'eliminate competition' and more to carve out a distinctive niche. Jain-founded enterprises have done this in many areas of the world, looking for gaps to fill within the local economy and establishing themselves as market leaders in these areas. Economic activity is part of the dual process of integration coupled with the retention of distinct characteristics and attitudes. There is no contradiction between these two positions because cultural distinctiveness helps an enterprise like Shambhu's to contribute to the majority culture and make a lasting impression on it. As a vegan company, Shambhu's is part of a larger western social movement offering an alternative vision of economics and the way in which human beings interact with the rest of nature. At the same time, it works within a capitalist structure, promoting a 'unique selling point' based on the cross-cultural adaptation of vegan cookery.

Nishma and Mahersh do not engage in political propaganda. Their activism takes place through education (another traditional Jain priority) living out their principles in order to exercise influence by example. Shambhu's has grown in size, range and influence since 2005. Despite its status as a market leader, the company maintains its original character as a family business. While it is actively embracing new opportunities and formulating new ideas, it does not aim to expand beyond a manageable size compatible with its aims and values. Preserving the essence of Shambhu's is therefore as important as change and growth, providing a basis of stability. Innovations are assessed against the founding principles of the company as well as their commercial viability. The balance between continuity and change characteristic of Jain philosophy finds practical expression in the workings of this young company.

Shambhu's practises Aparigraha by sponsoring 15 animal sanctuaries. Significantly, all these sanctuaries are in the United Kingdom, spread more or less evenly between regions and demonstrating the company's commitment to British civil society. Shambhu's has close personal links in particular with Hugletts Wood Farm in East Sussex, on England's south coast. Jain temples in northwest London and other areas of the country are encouraged to donate to Hugletts Wood, which is staffed by volunteers from a range of cultural backgrounds and faith traditions (Rankin 2010: p.65). Most of the volunteers are vegetarian or vegan in their diet. The sanctuary is founded on the principle of 'compassion for all life', which echoes the Jain concept of *Jiva Daya*: sympathy or identification with all sentient beings. In supporting animal sanctuaries, by financial sponsorship and promotion in their events and publications, Nishma and Mahersh Shah are adapting an Indian tradition, the Panjrapoor, to the new cultural setting, in which it is taking root and beginning to thrive.

Sigma Pharmaceuticals: preserving the balance

Sigma Pharmaceuticals PLC was founded in 1975 from a community pharmacy in Watford, just north of London, that had been established by the Shah family nine years earlier. Since then, it has become one of the largest distributors of pharmaceutical supplies and products in the United Kingdom, 'employing over 400 people, and servicing over 3000 pharmacies, 1000 hospitals and 600 dispensing doctors throughout the UK and Europe' (Sigma Pharmaceuticals 2014). Its vision is straightforward:

> The world of pharmacy is continually changing. In order to continue to thrive as a business, we must understand the trends and forces that will shape [us] in the future and move swiftly to prepare for what is to come.

In very much the same way, we want to help our customers prepare for tomorrow today with the services we provide.

(Sigma Pharmaceuticals 2014)

This clear and unadorned description of the business is reinforced by the company's mission statement: 'to continually grow (*sic*) a business where we have satisfied customers, satisfied suppliers and satisfied employees' (Sigma Pharmaceuticals 2014). These statements do not display the obvious (albeit) understated commitment to Jain principles of an ecological enterprise such as Shambhu's or an organisation like Veerayatan, part philanthropic agency, part-education and business facilitator. Sigma's founder and Managing Director Bharat Shah admits that setting up a pharmaceutical firm involved a process of 'compromise' because 'some products inevitably have animal sources and it is impossible to avoid completely anything that has been tested on animals' (B. Shah 2016). From a strict Digambar background himself, Bharat knows that some of the most devout Jains would raise objections to this practice, but he believes that members of his community should engage with the world in a practical way, taking 'what is there' and improving on it gradually by making a lasting commercial contribution. Therefore the company adopts a careful approach, constantly monitoring its stock and appraising its activities so that harm is reduced to a minimum. Bharat also views the pharmaceutical business, when operating within certain parameters, as 'ethical' because of its medical and curative dimensions. Those parameters include respect for the client, concern for the environment and a preference for products produced in conformity with Jain (and other animal welfare) ethics. Bharat regards modern Jainism as a practical philosophy of self-help and community work in which 'the original ideals are more important than the rituals'. He expresses concern that some (but by no means all) younger Diaspora Jains who are rediscovering their heritage 'put the rituals before everything else' (B. Shah 2016).

Sigma has succeeded in its field by maintaining its independence and 'staying within our means'. As Bharat explains, 'we have not got into debt and we do not want to go beyond our capacity'. Thus although the company's mission is to 'grow' and it has successfully fulfilled that objective, the growth takes place within limits and stages, with periods of decision-making and stock-taking. 'We have an annual meeting once a year of the whole family where we determine our future direction and talk through any problems we face and any changes we need or want to make' (B. Shah 2016). The firm is not 'cashing in' on its success, for Bharat and his fellow directors believe that their profits should be reinvested in the company to improve conditions for staff and efficiency for clients. Crucially, as with other Jain businesses we have considered, all the directors are from the same family, who made the transition from the Kenyan textile industry in the 1960s and 1970s: one branch of the family remains in Kenya. The Shahs arrive at decisions by consensus. 'I do not need to talk about leadership according to the standard business model', says Bharat. 'I express my views and advise and warn. Sometimes we try new things that I haven't expected and if they work we look at them again' (B. Shah 2016).

In one sense, familial control circumscribes the business by excluding external influences. Yet at another level it brings diversification as members of the family contribute their own areas of interest or expertise. Expansion into dental and veterinary products, for example, took place because 'new members of the family came on board' (B. Shah 2016). Aparigraha is also important to the family, which collectively decides what charities to support. The emphasis has been on education, health and disaster relief, with a particular bias towards Africa and India. One such charity is the Bangalore-based SHARAN (Sanctuary for Health and Reconnection to Animals and Nature), which promotes healthy forms of eating and naturopathic treatments for diabetes (now epidemic in India's emergent middle class) which avoid medicines tested on animals (see Chapter 8). As a pharmaceutical business, Sigma is inevitably involved with animal products or products tested on animals. Therefore, support for a charity like SHARAN is, from the karmic perspective, a way of cancelling out or seeking to minimise harm, as well as contributing to humane forms of research and therapy and divesting surplus funds as part of Aparigraha.

However, according to Bharat, 'the next generation increasingly wants to see an emphasis on local charities which benefit the communities in which they live, work and intend to remain' (B. Shah 2016). This shift of emphasis reflects a company, and a family, that has embedded itself in the British civil society and economy. Its practice of Aparigraha, and its emphasis on a personal rather than (in Bharat's words) a 'corporate and bureaucratic' service to its clients (many of them independent pharmacies like the Shahs' original business) depends on the family retaining control and the avoidance of expansion beyond a point where this control is sustainable.

Shambhu's Vegan Catering and Sigma Pharmaceuticals PLC occupy very different commercial arenas, but their business practices and the philosophy behind them are essentially the same. As with so much of Jain commercial activity, it is necessary to delve beneath the surface to find the distinguishing features. On the surface, they appear to fit the conventional business model, albeit in the case of Shambhu's appealing to a market that tends to be in favour of radical social and economic change. There are two critical differences from the 'textbook' business paradigm. The first of these is a sense that there are natural limits to the size of an enterprise if it is to retain its integrity. The second is that the business should not see itself as an independent actor but as enjoying a relationship of interdependence, 'bound together' with clients, customers and even rivals.

Both these principles are philosophical markers differentiating Jain businesses from the culture of competitive individualism in which they operate. They are part of what would best be described as an organic theory of commercial development, in which the structure and practices of the business take place with reference to human and environmental well-being. This is not, as a rule, publicised by Jain enterprises in the way in which many transnational corporations triumphantly announce their conversion to 'sustainability' and social justice. Such considerations are part of the foundations of the business and belief system behind it, rather than later additions which challenge and sometimes contradict its conventional activities.

In our case study of Shambhu's, we have seen that it regards its sponsorship of animal sanctuaries as integral to its commercial operations. Sigma Pharmaceuticals, meanwhile, eschews the conventional corporate model in favour of an emphasis on personal service and practical forms of charitable giving. The Jain business model is based on a series of obligations by the enterprise towards the community it serves, beginning with family and friendship networks and extending towards all members of society, human and non-human. It is understated, but no less radical for this, and its radicalism takes three closely connected forms. First, the business expands only in order to consolidate and contract. It grows organically, with an emphasis on its lasting impression or legacy instead of expansion into something unrecognisable to its founders. Whereas the dominant paradigm encourages an enterprise to be wholly centrifugal and favour continuous change, the Jain business model is favourably disposed to continuity, both of personnel and practice. Secondly, the attitude of management is one of borrowing and stewardship, in contrast to unconditional ownership and personal autonomy. The third and most radical aspect of this model is its underlying commitment to social transformation, as part of the divestment process of Aparigraha. This we shall consider in more detail in the next chapter, including the tension that can arise between control over (often substantial) resources by a family group and the process of 'letting go' which is essential to the vow of non-possessiveness.

6 Ethical investment

Social and environmental transformation and Jain business

Atul Shah

In contemporary finance theory and teaching, investment is seen primarily in monetary terms – the objective is to choose that investment which generates the greatest return or value. If and when other criteria such as social or environmental objectives are included, they are a supplement to the core financial goals, and not allowed to interfere with the overwhelming goal of wealth and value maximisation. In reality, business is a component of nature and society rather than separate from or above it (Ekins *et al.* 1992; Elkington 1999; Hawken 1994). It is an essential engine for providing necessary foods, products and services, and for creating jobs and sustaining families and communities. Somehow, this primary purpose of business has been lost in contemporary finance, and instead become overwhelmed by the desire to maximise wealth at any cost. In the process of creating the 'science' of finance, the experts have ended up separating it from culture, nature and society. Scholars have called this an 'era of financialisation' where the language and power of finance have come to overwhelm industry and enterprise (Zwan 2014). Even everyday life and survival have become primarily financial, influencing food, shelter, relationships and health arguably more than ever before.

Instead of supporting business and investment, finance is today seen as an important and direct creator of value. This is paradoxical, given that money is itself a fictional commodity with no fundamental or inherent value of its own. There is a strong bias towards investment calculation, evaluation and measurement, as if these are the only rational means of measuring progress and value.

Reflecting on the history of Jain business, the choice of trades and professions were restricted by their ethics and values – e.g. Jains refrained from the meat industry or dealing with animal products, and instead concentrated on agriculture, trading, manufacturing or professional work and services. Growth was often determined organically, rather than through external investment or finance. As an example, starting a small shop would be initially motivated by the desire to feed the family and provide a service, rather than a long-term calculation of risk, investment and return. If the business succeeded and grew, then greater professionalism might be applied to the evaluation of risk and return, and the raising of external finance. Otherwise, owners might be contented and limit growth to a scale that is more manageable for them personally.

Somehow, such changes in knowledge, expectations and investment behaviour over time are not seen as important in contemporary finance education.

Where businesses had been passed down over generations, as in traditional Jain communities, the necessary skills of investment and management would also have been nurtured within families and communities. The nuances of finance would traditionally have been learnt more through personal experience and social networks then through external training or specific professional education. Networks are an important repository of collective wisdom and experience, something which has really helped the community to grow and prosper over generations. Contemporary finance has no role for networks in the collection and evaluation of investment prospects or the building of relevant skills and experience. There is an ignorance and by implication, a denial of their very existence and importance.

Understanding the nature of investment

Sadly, the way finance is written about and taught, there are major gaps in the understanding of the fundamental nature and impact of investment, and the ingredients for its success and sustainability. The Jains have succeeded in investment without learning finance from school or a textbook, and perhaps that has been their secret formula. For most people, it is possible that the schooling of finance disempowers them from sustainable and profitable investment and instead promotes narrow self-interest.

Studying investment and understanding the nature of investment can be two very different things. Understanding the nature of investment requires a combination of lived experience, of seeing the links between risk and return, of studying intergenerational businesses and the variety of sources of information and analysis used by such businesses. Whilst a classroom can teach calculation and evaluation, it is more difficult to translate the nature of ethical investment into a textbook or lecture. There is a further bias that most business schools believe that people come to study how to grow wealth and profit through enterprise, not to critique or question business practices and investment decisions. As a result, business schools often find it difficult to teach the importance of tacit skills and knowledge, and why greed should be hampered by contentment and fairness. These are not personal value judgements, but the call of the hour if we are to build a sustainable planet.

One of the main obsessions of corporate finance theory is to ensure that managers are incentivised to act in the best interests of shareholders. Here again is a denial of the existence or importance of other stakeholders and by implication, significant power and influence is given to managers. There is an assumption that managers would be greedy and selfish, and they need to be contractually monitored and restrained such that their actions align with those desirable by shareholders. Tax avoidance and minimisation are seen as the required act of corporate businesses if they are to maximise firm value – there is no moral dimension needed in relation to taxation. As already explained, Jains have generally not gone for stock market listings of their businesses, preferring to control and manage their own businesses, and keep them manageable rather than to go for growth for growth's sake. Even businesses generating billion dollar annual revenues, such as some in the diamond industry, are kept within the family. Whilst debt and borrowings may be used to finance investments, there is a general tendency towards prudence and away from high-risk investment which may end up completely bankrupting the family name if the risk turns sour.

This assumption of managerial greed, at the heart of contemporary finance teaching and education, is deeply problematic. For one, it makes a significant cultural assumption, which is not true across different countries and communities. For example, in some cultures, managers would be very grateful to have a job, and their own ethics would encourage them to act in a responsible and trustworthy manner, and not to be overwhelmed by greed and selfishness. The other major unstated assumption this 'agency' theory makes is that most businesses, especially large ones, are stock market quoted and therefore there is a separation of ownership and control – the managers often run the show. This is not true – for example in India, there are still many very large national and international family-owned businesses. These have chosen not to be quoted in a stock market, and grown organically, because of their ethics, professionalism and reliability, and there is no desire to cash in and hand over control to what are perceived as distant and irresponsible shareholders. Furthermore, there is little attempt to teach separately the financial concerns of thousands of smaller family-owned businesses, which also have a huge impact on society through their products and services and job creation. Through conscious or unconscious bias, students of finance are told to assume that the theory of managerial greed is generic across all businesses, cultures and societies.

Purpose and culture

The late Deepchand Gardi is an example of a Jain businessman and investor who was wise and eminently successful (Vibhakar 2013), but always dressed and lived simply, and regularly gave to charity. Born to a modest family in Gujarat, he qualified as a lawyer, and then went into property investment, building a land portfolio which at one time consisted of nearly 4,000 acres of Mumbai. Mr Gardi did not engage in construction and development, simply buying and holding land, and now and again switching between different property investments. As he explained in a 2013 interview:

> Unfortunately, in this era the importance is given more to money than to humans. It is wrong. Money is the medium, not destination. If money is used wisely, the society receives good fruits from it. The same money creates troubles if it is used unwisely. When we donate money, we should not expect anything in return. Donate only for the sake of self-satisfaction.
>
> (Vibhakar 2013)

Gardi lived to the age of 99, and donated regularly to charity – I once had the good fortune to have lunch in his home in Mumbai, where he explained to me his business philosophy. He was a major community leader and highly respected – and very clear and simple in his thinking. Mr Gardi became a patron or trustee of many large Jain organisations.

Debt and borrowings never played a significant part of his investment portfolio – something which is central to modern property investment and speculation. In fact he was an investor not a speculator – Mr Gardi had an understanding of strategic locations and a faith in the future demand for property in Mumbai. If you saw him walking in the street, you would not have known that he was a billionaire – such was his humility and grace. His risk-taking in terms of land ownership was tempered by his faith in his own judgement and self-confidence in his investment analysis. Very little external finance and borrowings were used to finance his acquisitions – the business grew organically, without leverage. He adhered to the maxim of prudence and the general abhorrence of debt as a method of financing speedy growth and expansion. He was also very careful in who he transacted with, as in business, there can be many fraudsters and tricksters. This is where he used his legal skills to the maximum.

When investments are made on the basis of calculations, then it is easier for the ultimate purpose to get lost. For example, in the quest for value, the need to train and empower employees may get lost, and short-sightedness can lead to stunted growth or high staff turnover. The social and environmental damage often caused by large mergers and acquisitions (Korten 1995; Bakan 2004) is all too often underplayed in financial education as the focus is on shareholder value creation. Calculations have a way of concretising certain aspects of a business, and diminishing the value of elements which are not easily measurable or quantifiable (Ekins *et al.* 1992; Froud *et al.* 2006), but nevertheless equally important. Sustainable investment requires that purpose be clear and sustainable – hence investments are chosen on the basis of their impact on people and the environment, and the chances of them surviving over the long term.

When contemporary finance focuses on value and wealth maximisation as its core purpose, it ignores what can happen to a person after the value crystallises, say by the selling of a business to a large conglomerate. What does a person do with all this money? Do they invest in other shares and commodities, and instead of running a business, become distant speculators and investors? What happens to their real lives and relationships after liquidating an investment? What about the jobs for the extended family and their livelihoods? Here again, the tacit implication is that lazy effortless investment is the ideal – work is a hassle and not value maximising. The serious implication of such thinking is that it produces graduates who do not care about purpose and meaning, and instead focus on the quickest way to make enough to retire early in life, and do nothing.

Purposeful investment requires knowledge from a range of disciplines, and should be done with sleeves rolled up, rather than by managers or financial engineers sitting in offices and shaping clever deals which involve mergers and acquisitions, or tax arbitrage and avoidance. It requires managers to have a good understanding of the products, the markets, the logistics and technological skills required, and the culture and environment of production, sales and distribution. Such combined knowledge and understanding cannot easily be put into a formula which can be sold at a business school. It is often tacit, built on years of experience, of trusted relationships and networks, and a desire to not make rash or short-term decisions, but to stay in the business for the long term. Decisions are often taken after careful observation, listening, judgement of people and products, and do not involve excessive leaps or gambles which would bankrupt the investors. An open, holistic way of thinking is essential for investment to be purposeful and lasting.

Case study: Jain Irrigation vs. Monsanto

One hugely admired global Jain business was founded in India over a hundred years ago and is called Jain Irrigation. It is widely cited as a pioneer in agriculture, and one which has grown organically and sustainably, with a very good understanding of its products and markets. It works with farmers to help them improve their harvests by providing them with training, equipment, seeds, irrigation and finance, and then buys and markets their produce completing the full value chain. Today it is a multimillion (US) dollar business quoted in the Mumbai Stock Exchange, but still family-owned and controlled. Its slogan is 'to leave this world better than you found it'.

In essence, Jain Irrigation is a relationship-based business treating small farmers as stakeholders rather than customers or suppliers to be ripped off and exploited through its vast power and influence. Their stake may not be legalised through shares and legal contracts, but was understood and respected at a much deeper level by the founder Mr Bhavarlal Jain. He had understood the whole process of food production, distribution and sales, but not lost his respect for the land. The farmers, through the training, equipment and support obtained from Jain Irrigation, have experienced very high crop yields with highly efficient use of water via the Micro Irrigation Systems invented and supplied by the company. Through this work, Jain Irrigation has cultivated strong relationships with over 10,000 farmers, who regularly supply produce of good quality and in return get support and training from Jain Irrigation. A significant investment is made in research and development to ensure efficient land use, minimal waste and sustainable productivity and harvesting. A lot of this research is cutting edge and copied and implemented by the rest of the world. The business attracted a $60 (US) million loan from the World Bank to finance its growth and sustainable agriculture, and now has establishments or joint ventures all over the world.

In stark contrast, Monsanto, a similar business headquartered in the US, has gone for a very different investment model (Robin 2008). Its aim is to maximise profit and value by patenting its research, contractually binding its farmers to only buy seeds from itself, and then also using its power and size to determine seed and produce prices. Through patenting and strict seed enforcement, Monsanto squeezes maximum returns from its research and development – a kind of exploitative rentier practice. It is a business that is widely hated all over the world by activists and farmers alike, who find that all the risk of investment has been put onto their shoulders, and they have little freedom in their own business and feel like slaves to Monsanto. Any benefits from improvements in productivity are sucked by Monsanto through its contracts and restrictive practices. Instead of building good relationships and harmony with its farmers, Monsanto's aggressive financialisation has often destroyed their farms and livelihoods, and enslaved them in the process. Primarily, it is a finance business disguised as an agricultural enterprise. Nature – both human and environmental – is a resource to be squeezed and exploited to the maximum in pursuit of shareholder value. Many farmers have gone out of business in this way, or are pulling out of farming as they no longer feel respected or supported. Extreme finance has dehumanised them.

One of the most critical stakeholders in the farming business is land. Land may not be able to speak or demand returns for its efforts, but the truth is it is the soil which grows the produce, and the combination of water and sun which helps nurture the fruits and vegetables. The behaviour and conduct of Jain Irrigation is such that it respects nature and the interdependence of investment. Its very conduct and character is in harmony with nature. It is humble and holistic in its outlook, recognising that success comes through interdependence and partnership, not ownership and exploitation. In turn this respect is extended to farmers, who may be customers and suppliers to a big and powerful business, but are supported and nurtured rather than exploited and squeezed. The farmers are seen as partners in a joint enterprise, an ethical approach which is wholly in line with Jain values and philosophy. In contrast, Monsanto's behaviour seems to be extremely financialised, where the only important factor is profit maximisation at any cost, including a lack of respect for the land, the farmers and even perhaps the seeds and produce. All that matters is money and finance – everything else is in service to this extreme greed machine. The business is mechanistic and transactional, as opposed to human and sustainable. Whereas one business builds and nurtures social and ecological capital, the other business destroys it – there is no understanding or recognition of interdependence. The main difference between Jain Irrigation and Monsanto is the ownership, investment culture and ethics. The two busi-nesses seem to have very different 'cultural DNA', even though they operate within the same industry.

Real options arise when there are ongoing choices for investment depending on knowledge and experience. These can be modelled to support financial evaluation. Given the size and scale of their businesses, it is possible that Jains use unsophisticated methods to take investment decisions, and monitor the outcomes regularly through experience. The absence of a 'scientific' basis underlying their decision-making may mean that they lose out on certain opportunities – or it may be that they are improving their toolkit with the help of modern science and innovation. What seems clear is that they are not obsessive and hungry for growth and profit at any cost – there is a patience which is personal and profound, where important decisions are made after careful reflection and consideration, and numbers are not the only drivers. Competition is a threat, but the cultivation of relationships helps them to sustain customers due to loyalty and trust. Over time, they can respond to new competition armed with tacit knowledge within their own customer and supply chain.

Ethical humility: The acknowledgement of weaknesses and imperfections

In the last few decades, there has been a growing concern about 'ethical' investment, and there are also managed investment funds designed with specific ethical criteria to ensure that the monies invested on behalf of others follow these rules. There are a wide variety of 'ethical screens' from green investment funds, where environmental protection and sustainability are key drivers, to 'social justice' types of funds where human rights are valued and protected by the businesses in these funds. One of the challenges of such funds is that ethical criteria do encounter compromises that are made in the real world, and there are few companies which are 'perfectly' green or 'perfectly' socially responsible. In the same way, Jains are never 'perfectly' ethical, as the idea of ethical perfection is culturally subjective. Still, such investments do have some influence on the actions of companies and the ways in which management direct their finances.

Jains generally do not make any grand claims about their ethics, or the ethicality of their businesses. In fact, they also do not wear their cultural badge externally and show off their Dharma or faith – they are often very private in these matters. Even when asked, it is clear that Jains do not want to divulge more about their values or faith than is necessary. This comes partly from humility, but also from generations of experience of being a minority community trying to fit in to the wider society. Jain entrepreneurs practice their ethics through the processes of conscience and conduct, and fully accept the contradictions of modern life, and their own limitations and imperfections as humans. This may also be a reason why they do not 'show off' their faith and values.

I have often been asked questions about the Jain role in the diamond industry. Given the evidence of harsh labour conditions in diamond mining, and also the huge amount of smuggling, violence and conflict that goes on in the industry, especially across the African continent, are the Jains not ashamed to be in this business? What is their position on 'conflict diamonds'? The answer is more complex. Jains do not participate in diamond mining, and their business is based on trading and polishing – so they are not directly involved in the injustice. We have seen how their trustworthiness and social capital adds hugely to the credibility in the industry, and helps protect its integrity. Given the major recent fiascos around drugs in sport and athletics, corruption in football, fraud in banking, one may ask why it is that the diamond trade has been so little affected by financial scandal. Diamonds are complex products, whose condition and value depends on independent and objective expert analysis and evaluation. It must be because of the ethicality and self-regulation of the Jewish and Jain communities who operate in the diamond trading industry, that the polishing and sales industry has been relatively scandal free. However, the power and influence that Jains command in the diamond polishing and distribution industry could be used to influence ethical mining practices and supplier sourcing. This is an area where arguably, some Jains are violating their own ideals, as ends do not justify means. At the very least, Jains should collectively be engaging in a dialogue about how they could use their influence to help the diamond mining industry become more fair and transparent, and less corrupt.

In trying to judge the Jains by western ethical standards, there are subconscious cultural biases in the questioning and evaluation. As already explained, the Jains do not want to claim perfection in ethical character or conduct. They embrace the complexities and contradictions of life without challenging them, and for them the highest ethical standard is personal and soul-referential – am I doing something which will harm my reputation and karma? If not, I will carry on. I do not seek to prove my ethics to anyone. It is therefore not surprising that Jains do not have objective ethical screens about their products and services. Their activities may lead to pollution, or environmental unsustainability, or even social injustice in some people's eyes. They are simply doing what they know and feels right for them, and being reflective about their conduct and impact on people and planet – that is all. There are no grand management or ethical formulae, or claims to ethical perfection. In truth, ethical business is often very personal and subjective.

Furthermore, what happens if companies claim to comply with 'objective' criteria such as being environment-friendly, but their culture is such that people are evaluated solely on financial performance, and feel bullied or exploited? One definition of environment-friendly behaviour is caring for all living beings, not just clean air or clean water. Even objective criteria have their flaws, and there have been examples of companies who have fallen short of their ethical claims in other areas as well, such as using contract labour, or exploiting children (Fleming and Jones 2012). Companies have been found to deliberately use contractors to do their unethical work for them, and if they are found out, they blame the contractors or suppliers for the misdemeanours. In the case of football sponsorship, big companies were willing to continue sponsorship despite controversies. Even when there were many rumours about corruption in FIFA, major sponsors acted only after the evidence came into the open and could no longer be defended. They colluded in the corruption for a long time.

Long-termism

There have been constant claims about the short-termism of big business, and the effect this short-termism has on investment decision making, risk, and culture and management behaviour (Das 2011; Luyendijk 2015; Hawken 1994). Being family-owned, Jain businesses have often lasted for several generations, and this evidence itself proves that they must have had a long-term ethical orientation. One of the key qualities of sustainable businesses is that they understand the long term and respect future generations, and we should therefore be celebrating long-term businesses and their achievements. Sustainable investment is as much about track record as it is about promises and formulae or technological fixes. Jains have a long track record in maintaining ownership and control of their businesses, sometimes over hundreds of years, with some businesses lasting hundreds of years. One of the largest newspapers in the world, *The Times of India*, has been owned by a Jain family for over three generations. This cannot be said for most multinational corporations today.

Finance education is silent about the reality of human death and its consequences for business. In contrast, the Jains have a profound understanding of death, and through this understanding, they have transformed their whole approach to business and investment. As death is inevitable, investments need to keep future generations in mind, as otherwise they would be fruitless for the entrepreneur. With such a mindset, there is a sense of handover and passing the baton to others, ensuring the business and investment is in a good condition and therefore sustainable. This deeper engagement and understanding of death helps finance leaders to have a very different attitude and approach to investment.

Family-owned businesses have a reputation to protect, and when they belong to a community, this honour is especially relevant and important. The result of a combination of factors, including the Jain philosophy and respect for nature, is that the orientation of business tends to be long-term. The lack of external ownership and stock-market visibility gives them the opportunity not to have to report constant profits and growth, and Jain businesses tend to prefer this independence and privacy. Prudence allows them to absorb difficult or bad years, and family unity and faith help them to ride recessions without having to fire themselves.

My own community, the Halari Visa Oshwal Jains, were primarily farmers before they became merchants, and I was often reminded that this gave them a deep respect for nature, and a sense of humility towards it. The culture of farming rubbed into their own personal values and nature, helping them to understand that even when they get a bounty harvest in terms of huge profits, they did not create it all. Nature also played its part. As a result, in their early years of business success in Kenya, they shared the bounty through the building of schools, hospitals and community centres all over the country, a legacy which survives to this day. I distinctly remember a Jain entrepreneur Mr Maganlal Doshi coming to my father in Mombasa in 1950, explaining that if a temple was built in the town, he would like to pledge 51,000 shillings, a considerable sum at that time. The donation was pledged even before the project was announced! Suffice to say that the Mombasa Jain temple then came to take on historical importance in building a pioneering business community throughout Kenya. For decades, my father was the temple's unpaid chairman and CEO, working selflessly, driven by purpose and a desire to build a cohesive community. He never calculated the personal investment of his time, or the return for his efforts, or the risk to his family or career. It was a duty to be fulfilled, and an investment to be enjoyed.

Knowing and understanding the business limits to growth and scale can also help guide sustainable investment decision-making. Contemporary finance education and theory rarely considers this, and its key criterion is financial value generation – if an investment generates a positive Net Present Value, then it should be undertaken. Coming from a holistic culture, Jains evaluate all aspects of an investment project, not just the financial, and in particular are not in a hurry to grow and expand for the sake of it. I sense a measured contentment, and careful decision-making. Research has shown that large businesses can be very difficult to manage and sometimes growth creates its own new challenges which some companies fail to cope with. This problem can be particularly acute for global businesses, which need to operate cross-culturally, but often try to impose a particular operating and performance culture on differing local subsidiaries in different countries. To succeed in different environments, a new and important skill is needed – an ability to cultivate cultural intelligence and sensitivity and operate differently in different countries.

Intimate investment

Finance theory has no place for 'intimacy' in investment. This is because it is obsessed with creating an objective rational science, detached from 'ordinary' human concerns and emotions, whose findings can be universally applied. The reality of investment experience all over the world is that its success depends on many other things than good forecasting or calculation. We would like to introduce a new category called 'Intimate Investment' as a criterion for success. I have observed through my years of working with the Jain business community that their connection with the grassroots of society, combined with their social capital and tacit knowledge about customers and markets, helps them to make very good investment decisions. The combination of direct investment ownership, risk-taking, and personal responsibility and accountability with the Jain values of equality and sustainability really helps them to take win-win decisions. In addition, they evaluate all the dimensions of their investments carefully before embarking on a new project, instead of just the financial calculations. There is no rush to make decisions and 'seize' opportunities as greed is tempered by contentment and ethics.

For intimate investment decisions, the following factors need to be taken into account:

- Knowledge of the product and its market
- Operational and managerial feasibility

- Long-term success and viability
- Obtaining wider information from networks about the local market, demands and culture
- Key relationships and stakeholders who need to come together and stay together to make a successful investment
- Funding needs, availability and returns on capital
- Project risks and hedging possibilities
- An active conscience and continuing conscientiousness

As investment horizons and experiences change after the decision is taken, firms need to review their decisions and perhaps even withdraw, sell or close down failing projects or investments. Where there is an active review process, and the experiences of customers and suppliers are heard through the relationship culture, ongoing decisions are also taken holistically. Instead of losing the control and engagement with stakeholders through bureaucracy and irresponsibility, family-owned Jain businesses monitor progress and revise their actions to ensure stakeholders are not exploited.

For service-oriented businesses, a key success factor has to be their culture and behaviour. How employees and customers are treated is a key to retaining skills, developing new services, and employee motivation and performance. Where such businesses have a measurement or transactional culture, they are more likely to use financial performance metrics as a key method of evaluation, thereby reducing the quality of cohesiveness and employee morale. If on the other hand such businesses prioritise good culture and behaviour, and have a longer-term outlook where even employees are respected, then the likelihood of sustainable success is much higher. Such businesses do not just value external relationships, but genuinely see employees as key stakeholders, and build systems and processes which recognise this. In such cases, success is likely to come naturally and organically, and even last longer and be more consistent. My friend Bharat Dhanani is a major community leader and an accountant by profession who runs his own London practice – his clients only come through recommendations, and employees are happy and motivated. He effortlessly combines his business and community service, and succeeds in both.

The commercial world has the capacity to provide a range of opportunities for ethical conduct and investment. Providing needed goods and services to customers can transform their lives and opportunities. Creating jobs can help whole families obtain a livelihood. For business owners, the freedom and creativity that business can provide can be priceless, and if greed is set aside, then the joy of being useful and achieving a lasting sense of purpose can know no bounds. Successful business can generate important skills and resources for improving society and even transforming it. The values of humility and contentment can add to the satisfaction of the investor, and when running the business, they are directly in control of their actions instead of reporting to external bosses. As Jain culture emphasises self-discipline and self-control, it is suited to business ownership, and over time through family and tradition, skills of entrepreneurship and investment have been passed down the family tree.

Nurturing skills and talent

Successful investment skills can be nurtured through family ownership and management over time. When a person is moving from one business to another, their personal and skills development can depend on the whim of the bosses that they encounter. It may not be consistent, and there may even be little mentoring and support as in the contemporary world, selfishness is overwhelming and loyalties and trust are in sharp decline. In a family business, elders and more experienced family members can take an active interest in skills development and nurturing, and over time, this support can become invaluable. Instead of external investment in new products and services, attention is paid to skills development and mentoring. This is a priceless investment in potential future leaders, and can make a huge impact on the future business trajectory and its sustainability. Where such skills are not obtainable within, Jain entrepreneurs often send family members to work in other businesses to develop new skills and ideas and bring them into the organisation. They can be very open-minded and willing to challenge their own thinking and processes. I know many families who have thrived in this way, and their businesses have climbed new heights after the investment in fresh skills and technology or new systems and operating processes. One such example is my cousin Sachen Gudka who runs Rodwell Press in Kenya and has taken the business global and is now a serial entrepreneur. He trained at the London School of Economics and Price Waterhouse in London, and has combined his professional skills with relationship building and marketing to build a significant business.

Investing in skills, talent and leadership is as important as investing in technology or marketing. Big businesses talk about 'Talent Management' but often this energy and resource is focussed on those who are already skilled and are 'rising stars', rather than on expanding opportunity to everyone and recruiting from a diverse pool. Also if such investment is performance driven and financially motivated, then its processes may reduce creativity and risk-taking. There is plenty of evidence of big companies stifling innovation and talent, rather than nurturing or enabling it. Some of this is due to size and bureaucracy, some due to culture and micro-management, and some due to fears of risk-taking and systems which do not allow for failure and experimentation. Good investment depends on leadership and talent, and a proactive nurturing of this talent. It also needs to allow for experimentation and failure. In the case of family-owned businesses, the failure is contained within the business, so the risk-taker is not necessarily punished or fired, and the learning from the experience stays within the business. Good quality leadership is truly priceless, and many books on leadership say that integrity, good character, ethical conduct and selflessness are keys to lasting success. As the Jain culture is so exacting, demanding strong self-discipline, it regularly breeds leaders and talent, and allows the flourishing of this through family networks and social capital. This is how in spite of being a very small community, it has been so successful in business investment worldwide. It is very surprising therefore that contemporary finance textbooks devote so little space to the role of good leadership and skills in sustainable finance.

The value of the right leadership in terms of sound investment decision-making is also ignored by contemporary finance theory. This may be because it cannot be quantified or measured, but also because at root, finance denies the importance of character, skill and tacit knowledge without explicitly admitting it. Even when projects involve significant risks, the right leadership can help reduce and manage the risks, or even convert them into opportunities. Good leadership can make a huge difference in how project aspirations are fulfilled through motivated and empowered teams. When finance theory measures risk based on history or past experiences, or future forecasts and expectations, it loses a very key quality which is the lived and living experience of risk and its management. This is not easy to quantify or even define, but I have seen the difference it makes in decades of engagement with the Jain business community. Where project leaders have these skills, the ways in which risks are undertaken, tackled or transformed can have a huge impact on the success or failure of an investment decision. As Beck (1992) and Douglas and Wildavsky (1982) have said, risk is primarily a social phenomenon, and people and communities can transform its impact by the ways in which they engage with it and mitigate it.

Sustainable finance

Finance teaching gives a lot of attention to capital structure and dividend policy, as these may influence the value of the firm, which is a primary objective of business. The theory predicts that as debt interest has tax benefits, it is preferable to finance investment projects with debt finance. In contrast however, Jain businesses are not obsessed about their value, primarily because they are not run and managed for resale – instead the motive is to keep and build the business organically, and help grow its profitability over time so that it can be passed to future generations. Therefore the focus is on income generation, rather than value or wealth maximisation. Debt finance is undertaken and not ignored, but such finance need not come from external banks or financial institutions, but from lending within the community networks. This may be because they can get better repayment terms, or because such funding is more intimate and flexible than that of commercial banks which can be very distant and bureaucratic. Also it has been already explained that given the organic nature of Jain businesses, a lot of funding can be generated from within, and borrowing is avoided in spite of the tax benefits. Finance theory explicitly encourages tax avoidance and tax exploitation, without any concern for the wider impacts on political economy. Matters of the choice of dividend policy are irrelevant for family-owned businesses, as there are no external shareholders to worry about.

Any discussion on sustainable finance cannot exclude the role of culture, leadership and values. To do so would be to assume that ethics can be transactionalised and instrumentalised, and sustainability is a formula or technology, rather than a lived culture and philosophy. In our view, sustainability cannot be sustained without cultural and behavioural transformation at its very core. We have seen in this chapter how the Jains apply sustainable thinking to their investment decision-making. In doing so, they bring a combination of personal values, lived community experience and an active desire to protect nature and future generations. They are not correct or perfect, but through active reflexivity, the Jains have developed a way of sustaining their families and communities for thousands of years, and that experience is surely very relevant to this topic. Culture can never be a success formula which can be copied and replicated by students of business – but if openly shared, it can help others see different ways of investing and risk management, and learn from successful cultures about their inner secrets and experiences.

When corporate finance research and education ignores or suppresses culture and ethics, there is a vast damage to society, and we have already experienced this through the various corporate and banking crises which have bankrupted whole economies. Objective research and calculations have a place, but to claim that they are of overwhelming importance to good investment decision-making is to distort the truth. The limits of objectivity and calculation must be acknowledged and understood, and the ethical behaviour and conscience of academics is critical to the outcome of their research. Increasingly, philosophical and scientific analyses are applied to refute the idea that the prevailing approach to finance theory is genuinely 'objective'(Frankfurter and McGoun 2002; Daly and Cobb 1994). It has even been argued that finance academics are living in denial of their responsibility in the global financial crash through their ideology of free and efficient unregulated markets (Kay 2015: Das 2011).

Beck's questioning of expert bias in the evaluation of risk is very pertinent in finance (Beck, 1992). Research has exposed how experts are funded by financial institutions through consultancy and advisory work, and this has influenced their actions and scientific papers (Ferguson 2012). Research has also shown how the knowledge base developed in the discipline of finance has had a major influence on the creation of financial products and markets, and the spreading of the gospel of unfettered de-regulation as the best formula for success (Mackenzie 2006). This chapter has shown that academic experts on finance are hampered by their denial of culture and ethics in investment decision-making, and this must change. Furthermore, there needs to be more education around the political economy and the wider impact of finance theory and predictions on social justice, inequality and the exploitation of the state and its tax receipts and income. The obsession with greed as a driver for business is proving to be increasingly socially debilitating and divisive. The normative assumptions of finance theory should not be ignored – even if greed were to dominate investment decision-making, it is the obligation of finance academics to show a different way to help create a sustainable planet. They cannot lead us to destruction and claim that they are ethically neutral in doing so.

Organic investment

In general, Jains prefer organic investment to acquisitions or high-speed growth and expansion. For example, Jain Irrigation, one of the largest global businesses in the agriculture industry, has made only a couple of acquisitions to date. They have actively built their own science and research base, from which farmers can benefit through better seeds, fertilisation, irrigation and harvest yields. It has preferred joint ventures instead of acquisitions, like the one with Coca Cola which is a major buyer of their fruit and vegetable produce. Like the land that it irrigates, it is in no rush for growth or expansion, patiently making careful investments which it can control and monitor. Given that the Jains value intimacy in their business affairs and relationships, organic growth is in harmony with their principles and preferences. When necessary, joint ventures are preferred to outright acquisitions. There is plenty of research which exposes the problems of integration for large acquisitions, and the importance of paying attention to people and culture, especially when the acquisition is transnational. In fact, many expensive acquisitions have failed and continue to fail because of poor integration. Perhaps the Jains already know this, and being prudent and careful investors, avoid it.

Tharoor (1997) has argued that 'every Indian is a minority from birth'. This creates a natural intercultural intelligence, which helps them to integrate wherever they are and succeed and prosper (Kamdar 2007). Many of the top global companies like Google, Microsoft and Pepsico are led by Indians today. The current Dean of Harvard Business School, Professor Nitin Nohria, is of Indian heritage. There is a widespread recognition of the importance of cultural and contextual intelligence to successful global and business leadership. However, very few leaders possess it or are able to leverage it for success. For the Jains, the ways in which they became dominant players in the global diamond industry over the past half century have provided a case study in their ability to make peaceful and unceremonious use of their cultural and social capital. They are able to fit in without being very visible or hubristic. In East Africa, we integrated very well with the Africans, often giving them jobs for life, and as a result, they have become very loyal and supportive of our community. We have treated them with respect even when they have occupied lower level jobs or been less skilled. There has been a recognition that our success has depended on their hard work and sacrifice, and there are many stories where when the employees face personal or health difficulties, the bosses are there to provide immediate support. Employee trust and loyalty has been actively nurtured, not just for commercial motives, but because it has been found to be the right way to conduct business.

7 The implications of 'many-sidedness'

Aidan Rankin

Jaina logic of *anekanta* is based not on abstract intellectualism but on experience and realism leading to a non-absolutistic attitude of mind. Multiplicity and unity, definability and non-definability ... which apparently seem to be contradictory characteristics of reality are interpreted to co-exist in the same object from different points of view without any offence to logic. They seem to be contradictory of each other simply because one of them is mistaken [for] the whole truth. In fact, [the] integrity of truth consists in this very variety of its aspects, within the rational unity of an all-comprehensive ... principle.

Ramjee Singh, '*Relevance of Anekanta in Modern Times*'
(in Shah 2000: p.126)

The capacity for many-sided thinking is part of the ancient culture of the Jains. It is closely associated with Ahimsa, for the practice of non-injury arises from respect for the viewpoint of each life form. Aparigraha, one of the main themes of this study, is also linked to many-sidedness because the renunciation of unnecessary wealth is based on seeing oneself, one's achievements and possessions in a wider context. Wealth divested in this way is put to social use within Jain communities and outside them. The donors can be individuals or businesses, most of which are family-run with collective decisions being made about which charities to support. In a world where western economic hegemony is no longer by any means assured, many-sidedness is valuable because it offers a non-western approach to pluralism, tolerance and reason. It derived from values that elide with but often differ markedly from those of western liberalism. Therefore, it follows that the theory of many-sidedness should be assessed on its own terms rather than made to fit into a western straitjacket, a tendency adopted by some Indologists (for example Dundas, in Sethia 2004: pp.123–137). Equally, it is missing the point to view many-sidedness as a form of post-modern relativism, in which all ideas are equally valid and there is no inherent truth. That view, if anything, is the opposite of this Jain doctrine. Truth is held to exist and is identified with Dharma, the workings of the universe as a whole which only those who have achieved enlightenment can fully appreciate. The quest for truth must therefore be undertaken with humility, and this involves respect for those who approach it from a variety of angles.

The doctrine of many-sidedness remains mysterious to most non-Jains because it is usually studied as an abstract theory and its tenets can seem complex esoteric. It is rarely assessed in the context of everyday life, including the business affairs of Jain communities. This omission is unfortunate because the many-sided position is at once theoretical and practical. At the commercial level, it translates into flexibility and adaptation to a wide range of economic and cultural settings, an approach that has contributed to the quiet success of Jain businesses in the varied settings of the Diaspora. It has also enabled Jain culture to survive as a minority tradition in India and abroad under a range of political conditions, displaying a latitudinarian tolerance to surrounding cultures while maintaining its integrity. Many-sidedness also provides a sense of perspective, reminding us that business and financial transactions do not take place in a vacuum but have a larger context that includes the environment, society and the careful evaluation of all activities with regard to their longer-term effects.

Many-Sidedness and Careful Action

The doctrine of Anekantavada, which is also referred to widely as 'Anekant' or 'Anekanta', is arguably the most attractive and compelling feature of Jainism in the twenty-first century. With its emphasis on 'both/and' in place of 'either/or', and its acknowledgement of multiple possibilities rather than fixed certainties, Anekant can be a useful intellectual and practical tool for business activity and also contribute to the development of a distinctive commercial ethos. Its potential uses are not confined to the Jain business community, for which it exists as a prominent backdrop. They can also find universal application or at least be worthy of consideration for non-Jains. Nor are its uses confined to business in the sense of 'pure' commerce, abstracted from all other areas of human interplay. The insights of many-sidedness can equally be brought to bear on the relationship between business and society, the attempt to overcome or transcend cultural differences and even the conduct of politics. Anekantavada is a complex doctrine, rooted in abstract reasoning and speculations about the nature of the universe. Its relevance to business can be hard to understand immediately, especially for those who have been educated or conditioned to separate abstract thought from practical actions. Jain culture admits of no distinctions of this kind. To understand Anekantavada, we should view theory and practice as a continuum, instead of perceiving them as separate spheres that are rarely expected to collide.

Many studies and descriptions of Jainism (both by Jains and non-Jains) are excessively preoccupied with dietary issues or ascetic practices. This focus unwittingly creates the impression of a puritanical or otherworldly philosophy. Yet the vegetarian diet practised by Jains has a close connection with the doctrine of Anekantavada, because it is founded upon the idea that all conscious beings have their own 'naya' or point of view, the strength and validity of which in non-human animals approximates to those of human beings.

Because the doctrine of Anekantavada enjoins us to consider all viewpoints and experiences as aspects of a larger reality, it 'legitimizes considerations from non-human perspectives, enabling [human beings] to consider the effects of our actions on non-human life forms and environments' (Koller, in Chapple 2002: p.20). However, the aspect of Jain philosophy and practice most relevant to non-Jains – and most likely to acquire universal influence – is not the dietary regime but the mental attitude associated with many-sidedness.

Anekantavada is also the philosophical means by which otherworldliness and the cult of asceticism are reconciled with involvement in the material world, including or perhaps especially business and finance. Asceticism and worldliness express two parallel truths and are recognised as two aspects of the human condition and are recognised as overlapping rather than in conflict with each other. In previous chapters, we have noted that the setting of limits to a company's growth is a frequent practice among Jain businesses. From the conventional or 'western' standpoint, this is counterintuitive because growth is perceived as the *raison d'être* of any commercial enterprise. From a Jain standpoint, the growth of the firm is only one 'naya'. Other significant viewpoints include preserving the firm's ethos and expertise and retaining the links to an extended family and local community that give it character and purpose. Of equal importance is the policy of charitable giving, whereby a proportion of the company's profits are ploughed back into the community through educational or welfare (including animal welfare) projects. Growth is not seen to take place in a vacuum or to be a force that exists independently of all other considerations. Central to the Jain commercial ethos is the balancing of growth with the protection of the environment and the practices of non-violence and Careful Action. Although this is achieved with varying success by Jain enterprises, as they are themselves the first to admit, it remains a goal against which other achievements are critically evaluated and establishes a clear framework for business practice.

Moreover, there is a recognition that personal and ethical priorities change, that different 'modes' or aspects of reality assume greater importance at different stages of life. In the case of an individual, priority can shift from education to career, or sometimes from career to family commitments. Over a lifetime, or during the progress of a career, there can be a shift of emphasis from material concerns (including immediate provision for family and community) towards divestment of material possessions through Aparigraha. A comparable process can as easily occur with a business, as the emphasis shifts from mere survival to expansion to consolidation. The latter includes the retention of the firm's distinctive identity and the use of its resources for social benefit, a form of collective Aparigraha.

At personal and corporate levels, these shifts of emphasis do not represent a change of values. The responsibilities of the householder and the businessman or woman, the lay Jain as opposed to the ascetic, are viewed as evolving with age, experience and accumulation of knowledge or resources. Individual circumstances – and the fortunes of a business – also compel different forms of behaviour, as long as violent actions or exploitative relationships are avoided. The accumulation of resources and the practice of Aparigraha turn out to be fully compatible, because in Jain ethics Aparigraha is one of the main aims, indeed arguably the most important aim, of the processes associated with wealth accumulation. Commercial activity is perceived in cyclical terms, with small-scale origins followed by growth and then return to first principles (see Chapter 5). An ability to set limits to growth is seen as a measure of success, as opposed to uncontrolled expansionism and consequent loss of identity.

The personal 'journey' from student to householder to charitable donor and the commercial 'journey' from expansion to return to point of origin have important parallels with the Jain view of the universe as a series of repetitive cycles, progressive and regressive. By the same reasoning, the continuous reincarnation of each individual jiva through various stages of material and intellectual evolution is also cyclical, because the ultimate goal of liberation and enlightenment is also perceived as a return to the point of origin. Constant, and yet continuously changing, the lokakasa ('inhabited universe') is composed of multiple aspects of reality. Many of these on first appearance seem to be in conflict or cancel each other out. However, they are all parts of a larger, overarching truth. For the practising Jain, all areas of life are influenced by the awareness that 'reality' has multiple forms and that there are many aspects of 'truth'. The ascetic, who renounces all possessions, and the materially successful businessman or woman represent different permutations of the truth. The creative interplay between these two aspects of the Jain way of life is a practical expression of the doctrine of many-sidedness, by which differing priorities and points of view are reconciled or coexist as part of a unified whole. Perceiving and recognising that underlying unity is equated with enlightenment, the pursuit of which takes place (in familiar western terms) simultaneously at spiritual and scientific levels.

There are several English translations for the term Anekantavada (hereafter Anekant, a popular abbreviation). 'Many-sidedness' is, perhaps, the most frequent because it expresses the positive and inclusive aspects of the doctrine. 'Non-absolutism' is also used, although this rendering is undermined by the fact that Jains frequently appear 'dogmatic about non-dogmatism' (Matilal, in Shah 2000: p.16). Many-sidedness is the definition favoured here, since it is the one most readily applicable to economic and political activity, despite having potentially radical implications for both. That said, a more accurate rendering might be the cumbersome 'non-one-sidedness'. The doctrine requires the conscious avoidance of one-sided or doctrinaire positions, rather than the mere acceptance of all possible aspects of the truth, which could be caricatured as blasé indifference. Anekant is a form of mental investigation, a weighing up of possibilities, but it also takes into account the limitations of human (and all other) knowledge. Our understanding of the world comes through 'holes' in a 'veil of ignorance' (Tatia, in Chapple 2002: pp.9–10) and the knowledge we acquire is held in check by an awareness of how much we (individually and collectively) have still to learn about the way the universe works – and about ourselves:

> Ordinary, non-omniscient knowledge claims are always limited by the particular standpoint on which they are based. Consequently, claims from one perspective must always be balanced and complemented by claims from other perspectives.
>
> (Koller, in Chapple 2002: p.20)

Knowledge is acquired through rational thought, experiment and intuition. The intuitive aspect complements and reinforces the more abstract and rational framework of knowledge. No western-style dichotomy between rational and intuitive forms of thought is acknowledged, any more than there is seen to be a division between the scientific and religious (or more accurately Dharmic) spheres. This approach also helps us to understand the way in which highly abstract and speculative elements in Jain thought suddenly give way to practical considerations for how the lay man and woman should live in the world. The sense of a division between abstract and practical reasoning is also largely absent from Jain thinking, as is the idea that one is a 'higher' or 'lower' form of thought than the other. Thus a seemingly abstruse theory translates into daily life and also becomes relevant to the choices and judgements of businesspeople and policy-makers.

The practice of Careful Action (irya-samiti), examined in Chapter 2, is codified as part of a series of guidelines for the ways in which ascetics should move from one location to another. However it is also an integral part of the daily lives of lay Jains and is expected to form part of each decision they make. Careful Action is an extension of the vow of Ahimsa. It requires the practitioner to avoid or reduce to minimum any actions which cause harm to other living beings, and to plan ahead consciously to avoid actions that cause harm. There is no clear division between thought and action. From the standpoint of karmic accumulation, thoughts are a form of action: they are inner activities which, like outward activities generate positive or negative forms of karma. Thoughts also translate themselves into actions. Racial prejudices, for example, find ready expression in discriminatory or overtly violent acts, while creative thought inspires works of art or lead to scientific breakthroughs. Careful Action involves an emphasis on long-term thinking, not dissimilar to the Seventh Generation Principle adopted by some Native North American peoples, whereby decisions are evaluated by their possible effect on distant descendants (Rankin 2010: p.133). In an address to the United Nations General Assembly in 1992, Oren Lyons, a chief of the Haudenosaunee (Iroquois) Nation expresses the concept in terms that echo almost precisely the injunction of irya-samiti. His words refer explicitly to careful movement and the ecological consequences of each action:

> We say that the faces of coming generations are looking up from the earth. So when you put your feet down, you put them down very

carefully – because there are generations coming one after the other. If you think in these terms, then you'll walk a lot more carefully [and] be more respectful of this earth.

(Rankin 2010: p.133)

We have seen that a similar thought process informs the practice of Aparigraha, and hence the way in which Jain businesses are often organised. Instead of viewing the commercial activity as an independent 'end in itself', it is viewed as part of a network of connections, initially familial and communal, but encompassing the rest of humanity and, ultimately, the potential effects on the environment and future generations. Careful Action extends to financial transactions. These are viewed as transient and as means to a limited end, but the ways in which they are conducted either reduce or increase himsa (harm) and so must be addressed with care and subtlety. Because the business is not viewed as an isolated unit, as tends to be the case with the conventional western model, its need for growth is seen as one 'viewpoint' among many. The results of that growth can include economic security, personal and familial wealth and wider social benefits, including charitable giving and philanthropic (or animal welfare) projects. All these, in their own ways, are considered to be valuable aspects of lay Jain life. However each of them generates forms of attachment that, from a religious point of view, obscure understanding of reality and, from a secular or worldly viewpoint, induce artificial certainties or inflexible patterns of behaviour that work against creativity and dynamism. The expansion of a business, for example, can lead to increased bureaucracy, impersonal relationships between the business and its clients (as well as within the company's own structure) and a loss of the original ethos and values. Even the charitable or philanthropic outgrowths of commercial activity – although among the most important aspects of Aparigraha – can become self-serving, when the original intentions of the charitable endeavours are forgotten or become inflexible and fail to evolve. These factors, as well as the environmental and social impacts of the company's overall activities, are viewpoints that need to be taken into account and have more significance over time than the temporary need to expand. Expansion therefore yields to consolidation and eventual divestment of wealth so that the business can retain its original ethos and the cycle of growth, consolidation and divestment can start again with the next generation. This circular process of renewal takes into account the interests of future generations as well as the need to 'walk carefully', avoid unnecessary harm and unsustainable attachments.

Jainism is not an earth-centred philosophy, because its ultimate goal is transcendence or escape from the constraints of the body and the material world. Yet it shares with indigenous traditions such as that of the Haudenosaunee an intuitive sense that 'everything is alive', including plants, microorganisms and inanimate structures such as rocks, which contain traces of life or are descended from living matter. This sensibility is retained from Jainism's ancient, pre-literate roots. The scholarly and scientific traditions that later emerged have not supplanted or obliterated the intuitive sense of 'binding together', but instead have reinforced them. Possession of jiva, the life force or unit of life, is an experience that binds together species that have little apparently in common and might be mutually hostile. This poetic insight is the basis for layers of scientific investigation and the hierarchical conception of life distinctive to Jainism, whereby species have numbers and qualities of 'senses' corresponding to their supposed levels of intellectual and ethical development. The more evolved a species or individual being, the more obligations are expected, especially those associated with acting carefully. The idea of Anekant, as an acknowledgement and negotiation of 'multiple viewpoints', intersects with the practices of irya-samiti and Ahimsa. One of the main reasons why Careful Action and non-injury are so important is that each being has its viewpoint, which can be interpreted as its place within the 'ecosystem' or more positively, its point of view and way of looking at the world. With the loss of an animal or plant species through the destruction of its habitat, a potential area of knowledge is lost. Acting with care means recognising the importance of every 'naya', each point of view, including but not confined to fellow humans. The second century CE ascetic and scholar Umasvati expresses the idea in these terms:

> Each soul has its own view of the world, which differs from the view of other souls. No view is perfect, although each has its own utility. Thus the world is not as it seems to be, and therefore it is not untrue to think that, if we shut our eyes, the objects we had been seeing do not remain as they appeared to us.
>
> (Tatia 1994: p.10)

A modern Jain translator of Umasvati's *Tattvartha Sutra* and other sacred texts, Nathmal Tatia makes clear that it is each individual being, as well as each species, that has 'its own view of the world'. Loss of biodiversity is part of the loss of knowledge and understanding brought about by careless actions. Such actions are usually associated with short-term economic expansion without consideration of consequences for the immediate and more distant future. The reduction in the number of Amazonian plant species can mean that opportunities for increased medical knowledge are also lost. The corresponding cultural loss of indigenous knowledge or 'plant wisdom' can mean that local knowledge which could have universal significance is allowed to fade into obscurity (see, for example, Beyer 2009; Dobkin de Rios 1992). Many-sidedness takes as its first premise that 'no view is perfect', and much is unknown to 'ordinary' man and women, however well-educated or outwardly successful they might be. From this starting point, it follows that no potential channels of knowledge should be wilfully blocked.

Although Anekant is often interpreted as a system of 'relative pluralism', it does not adopt a relativistic attitude towards truth, which is considered as absolute if ungraspable. Therefore the doctrine of many-sidedness does not slot neatly into the New Age eclecticism of spiritual entrepreneurs. It is concerned with the rigorous evaluation and testing of all areas of knowledge rather than picking and mixing those that seem most attractive or convenient. The confusion with relativism arises from the apparent tolerance that Jains show towards other religious or cultural traditions and philosophical standpoints. Thus, although Jain Dharma is specifically nontheistic, for there is no *Ishvara*, the personal god, Supreme Being or creative deity of many schools of Hinduism, Jains in India participate in ceremonies and festivals in honour of local Hindu gods and goddesses and that some deities are highly esteemed in Jain culture (Jain 1998). Saraswati (or Sarasvati), the goddess associated with learning, the search for self-knowledge and the benevolent healing power of water is revered by Jains as much as Hindus (von Glasenapp 1999 [1925]: p. 50).

Reverence for deities might seem contradictory for a nontheistic religion. However it is part of the reasoning process of Anekant, because each deity denotes a facet of the truth. In this way, a niche is carved out for deities in the Jain universe, as aspects of reality rather than glimpses of the ultimate creative power. They can also be perceived as symbolic representations of an aspect of reality, such as a force within nature (for example water, trees or weather conditions), a concept or emotion (knowledge, love), an activity or practice (commerce, law or teaching). Reverence, even worship, need not imply literal belief and is unlikely to mean more than respectful acknowledgement of a partial truth. This conception of deities helps the western reader to understand an otherwise puzzling summary of the ecological aspects of the *Adipurana* by Sadhvi Shilapi, a female ascetic. Sadhvi Shilapi combines asceticism with social activism and is Director of Education for the environmental NGO Veerayatan in Bihar (see Chapter 5). Veerayatan has diverse interests today, but its original concern was the planting of trees and the preservation of forests, which it identifies as critical to the survival of local communities and businesses, as well as the overall ecology of the region. The *Adipurana* is a ninth-century CE text in honour of Rishava, the first Tirthankara, who in the spirit of many-sidedness is also an aspect of Shiva (see Chapter 2):

> The text emphasizes that forests moderate the climate, check thunderstorms and floods, protect the neighbouring areas from cold winds, and enable the constant flow of rivers. ... The *Adipurana* says that forests are like saints, or *munis*, who, overcoming all obstacles, create a better welfare for all. ... As in the relationship between bride and bridegroom, it is the duty of all of us to protect and preserve the forest. To live a peaceful life and earn positive karma, the *Adipurana* suggests the planting of a tree. It is said that one who plants a tree remains steadfastly close to God.
>
> (Shilapi, in Chapple 2002: p.162)

The essay by Sadhvi Shilapi cited above was adapted from a lecture to a predominantly western audience. It follows that the ascetic's use of 'God' stems from a desire to use theological language with which that audience would be familiar. Furthermore, Jain thought and practice has not developed in a vacuum, but has interacted with surrounding cultures and belief systems. For example, the Hindu practices of devotion (*bhakti*) have influenced Jains from the seventh century CE onwards, as have encounters with Islam and western ideologies, religious and political. The form of social activism in which Sadhvi Shilapi and her colleagues are involved resembles in some ways the actions of Christian religious orders. Since even devout Jains recognise other religious and philosophical concepts as worthy of consideration, they have no necessary reason to object to the use of 'God' as a synonym for the universal order, Dharma or ultimate truth that is unknowable in its entirety.

Veerayatan itself is officially a non-sectarian organisation, although its values are informed by the 'teachings of Mahavira' (namely Jain doctrines) and an activist interpretation of Ahimsa. Its environmental work has broadened into educational projects to provide sustainable careers for young men and women, lifting them out of poverty. For this, the organisation has received financial support from the New York-based Diamond Empowerment Fund (DEF), specifically for its Colleges of Pharmacy, Engineering and Business Administration. Founded in 2007, the DEF's stated mission is to 'support initiatives that empower people in diamond communities worldwide' (DEF 2016). DEF's support network includes 'global partners' such as De Beers, Rio Tinto, Hong Kong-based Chow Tai Fook and Mumbai-based Asian Star. We have referred above to the close connections between Jain culture and the jewellery trade, including diamond production and the way in which it combines traditional forms of apprenticeship with modern technology and production methods. Veerayatan is influenced by Anekant in that it recognises no barrier between business and commerce and charitable programmes or environmental education. These activities intersect and complement each other. The emphasis of the organisation's charitable and ecological work is on individual self-reliance and collective maintenance of the local environment, values associated with the Jain business community. Similarly, the establishment of successful businesses with strong local roots is viewed as one of the most effective ways of conserving local environments and lifting communities out of poverty without inflicting instability or imposing unsuitable changes from outside.

The journey of an organisation or social movement like Veerayatan from environmental NGO to provider of education in commercial activities is, in itself, an example of Anekant translated into practical activity. Environmental concerns are about more than the protection of forests and habitats. While these are of paramount importance, they are closely connected to questions of social equity. Poverty and the lack of opportunity it causes are ecological issues, because they create a deprived and polluted environment and make ecological responsibility difficult or impossible. Liberation from poverty encourages behaviour based on non-violence towards the environment, and the longer-term planning required for Aparigraha. This holistic concept of ecological conservation differs from 'niche' environmentalism, revolving around narrowly focussed campaigns that deny or overlook connections with other areas of life, including the values of the surrounding society. Equally, it differs from much of green politics in Europe and North America, where the critique of neo-liberal ideology and the workings of modern capitalism has led to a more generalised opposition to commercial activity. The Anekant-based approach that has guided Veerayatan's development is at once 'pro-business' and in favour of increasingly self-sufficient village communities on the Gandhian model. It does not perceive that there is a necessary or inherent contradiction between ecological goals and promoting skills associated with industry and finance. Instead, it recognises the value of wealth creation, which gives families and communities the freedom to make responsible choices. Simultaneously, this model recognises the need to live within ecological limits, because of the intrinsic value of the environment and because pluralism extends to other species and organisms.

In this stance, we can see that the divisions that characterise the prevailing modes of academic discourse do not influence the underlying world view of the Jains. The western paradigm tends to favour compartmentalising interests such as business and environmental campaigns, sustainable living and wealth creation, so that reconciling them requires painstaking and by no means universally successful negotiation. The many-sided approach begins from a position that there is common ground between these interests, that they are shared and overlapping rather than disparate or opposed. In practice, Anekant is about blurring and eliding divisions. This can easily be mistaken for a generalised, latitudinarian tolerance or the 'fuzzy logic' beloved of some New Age movements. But this is a misleading impression because Jains view their acceptance of multiple facets of reality as an indication of intellectual rigour and a scientific approach, even where the limitations of current scientific thinking are revealed. Many-sided logic suggests that it is more rigorous to arrive at a conclusion of not-knowing or only half-knowing than to adopt a position of intellectual certainty deriving from only partial knowledge In Umasvati's words:

> There is no viewpoint that is perfect and there is no science that is complete. ... [All] philosophies are imperfect although they are the glorious blocks that build the grand edifice of philosophy. ... And as there can be reality that science does not encompass, so there can be problems that are not solved by philosophy which is an endless quest.
>
> (Tatia 1994: p.139)

The scriptural language above is reflected in the lives of practising Jains through a process that can be likened to meditation. Actions are evaluated against possible consequences and the mind is cleared of preconceptions and prejudices, for these lead to negative actions and negative karma. The intention behind an action becomes at least as important as the action itself, for it frequently determines the outcome. While not all Jains engage in this type of mental exercise, and few other than ascetics would claim to do so consistently, it is a strong cultural influence, affecting attitudes towards business and other social activities. The state of equanimity or 'non-violence of the mind' (Rankin 2006: pp. 159–193) produced by Anekant seems, at first glance, to militate against or at least neutralise the entrepreneurial impulse. Yet a sense of multiple possibilities points in the opposite direction, towards innovation, variety and a simultaneous awareness that commercial activity exists in a social context.

Outside of Jain communities, Anekant remains a little known and under-researched doctrine. It is therefore largely untested as a way of working and problem-solving. Yet its flexibility and quest for underlying unity equip it for an increasingly globally-based business community where borders are routinely transcended but cultural sensitivities are higher than ever. Before exploring possible areas in which Anekant interacts with and can influence commercial ethics, it is worth briefly examining the basis of this philosophical system, which offers us a significant non-western approach to pluralism.

The philosophical basis of Anekant

Many-sidedness is a sensibility, that is to say an attitude of mind or frame of reference that can guide daily decision-making. In this sense, it is rooted in 'experience and realism' (Singh, in Shah (ed.) 2000: p.126). The origins of Anekant are also found in complex intellectual speculations which have little apparent relevance to the lives of most Jain householders and the way the economy is organised. In the same way as the highly abstract theory of karmic accumulation translates into the practice of Aparigraha and underlies the culture of philanthropy, a subtle and multilayered discourse on the nature of reality has given rise to a culture of tolerance. Such 'tolerance', far from implying easy compromise between competing or hostile ideas, involves acceptance that alternative views deserve critical evaluation and ideas should triumph because of their intellectual worth and practical use rather than be imposed by force.

The second proposition can seem hopelessly utopian when looked at through the lens of history, or viewed in our present time of accentuated cultural conflict as a byproduct of globalisation. In the commercial sphere, where business concepts are constantly tested against each other, it acquires practical relevance. It has a similar relevance for the processes associated with scientific experiment. However, one of the strongest elements of the Jain culture of tolerance has always been survival as a minority population surrounded by numerically strong and well-armed rival ideologies. This is an important reason why so many key Jain ideas have remained untried in the outer world, and why Jain communities can appear introspective or sometimes unwilling to reveal their beliefs and insights. Minority status, in the Diaspora even more than India, has combined with an underlying philosophical position of equanimity to bring a degree of humility to the way questions of faith are addressed.

Anekant is an inclusive doctrine of 'both/and' in place of 'either/or'. It is also a doctrine of 'perhaps' and 'maybe', a process of perpetual questioning and qualification in place of assertions of certainty. What is invisible is at least as important as what can be grasped and perceived. Proponents of Anekant admit of an infinite variety of possibilities, but simultaneously emphasise the limits of human knowledge, and hence the amount that we do not – and probably cannot – know.

Anekant as a concept arose out of an attempt by ascetics and scholars to define and explain the nature of reality, whether visible or invisible, finite or eternal. The result of these speculations was a 'denial of absolute existence or absolute non-existence, absolute permanence or absolute impermanence' (Tatia 1994: pp.134–140). In other words, existence is neither a continuous state of flux nor a state of rigid immutability. It is changing all the time, and these changes involved perpetual progress and regression, expansion and contraction, decay and renewal. This process of change is balanced by a continuity that is equally important. An object or a person changes with age and surrounding conditions, but retains a fixed identity. The universe does the same, constantly evolving but retaining its innate characteristics.

This view of reality corresponds with the cyclical view of time and the idea of the universe as passing through long forward and reverse cycles lasting for aeons. Moreover that which is 'real' (tattva) has two aspects, the eternal and the non-eternal or transient. It is permanent 'with respect to its essential substance and impermanent with respect to [the] modes [of existence] through which it is ceaselessly passing' (Tatia 1994: pp.134–140). One 'mode' – one phase or aspect of existence – may also 'be grasped at the expense of others': the 'grasped mode' is 'brought to light' while other attributes remain in the background (Tatia 1994: pp.134–140). Here we can draw partial parallels with more familiar forms of dualism, such as the polarities of Yin and Yang in Daoist and other classical Chinese thought, but in the Jain interpretation there is not necessarily creative tension, merely coexistence. Nor are there only two aspects, one of which is seen and the other hidden, but multiple aspects with different degrees of visibility and invisibility, these aspects continuously manifesting or concealing themselves according to circumstance and context. This is why the reasoning process of Anekant is popularly likened to the experience of light reflected in a cut diamond from a multiplicity of angles. In homage to this analogy, there is even a company in Jaipur called Anekant Diamond Products. Existence is composed of 'origination, cessation and persistence' (Tatia 1994: pp.134–140). This definition mirrors the business model founded on expansion, consolidation and return to point of origin, and Aparigraha as the transformation of wealth into social capital.

The process of reinvention is eternal, in that although individuals and objects perish, every aspect of the inhabited universe is recycled and emerges in a new form, including the cosmos itself when it enters a new cycle. The future is 'endless' and the past 'beginningless', but nothing within that framework remains static. The 'non-omniscient person' cannot 'perceive the existent in its reality':

> At a single moment he can be aware either of the persisting unity (*ekatva*) of the substance [or object, person, animal, plant, etc.] and the transient multiplicity (*anekatva*) of its modes.
>
> (Jaini 2001: pp.90–91)

It would be easy to mistake this scientific approach, which admits of many possible answers to questions of existence, with a form of scepticism that accepts all modes of thought as equally valid. In fact, *Ajnanavada* or scepticism is rejected by the *Sutrakrita*, the second *Anga* (Limb) of the Jain canon (also called the *Sutrakritanga*), as one of the paths 'opposed to the Jina'. The other paths, which are described in unequivocal terms as 'wrong' or 'false', include *Nijativada* (fatalism), *Akriyavada* (non-action), *Samkhya* (eternalism) and Charvaka (annihilationism: the idea that there is 'nothing beyond the senses' and only material beings and objects exist). All of these are versions of *ekanta-vada*, one-sidedness, and are 'thus inferior to the comprehensive (*anekanta*) Jaina view of reality (Jaini 2001: p. 53). The *Stotras*, a series of poetic hymns to the Jinas, also criticise 'ekantavadins' who 'hold absolutist doctrines' and are therefore opposed to the 'doctrine of manifold aspects' (Jaini 2001: pp. 85–86).

As with so many aspects of Jain Dharma, there is an internal logic behind this apparent contradiction between acceptance of ideas and the rejection of competing doctrines as 'false'. For the falsity is held to arise from incompleteness or the refusal to acknowledge other facets of reality. A fatalistic position fails to take into account the importance of individual (and for that matter collective) action. At the social level, it generates apathy and works against education, enterprise and constructive reform. Open-ended scepticism is held to undermine the sense that there are absolute truths such as the centrality of Ahimsa. Non-action might be an ultimate goal of transcendence, but for the 'non-omniscient' person it blocks the quest for knowledge and prevents the accretion of positive karmas. In this respect, it is the opposite of Careful Action. The quest for knowledge is a search for completeness, the attempt to put together a universal jigsaw, when many of the pieces are missing or hidden from view. These missing pieces compel an element of doubt, a logic built on possibility and conditionality. From the premise of partial or at best highly qualified definition arises the system known as *Syadvada*. The word *syat* literally means 'might be', which is why Syadvada is at times referred to as 'maybe-ism', but in Jain logic it is used to convey the idea of 'in some respect' (Jaini 2001: p. 94). Syat is further qualified by the word *eva*. This means 'in fact', but its use in the context of Syadvada conveys the 'fact' as experienced by the speaker, in contrast to other interpretations (nayas):

> Thus the statement 'the soul is eternal', when read with syat and eva, would mean: 'In some respect – namely, that of substance and not of

modes – the soul is in fact eternal'. By qualifying the statement in this manner, the Jaina (*sic*) not only makes a meaningful assertion, but leaves room for other possible statements (for example, "it is not eternal") that can be made about the soul.

(Jaini 2001: p. 94)

Syadvada as an organised system of thought is one of the distinguishing characteristics of Jain thought. Yet as a mode of argument or discourse it occurs spontaneously in many cultural settings. A good example of unwitting use of Syadvada is found in Sean O'Casey's play, *Juno and the Paycock*, written in 1924 but set two years earlier in a Dublin tenement shortly after the start of the Irish Civil War and written largely in the dialect of that city (O'Casey 1998: pp.63–149). One character, Mrs Madigan, exclaims in exasperation of the police: 'For you're the same as yous were undher the British Government – never where yous are wanted! As far as I can see, the Polis as Polis, in this city, is Null an' Void'(O'Casey 1998: p.146). Irrespective of political change, the lives of the city's working class residents and their relationship to authority remain essentially the same. That said, although the police are therefore 'null and void' as a collective body, the possibility is left open that individual police officers might lead constructive and useful lives outside their role as agents of the state. Most Jains, practising or otherwise, would be entirely at home with this concept of a multifaceted identity.

To return to the example of the 'eternal soul', the jiva, or life unit (analogous to the 'soul'), is eternal in that it never ceases to exist and so its 'substance' remains. However it changes its 'mode' with karmic influence and the cycles of reincarnation through which it passes. It is, like everything in the Jain universe, at once permanent and impermanent, depending on context. Syadvada is a way of navigating between competing or conflicting nayas, not by surrendering an argument but by admitting that many perspectives can exist and that any proposition can be viewed from two or more angles:

> The spirit of this approach guards [the Jain] at all times from extreme viewpoints. ... Jainas (*sic*) are encouraged to read extensively in the treatises of other schools [of thought]. ... It also seems likely that the failure of any doctrinal heresy to appear during nearly 3,000 years of Jaina tradition can be largely attributed to this highly developed critical analysis and partial accommodation.

(Jaini 2001: p. 96)

There is a circular relationship between Syadvada and Anekant. The process of constant questioning ('syat' and 'eva') induces an attitude of open-mindedness and a refusal to dismiss alternative views. The belief in 'many paths' towards the same ultimate truth also fosters a spirit of inquiry and self-examination.

From the 'naya' of business, these theological speculations might appear to be irrelevant curiosities. In Jain culture, there is no arbitrary distinction between philosophical speculation and the demands of mundane existence, including business planning and financial transactions. The speculative aspects of Jainism provide a background influence, guiding everyday decisions and acting as a reminder of long-term interests. Even the most abstract areas of Jain thought find practical expression in the idea that all life is 'bound together', which is easily understood as a reminder to 'live lightly on the Earth' (Schwarz and Schwarz 1998). The concept of 'binding together' includes past and future as well as the considerations of the present or the short term. In many respects, it echoes the idea of a 'contract' between generations expressed in 1790 by the Anglo-Irish politician and philosopher Edmund Burke:

> Society is ... a partnership not only between those who are living, those who are dead, and those who are yet to be born.
>
> (Burke 1968: p.194)

Jainism takes this idea further so that 'society' encompasses all forms of life, so that the interest of humanity is seen one among many and hence needs to be balanced against competing viewpoints. Failure to take account of other viewpoints within nature, such as those of animal and plant species, can threaten the resilience of human communities or human survival itself. The disconnection between humanity and nature can inhibit economic constructive activities, thus perpetuating deprivation and inequality. The work undertaken by Veerayatan in the communities of rural Bihar addresses this problem by including environmental awareness as part of its programme of poverty reduction, education and training. Poverty in that context means eking out a basic existence at the mercy of natural as much as economic forces, both of which are seen as potential enemies to be appeased by acts of submission. For these communities, economic independence involves developing a more balanced relationship with nature and acquiring the resources (educational and material) to work with it rather than living in fear. Conversely, the sponsorship of educational foundations and animal sanctuaries by global financial concerns like the Jain-owned Meghraj Group or long-established local businesses like Vardhaman Gems of Jaipur (see Chapter 2) is a way of reminding the owners of these enterprises of their wider social obligations, in a literal sense 'bringing them down to earth'. In each case, awareness of multiple viewpoints points us towards a more balanced relationship with the rest of nature and offers a long-term view of worldly considerations, including entrepreneurial success and its rewards.

In the current western paradigm, by contrast, there is an increasing tendency to draw a radical distinction between moral philosophy and commercial activity. These are seen to occupy separate spheres of interest which rarely if ever overlap. Despite the existence of strong traditions of ethical business and finance in western cultures, the prevalent model has become one of 'neutrality' or 'rising above divisions' arising out of religious or other 'beliefs', as opposed to economic 'facts'. Jainism does not draw this distinction: because commercial activities are aspects of Dharma, they cannot be neutral and do not lie outside the cyclical patterns of existence. Despite the impression of detachment, many-sidedness is in practice far from neutral, because it is a means of constant ethical evaluation guided by concern for future repercussions. Thus Anekant and its corollary Syadvada create a flexible attitude of mind and an ability to think ahead that resonates with the commercial environment. In the context of increasing interaction between cultures, they can offer both an intellectual framework and the practical means for negotiating differences.

A sense of possibility

As a system of values and a practical guide to day-to-day living, Anekant reminds the commercial and financial sectors that they do not operate in a void. They are not 'independent' of surrounding human communities and the environments where they live, but products of them and ultimately dependent on them for their survival and success. This challenges many of the prevailing assumptions about entrepreneurial independence or rugged resilience through isolation and self-belief. Although these are the stuff of cliché, they still underlie many of the concepts associated with business studies. Often, these stereotypes influence the way in which business and finance are constructed and they have made a deep impression on the popular consciousness. And yet this way of conceiving and 'doing' business (thought and action being coterminous) has done much to alienate the commercial sphere from the communities it ultimately serves. Artificial barriers are erected: between individual interests and collective endeavours; ecological considerations and commercial activity, and ultimately the individual and society (see, for example, Devall 1990; Klein 2008, 2015; Macy 2013; Sessions 1995). Competition is defined narrowly in terms of victory versus defeat, success in terms of triumphing over others and imposing one's own viewpoint.

In the late twentieth and early twenty-first centuries, the strongest critique of the separation of humanity and nature, business and environment has come from the philosophical movement known as Deep Ecology, which has influenced the intellectual landscape of the United States and Northern Europe, but had little practical bearing on the green political movement or environmental campaigns, including attempts to establish sustainable businesses. Deep Ecology, unlike much of 'mainstream' green thinking, transcends the boundaries of 'left' and 'right' and acknowledges the importance of spiritual insight and practice in influencing human priorities (see, for example, Devall 1990; Devall and Sessions 1985; Griffin 1984; Naess *et al.* 2010; Sessions 1995). There are many overlaps with Jain and other Asian thought: links with Buddhist and Daoist insights are, in particular, acknowledged and celebrated and the critique of 'industrial' society is balanced by a tacit acknowledgement of multiple viewpoints. Deep Ecology questions the philosophical assumptions behind unrestrained economic expansion, notably the anthropocentric or 'human-centred' bias that Jain thought also challenges. However Jainism, while respecting nature, does not idealise it and – as Veerayatan's work demonstrates – does not romanticise poverty and subsistence in civilian (i.e. non-ascetic) communities, as is a temptation for western ecologists. Non-ascetic Jains are also encouraged to play an active role in the economic life of the societies in which they live, balancing their activity with many-sidedness and restraint.

The problems associated with this model are manifold and arise as much because of its successes as in spite of them. Concentration on economic growth for its own sake, abstracted from more essential human or ecological needs has given rise to an array of environmental concerns. As well as the overarching theme of climate change, these include more immediate and tangible symptoms such as urban pollution, deforestation and the depletion of animal and plant species. Poverty can have as deleterious an effect on local environments as industrialised affluence. Subsistence farming was one of the causes of deforestation in rural Bihar addressed by Veerayatan's community programmes, which promoted more sympathetic approaches to the environment and (through education) alternatives to agriculture that involved clean technologies.

In their own ways, uncontrolled expansion and subsistence increase the artificial division between humanity and the rest of nature. Their interests are perceived as being diametrically opposed and immediate human interests, especially economic, take precedence over all else. Lack of co-operation and the absence of a sense of shared interests increase inequalities, whether at regional level or between 'competing' areas of the world. The divorce between economics and more essential human needs contributes to disenchantment with conventional politics, as well as business, and a desire for more fulfilling ways to live and work. Nonetheless, in the west, even in an age of austerity, increasing affluence allows for the possibility of reflection and the search for alternative approaches. Anekant is one such approach. From the standpoint of business, it offers the novel possibility that innovation can involve a process of creative engagement rather than the vanquishing of an opponent. There is also the possibility of viewing the business less as a self-contained unit and acknowledging other 'nayas', whether these come from the environment or community where the business operates, from employees and clients, or even rival organisations. Financial planning might take place with a view to the long term and a shift towards conservation and consolidation.

A fresh look at the way businesses are managed and financial transactions are conducted means un-learning many of the longstanding practices and mental processes associated with commercial enterprises. This applies to activities within the business organisation and the way it presents itself to the outside world. Philip Horvath, a Los Angeles based management consultant and Information Technology (IT) specialist, sees a connection between the 'big picture' (macroeconomics, ecological questions and social justice) and the way individual companies (and the individuals within them) interact. In making this connection, he is influenced by Jain philosophy and has come to view Anekant as a concept that can be usefully deployed in people management and beyond that, in the ways in which an enterprise and its employees view themselves:

> Far too many business meetings I have experienced over the years are highly competitive: apart from a lack of listening, there is an active, at times even aggressive, contest about "who is right". … Unfortunately, we have debate teams in high school rather than classes in active listening and communication. Considering that we spent the majority of our daily lives communicating with others, it is astonishing that we don't educate our young more rigorously in communication theory, basic semantics, logic and, most importantly, respect for other people's feelings.
>
> (Horvath 2014)

Such problems in communicating can arise in small- and medium-sized business as much as large corporations, and in private, public or even co-operative sectors. Horvath, whose clients have included NBC Universal, Experian and the late fashion designer Liz Claiborne, became interested in Jainism because of its ability to reconcile cultural differences and avoid conflict without abandoning its ethical core. He sees the Jain view of multifaceted reality and 'many paths' to the ultimate truth not as abstract or ethereal, but as peculiarly pertinent to a business environment in which interaction between cultures is becoming the norm more than the exception. Many workplaces are themselves multicultural and pluralist, with women and men working together at all levels, and equality between same-sex and heterosexual relationships celebrated and valued. At the same time, technological advancement operates as a double edged sword, facilitating communication but also erecting new barriers of bureaucratic and impersonal rigidity: 'computer says no'. In this working milieu, 'soft' skills such as empathy can prove more useful to a company's culture than an ideal of competitive individualism. Yet the transition from 'hard' to 'soft' skills, like the advancement of 'soft power' in politics, exists more at the level of theory than practice and can all too easily lapse into self-referential New Age fuzziness. Anekant, in contrast, offers a method of reasoning that transcends vague tolerance. It encourages a process of self-questioning along with listening to contrasting viewpoints. As a management tool, it is radical in the original sense of the word because it starts with small but crucial changes of perception and works upwards to influence the entire ethos of the company:

> For now, actively encouraging and training your staff in effective communication will do wonders. One of my clients saved himself 80% of his back-and-forth emails with his clients simply by adjusting his language and communication behavior, something that took about an hour to share with him
>
> In addition to cutting out unnecessary and combative communication, having respect for multiple viewpoints can inspire you [as manager] to facilitate some of the quiet voices in the room. In many meetings I have

been in, someone on the table … knew the solution to the problem we were discussing, but did not feel encouraged to participate. Asking and prompting your quieter, more introverted team members will work wonders. Try it.

(Horvath 2014)

The examples above illustrate the way in which Anekant can easily translate from a complex theoretical system to a practical way to resolve problems in the workplace and draw upon otherwise hidden resources. Horvath also uses a technique he refers to as the 'Ahimsa moment', whereby managers and staff take stock of the injuries they are causing to themselves and others. These injuries might be emotional or psychological, environmental or arising from the company's commercial activities, which might need to be re-evaluated. The format is light-hearted, but the outcome can be substantial. Again, the theoretical and practical merge and the distinction between overarching plan and daily reality (often made, consciously or otherwise in the western paradigm) is blurred beyond distinction:

Allow anyone in the organization to call an "Ahimsa" moment any time they feel there is aggression in the room. In that moment everyone has to stop and check in with themselves not "was I violent?" but "how was I violent just now?" – because we all are, by default, in every moment taking life in order to live ours. … I suggested this technique to a client … and helped to change the culture of [their] organization to be the non-violent atmosphere everyone was ultimately looking for. … This does not mean everyone is hyper politically correct and "nice". It means that there is no backstabbing, no manipulation, no harassing, or other means of hurting people who work in your organization and a zero tolerance towards these behaviors.

(Horvath 2014)

This use of Anekant-derived techniques in western management is a relatively small beginning, but it illustrates the flexibility of these techniques and their applicability across cultural lines. Projects such as Horvath's are, as yet, in their infancy and it would be easy to dismiss such thought experiments as an attempt to turn commercial enterprises into encounter groups. Such criticisms might arise from both ends of the western political spectrum: those who adhere to conventionally 'hard-headed' notions of how an enterprise should be run and those who believe that reform of our ways of working is a sideshow compared with changing the way the economic system itself is structured. In these contexts, it is important to note that, influenced by Jain theory, there are clear injunctions against certain forms of behaviour. These point towards a structured freedom rather than a free-for-all and are based on shared values and co-operation rather than mere self-empowerment. Horvath himself became interested in Jain philosophy and its practical uses through contact with a

Bangalore consultancy, Project Anveshan, founded by a group of young professionals who have benefitted from that city's rapid economic expansion and technological revolution:

> Our collective goal is to explore the tenets of Jainism and their relevance to society, both past and present. ... By rediscovering the essence of *parasparopagraho jivanam*, perhaps we can bring out the essence of an alternative way of thought.
>
> (Project Anveshan 2014)

The aims of Project Anveshan mirror those of Young Jains in Britain or JAINA in the United States and Canada. They aim to rediscover a cultural heritage that has been overlooked during their secular education and as they participate in a pluralist society. The purpose is cultural revival at one level, and at another to discover the extent to which the doctrines of Jainism can be applied in a modern context. In India, that context is a rapidly expanding economy that has achieved superpower status, but in its emergence onto the world stage finds its traditional values challenged or eclipsed. The principled and structured (as opposed to uncontrolled) tolerance of Anekant is an aspect of Jain doctrine that is especially suited to working with a pluralist framework and participating in a global community where fixed ideas and rigid practices are open to continual questioning. The fact that the pluralism of Anekant extends beyond humans enables it to enlarge our understanding of environmental issues, in particular the need to rebalance human economic activities to work with the grain of nature. In this sense, Anekant could be the basis or at least a powerful contributor to a non-western form of environmentalism that addresses from within the dilemmas faced by emergent economies. Chief among these dilemmas is that of increasing material prosperity while avoiding excessive material attachment and continuing to challenge (to use Anveshan's words) 'our apathy towards the greater impact of our actions' (Project Anveshan 2014).

In the setting of the west, the concept of many-sidedness can be adapted from Jain survival strategy, as a perpetual minority population to a way of working in a context where beliefs and values are contested rather than remaining fixed. The element of survival strategy in the doctrine of many-sidedness is often understated, but it is valuable nonetheless. Far from being compromised by experience, these Jain principles are refined when they are tested against competing world views and surrounding events that challenge certainties and fixed patterns of thought. A viable business strategy works in much the same way, with the original concept modified, improved upon and marketed by different means, but retaining its essence. Furthermore, in a working environment where the emphasis is increasingly on networks across cultures and regions, the concept of multiple possibilities can increase mutual understanding and provide the framework for creative exchanges and mediation between conflicting values. In an economy where technologies at once liberate and impose new constraints (including unemployment and under-employment) the many-sided approach can be used to devise ways of working that are more appropriate and effective.

At its most radical, many-sidedness challenges the academic paradigm of business and finance as disciplines subject to exclusive study, abstracted from lived experience. It guides us instead towards the more holistic view of commercial education outlined by the jeweller Jyoti Kothari (Kothari 2004, pp.48–50). There, the values of social and environmental concern are a key feature of the training of an apprentice, part of the acquisition of technical and financial skill, not a separate or additional feature. In a technological and highly pluralist age, the practical relevance of such 'ancient' methods of teaching and learning might become apparent once again.

There are many 'cans', 'mights' and 'maybes' in this conclusion, exemplifying the process of qualified definition, questioning and revision at the heart of Syadvada. The reason for this is that outside of Jain communities, Anekant is a largely untested resource. Within them, it has fostered a spirit of flexibility combined with the retention of core values: a balancing act between continuity and change. In the areas of business and finance, it encourages us to set our activities in a wider context and think more deeply about their future consequences, intended or otherwise.

8 Faith beyond finance

Cultivating detachment and humility

Atul Shah

From a Jain perspective, no human being can cope and survive in life without having a faith or belief of some kind. This faith may not be based on religion, or may even be against religion, but it would still be for something. Some have argued that even atheists have a strong faith (Bentley-Hart 2013). Elements of such faith would include ideas and values about health and happiness, life goals and aspirations, personal fulfilment, relationships, money and wealth, and personal attitudes to animals and the environment. The way finance is taught today in business schools, there are deep underlying values and beliefs, but these are rarely made explicit in the teaching and research or analysed (Shiller 2012). As a very simple example, the entire subject focuses on money and wealth creation, but there is no reflection about the nature and origins of money and its impact on people and society (Daly and Cobb 1994; Ekins *et al.* 1992; Shah 2016). It is simply assumed that money is very important, and of course so too is wealth, and the aim of business has to be about guiding wealth creation in the most efficient and productive way. There is little reflexivity about the meanings of words like profit, wealth, efficiency and productivity, and instead they are portrayed as being 'objectively' good things worth aiming for and achieving. As to politics, its significance and relevance seem to be downplayed if not denied altogether in much of contemporary financial literature.

Success in finance gives the financier or entrepreneur personal power and resources. In contemporary finance theory/ideology and research, there is a subtle denial of human culture and psychology. The assumption behind conventional finance theory is that it is not people who succeed, but projects, enterprises or investments that appear to act autonomously. Human agency is modelled in a clinical way – everyone is assumed to be greedy and selfish, whether or not they have less money or more money, and irrespective of their political power and influence in an organisation. Sadly, the reality of our experience with financial institutions is that people do matter and they have influence (Luyendijk 2015). Also behavioural finance research (Thaler 2013; Shefrin 2000) has demonstrated that not everyone is greedy or selfish or 'rational' all the time. People often get carried away by their financial power to commit massive frauds or take on huge risks without proper understanding, evaluation or calculation. There is also no discussion of the human and ecological limits of finance – when if ever is borrowing enough? In a 'perfect' world, Modigliani and Miller (1958) have shown maximum leverage is the best, and there have been many cycles in the last three decades where financial institutions have facilitated very high leverage for their clients and continue to do so (Das 2011; Coggan 2011). What profits and returns are enough? How does greed influence the performance of the project and investment, and its sustainability and social/cultural impact? Is it OK to rely on 'other people's money' to maximise your own profits, at their expense? These are the themes analysed in this chapter.

Access to finance is not available for all (Xu and Zia 2012). There is evidence of this amongst ordinary people where even in developed countries like the UK nearly two million people have no bank accounts, and the number for the US is ten million. The same applies to businesses and corporations. Small/medium businesses often are at the mercy of the bank manager who knows his/her power, and has often exploited it by squeezing his clients or even making them insolvent, as was the case with the Global Restructuring Group at RBS Group (Fraser 2015). Big businesses on the other hand, have plenty of access to finance at top rates, even when they don't need it. Their brand name, size and power influences the terms on which they can raise finance, and this is also why when big firms like Enron fail, the losses and frauds are truly spectacular. Credit risk for big firms is evaluated by credit-rating agencies, who have been shown to be conflicted and corrupt in their credit evaluations and judgements (Tett 2010; Das, 2011). All the above are anomalies in contemporary finance theory.

Coping with financial success

Given that the Jains have a deeper experience and understanding of finance, it is interesting to see how they personally cope with success, power and prosperity. There is no easy formula for this, but what is insightful is to learn about their rituals, relationships, myths and restraints.

For many Jains, the morning starts with some form of prayers or *Pooja* (Cort 2001; Babb 1996) – in fact in many businesses, there are also small temple shrines to bring divine blessings for the business. In India, most Jain merchants try to live walking distance from a Jain temple so that they can walk there barefoot to conduct their Pooja. Pooja is an act of bathing the images of the Tirthankaras (spiritual masters and guides), whilst reciting prayers such that the virtues of such selfless and compassionate leaders rub into their everyday lives. It is a regular 'shower' of good character and virtues necessary for living an ethical life. I have seen it act as a prevention mechanism, nourishing the conscience and preventing it from going astray by vices such as greed, avarice or fraud and corruption. I have visited these temples in the morning, and they are a hub of activity. There is no 'middleman' in this prayer ritual, and often there is a queue during the morning 'rush' hour, but I have never seen any argument or conflict inside the temple at this time. The other beauty, for me, is that whether someone is an office worker or a multi-millionaire CEO, they are all equal and have to wait in line – there are no short cuts. Also cell phones are switched off and not carried into the temple. It is only after this that the entrepreneur goes home to breakfast. Other Jains may conduct prayers at home after the morning shower in a home shrine. Some may meditate or read scriptures or sacred texts as part of their ritual.

There are many ways to analyse the impact of these actions. For one, it is a daily reminder that human life on earth is a blessing, not to be wasted away, and its purpose and meaning is much higher than just making money or creating wealth. It creates a spirit of 'equanimity' whereby even when one succeeds in a transaction or investment, there is a balanced response rather than a euphoria, or rise in personal ego and status. One of the acts in this Pooja is to bow down right to the floor and touch it with the head, asking for forgiveness for any hurt to others, knowingly or unknowingly. This is a daily action of humility, performed even by CEOs of huge family businesses. I have seen it on many occasions and it is remarkable and inspiring. Most importantly, it gives business leaders a daily dose of mindfulness, peace and equanimity in a world which is often noisy, chaotic, argumentative, selfish and greedy. It is also possible that the Pooja reawakens the conscience and improves intuition, leading to compassionate decision making.

Equality and interdependence

There is a morning prayer which asks for universal happiness for all living beings, even requesting that may all become busy in helping one another and removing each other's pain or suffering. This prayer recognises the fundamental interdependence of all life, Parasparopagraho Jivanam, and reminds financiers to include this universal truth in their actions and decision-making. It helps cultivate a win-win approach to finance, where profit sharing is central to a business transaction. It goes against the grain of profit-maximisation at any cost: success needs to be shared. Its orientation is towards the medium and long term, and not to the short term. Seeking and giving forgiveness is also a core part of daily ritual, through prayer and meditation. This has a very calming effect on the mind, and helps people to deal with anxiety and conflict, and not allow them to overwhelm their conduct. In the arena of competitive business, where forgiveness is rarely even discussed, let alone practised, such practices can have very important long-term effects.

The dress code for the temple-Pooja visit is plain, with a compulsory shower prior to the ritual, and clothes worn that have not been used elsewhere but for such worship. Often they are cream or white, or a single colour like saffron or purple. Once again there is no ostentatiousness or even an opportunity to show off one's wealth or success. Everyone is barefoot, so there is 'groundedness' in the worship. For the people who practice the Pooja as a daily 'peace' exercise, it makes a very important mark on their conscience and their subconscious thinking. Life is about more than business, more than money or profit, and this peaceful meditation reminds them of what it really feels like to be happy and stress-free. I know it makes an indelible impact on the actions that will emanate during the rest of the day as the entrepreneur has to juggle with day to day challenges, making important decisions, or keeping a team together and growing the business.

Community and social capital

In a similar way, given that communities are at the web of social and cultural life, building and managing community institutions is a major priority for the Jains. In fact, if I examine our earlier history in East Africa during the second half of the twentieth century (Shah 2016), it was a major honour to serve on boards of trustees, often more valued than being a successful businessman or financier. Business leaders took an active role in such institutions, not just through philanthropy, but also through active volunteering and governance, and they still do so. Once again, engaging in both business and community management helped Jains to become 'social entrepreneurs' long before the term was coined. It also helped business leaders to reinforce their sense of purpose and meaning in life, which enhanced their leadership drive and achievements. Today, the Jains in East Africa are regarded as one of the most successful business and finance communities, and this success has been cultivated over at least three generations and endured.

As an example, and there are hundreds of such stories, Mr Ashok Mepa Shah is founder and CEO of APA Insurance in Kenya, a company which has grown consistently since its birth in 1977, and he is well known and respected throughout the business sector in Kenya. Insurance is a risk based business and therefore trust is at the heart of its long-term success. As in many African states, bribery and corruption has been a social problem in Kenya, but Ashok Shah would not entertain such offers and is very clear about his own values and methods of doing business. He is incorruptible. As a result, he has built a certain reputation which means that he only attracts those partners who want to play a straight bat – so Ashok sets his own ethical standards, and that also becomes an attraction to those businesses who want to compete on a level playing field. The business is primarily owned by the family and has grown organically. Over the years, he has built a large number of very high quality relationships which have helped him to grow the business and generate new customers and finance. He does not believe in short cuts or quick short-term profiteering. His father Mr Mepa Shah, had a tremendous reputation, both as a business pioneer and also as a community leader and benefactor. In fact, his first love was *Sewa* (Seva) or community service. My own father, Mr Keshavji Rupshi Shah, dedicated his whole life to the service of the Jain community in Kenya, and has left a transformational legacy which has impacted three generations.

If one is part of a culture where individual, family and community are borderless, then holistic thinking and action become instinctive acts, often conducted quite subconsciously, as I have witnessed in my engagements with Jain entrepreneurs. The impact of such culture on the behaviour and decision-making of entrepreneurs and financiers should never be under-estimated. It may not always be directly visible or even measurable, but throughout my career, I have met many business leaders who have been really influenced by the culture in significant ways. In turn, this has helped build the financial and social capital of the community, and reinforced it over time.

A different frame of reference

The frame of reference and decision-making, both conscious and unconscious, is therefore very different for Jain finance leaders, as already explained in previous chapters. Given the strong family and community orientation, sharing is both natural and instinctive. Similarly, short-termism is rare, and instead focus is often not just on the long term, but intergenerational. Trust starts from within, and trusting one's own soul and spirit, and engaging with it, builds an inner strength and resilience. This courage often travels far and wide, and helps in cultivating trust in others and nurturing trustworthiness. The experience of family and community networks and sharing helps to build lasting relationships with others. Active involvement with community helps finance leaders directly observe the impacts of their actions on others, and understand the practical challenges faced by people from different walks of life, and also the diversity of skills and experiences needed to build a cohesive organisation or community.

Where the actions create equality and jobs which help families flourish, such direct experience encourages entrepreneurs to work harder and help more people. Community engagement and membership helps in reducing greed and ego, and in tampering material success with contentment and generosity. It is not 'all mine, and my achievements alone'. 'Besides', a Jain entrepreneur is likely to think, 'death is my final destiny, so why should we get too obsessed by wealth creation and accumulation?' Even among financiers, there is a direct engagement with mortality, not a running away or denial of it. Furthermore, the sense of purpose and meaning in life is also very different and given unique importance. If for any reason, some members of the community are greedy and selfish, they will not get much kudos in the community and this may hurt them, ending up transforming their behaviour, or at least checking it.

The conduct and behaviour of leaders have an important impact on the culture of an entire organisation. The deeper that culture and self-discipline, the more likely it is that others around them respect and learn to imbibe those values. Also this depth gets established inside the organisation, giving it a profound resilience. So many businesses struggle with culture change and building good behaviours and relationships. When Jains are in leadership, the ripple effect of their behaviours, seen by other subordinates or employees from other cultures and backgrounds, can and often does have a much more lasting impact without the need for any mission statements or speeches. There are plenty of examples of this happening in practice inside many significant Jain businesses. As a result, there is much more employee, supplier and customer loyalty. There is a steadiness and calmness around the organisation, and a feeling that everyone is respected and listened to.

Sustainable finance: no hurry to make money

From my experience, few Jains ever seem to be in a hurry to make money. And when they do earn windfalls, somehow they seem able to 'digest' them, rather than let it go to their head or run straight onto a spending spree. As the needs are simple, they are not used to ostentatiousness or showing off their wealth and riches. In fact if they do, it would question their Jain-ness. There is rarely any underlying insecurity which forces them to earn respect through boasting or showing off one's successes. Instead, I have often heard them sharing their success formulae, so that others may learn from them and imbibe them. The story of the founder of Jain Irrigation, Bhavarlal Jain, affectionately known as Bhau, is most inspiring in this respect. He was given India's highest honour, the Padma Bhushan, in 2008.

Born in a small village in 1937, he rose to become one of the world's leading social and environmental entrepreneurs, founding the second largest drip irrigation company in the world. Influenced early on by Mahatma Gandhi's philosophy of *Sarvodaya* – compassion to all, he built his business to support small farmers all over India with education, finance, tools and equipment and the best seeds and harvest returns, all the time preserving and respecting nature through use of minimum water irrigation methods. There were many hardships, challenges, ups and downs, but somehow he managed to grow and build the core business. He started work every day with a walk and meditation. He died in 2016 after a brief illness, and left behind a global business and many educational and training institutions, including international research institutes and collaborations in efficient agriculture.

It is known within India's Jain business community that Bhau acknowledged the need to prepare future generations to carry his legacy forward, and that he conveyed these feelings in a profound letter to his eldest grandson Athang. In this letter, he expressed his deepest empathy for India's farmers and his simple business mantra. He told his grandson to approach the company with love and realise that mutual interdependence is far more valuable than independence. He had gone on to explain that true wealth and success must be achieved by hard work, integrity, compassion and commitment to preserve and protect the environment, and that respect based on education and position needs to be earned and deserved rather than taken for granted.

Bhau's final legacy was not wealth or fortune but values and compassion. He fully recognised the importance of interdependence in spite of his huge personal fortune and success. He lived simply and passed away simply. His business became sustainable not through zero carbon technology or policy statements, but through writing a letter to his grandson to preserve the legacy and nurture truth, wisdom and compassion. Like many Jains, he believed that ultimately, it is only values and culture which can transcend generations.

Intergenerational faith

Intergenerational equity is not something that can easily be codified as a business method or technology. However, it is critical to a sustainable planet. When principles and values about a concern for present and future generations are deeply imbibed into the mind and actions of a finance leader, the outcomes are often completely different. In the above case, Bhau's letter to his eldest grandson shows how much he cares about the various stakeholders, including the farmers and nature. He did not wish that the success of the business be used to exploit the farmers or the land, something that can easily be done if the financier has a short-term greed horizon. Instead, the interdependence of life is at the core of his message, and something he wants the grandson to protect and preserve. Bhau's view of success differs radically from that of mainstream, western-led finance. However they are surely worth our consideration in an era when many business men and women from many cultural backgrounds are seeking to reconnect commercial activities to the environment and larger commitments to the human community.

Faith is needed in the finance world – not just to protect against adverse risks, but also to help make good decisions, to seize opportunities and to personally and emotionally deal with setbacks, failures and challenges. Contemporary finance theory and writing is totally silent about faith, and having been grounded in 'science', is beyond faith. Its core principles are reason and rationality, and every individual is assumed to act in their self-interest, gaining happiness through material income and wealth. One could argue that it encourages faith in greed, selfishness and materialism, helping people 'measure' their success and happiness. Scientific experiments and the growing literature on behavioural finance (Shefrin 2000; Thaler 2013) have shown that people are not always rational or selfish, but somehow, this has not been allowed to interfere with the beautiful inner world of finance and its logical science. In fact, there is no role in finance for the 'person' as such – it is obsessed about markets and institutions, and uses transactions and decisions to replace the person and any emotion or individual belief are seen as irrelevant.

If the risk-taker or decision-maker is a person, then they will have emotions, they will have family and other relationships, and be motivated by a range of factors – from purpose, to power, ambition, ego, status and personal values and goals. All this will undoubtedly influence their decision-making and risk-taking or investment planning. To deny that such factors exist or are relevant is to only see a partial truth, or the truth that the theory wants us to see because it fits in neatly with the models and the hypotheses. Such denial makes us seriously question the very basis of the academic finance enterprise and its power, influence and empirical or evidential frauds. One cannot practise science by denying the real world and its complexities (see Donaldson 1984), or assuming them away to carve out a niche and expert discipline based on sophisticated language and techniques. The more this happens, the more it makes us question the fundamental goals and motives of the finance academy and its teaching and research output. Instead of unravelling truth, it seems more about colonising the expert language and territory and policing the borders or boundaries.

Conquering power with humility

Success in finance often endows the business or bank owner with power and influence. When Graeber (2014) examined the 5000 year history of finance and debt, he determined that money and power are always entwined, and the powerful often dictate the terms and method of payment. Bankruptcies can be bailed out if one is powerful, but punished if one is not. The repayment of debt has often been optional in human history. He argues that finance is a moral obligation perverted by numbers and violence. Financiers are bullies, exploiters and often ruthless in the abuse of their position and influence. Rarely do Jains exercise power and might in this way, in spite of owning many large businesses. As we have seen, there have been stories in the past where Jains have opened up their treasuries to help kings fight wars, without any condition of repayment. For Jains, to use finance to bully or exploit is viewed as wholly unethical. Their character and actions actually help them to prevent the power from getting into their ego or making them aggressive. Instead, there are many examples where they have proactively used this power to empower others, either through debt cancellation, charity and philanthropy, or through job creation and helping other fledgling businesses grow and succeed.

How humans cope and adapt to the power of finance is worthy of investigation. There is some research on the financial crisis which suggests that many key individuals were overcome by hubris (Mcdonald and Robinson 2009; Kay 2015). This conduct resulted in the crisis – it was the leadership behaviour and character which had such a huge impact on the global economy. In the case of the Jains, faith and values exercise a restraining influence, creating greater scope for sustainability and sensible, equitable business and finance.

As monetary currency is often controlled by the state or king, leadership positions in finance require some form of co-operation or partnership with the state. In fact, the very licence to run a bank is given by the state, as money creation today is primarily in the hands of the private banking sector. There have been some fascinating historical cases where Jains have taken up such roles, but exercised them with unique humility and cultivated a highly trusted relationship, either as chief treasurers to kings or as issuers of the Royal Mint, as in the case of Jagat Sheth Manikchand in Bengal whose story has already been told. Once again, their own 'self-regulation', where they will not allow anything to compromise their integrity and values, has attracted them to these roles, and enabled vast sums of money to be moved and managed prudently and with the highest sense of trust and reliability. Integrity has often come instinctively to the Jains, as from a young age they have been taught to be honest and truthful and 'not cheat their own souls, as karma is always watching and recording their thoughts and actions'.

Understanding the limits of calculation

Contemporary finance theory and research has focussed increasingly on the measurable and the 'calculative' (Ekins *et al.* 1992). This in turn has promoted a calculative culture and mindset, which has led to finance experts developing particular biases and deficiencies about the way they view the world. It seems they have failed to understand the limits of calculation, and forgotten the grand assumptions often made behind the calculations, as happened in the case of US home mortgage securitisation. Some have even argued that the emphasis on selfishness and wealth maximisation has actually become a mantra for graduates of finance courses (Hendry 2013; Shiller, 2012), who then go out into the world practising this 'religion' and seeing it as the only right way. In this way the knowledge and techniques are actively used to police and control the practice, and also to exploit others. The 'science' has changed human behaviour, with consequences for our planet.

The real world is far more complex, and also involves non-calculative elements to decision-making which are equally important and should not be ignored. Calculation has often closed the window on alternative ethics and cultures, and the different ways in which they could influence the financial decisions and impact. Sadly faith is often seen as something totally outside the calculative space, although research shows that early mathematics was developed in faith communities (India invented the zero), with the Jains playing a critical role and having whole treatises on mathematics. Often, due to this bias, the important 'softer' aspects of strategic investment are ignored, to the peril of the whole organisation.

Calculative mindsets can become attuned to ignoring the 'softer' or intangible aspects of finance, even though they may be real and significant. Such programming becomes especially dangerous when such people have power and influence, in an industry like finance which is very critical to a good economy and society. This power can actually help them impose their biases and values on others, breeding a culture which is very partial and materialistic, as opposed to one which is holistic. It also prevents such leaders from seeing employees as people with culture and values, and a creative potential because of their difference.

Sewa as faith

The Indian word for service is Sewa. It actually means selfless service, without any expectation of return or reward. The western world has increasingly shifted towards a service economy, with manufacturing outsourced to the East, where labour is cheaper, and people less aspirational due to their poverty and illiteracy. This has meant that much of business is actually service-oriented, dependent on a good culture of customer and supplier relationships. When small family-owned businesses focus on service, they have a direct stake in the rewards, and as a result often go out of their way to provide good service. Companies like Sigma Pharmaceuticals, the fourth largest distributor of pharmaceuticals in Britain, have grown significantly because of their family ownership and service and relationship orientation. Bharat Shah, the CEO and founder, explains that it is this quality and reliability which has been a key secret of their success in pharmaceutical distribution. These values have played a key role in nurturing quality customers and suppliers over several decades, who have stuck with them in spite of the growing competition by big corporates in the industry. Service becomes potent, when combined with faith (see Chapter 5).

Faith and unity have been a key ingredient of success in the sustainability and longevity of Jain businesses like Sigma Pharmaceuticals PLC. The family owners are Digambar Jains, a sect which places a strong emphasis on study, knowledge and reflection. When we met Bharat Shah, it was clear that when the family took major decisions to expand the business or restructure it, a lot of research and thought had gone into it. There was no rush to move, and a holistic approach was adopted to ensure all factors, including the impact on the family, were considered before the expansion was taken on. It was important to him that everyone took ownership of the decision, and any concerns or challenges were listened to carefully (see Chapter 5).

When my co-author and I met him, Bharat had come across an NGO charity from India called SHARAN, which was having significant success in reversing diabetes without medical intervention or drugs. At one level, this would have a negative impact on his business, as the demand for drugs would reduce. However, he was instead much more generous and actually organised and sponsored SHARAN founders on a visit to the UK, running workshops and seminars for the community to help them recover from diabetes. The faith gave him an open-mindedness and a generosity of spirit where helping others is paramount. Faith can give entrepreneurs a deeper understanding of longevity and sustainability, and desire not to exploit or hurt present generations in the pursuit of their own welfare. Bharat rarely mentioned profits, returns or valuations. The conversation was primarily about ethics and sustainable business (see Chapter 5).

However, when large corporations control service industries, where the motive is to maximise absentee shareholder wealth, it is much more difficult to preserve a positive culture and values. We have often seen that when businesses are taken over by corporations, their service level goes down. It is critical that the supplier of a service bears some personal risk, and for family businesses, this is their secret to success. Alternatively, when large companies take over service industries, it is very critical that they develop a positive culture and values, and continue to invest in nurturing this culture. Otherwise, the quality of output will deteriorate, leading to poor returns.

Groundedness

Another fascinating Jain business in the UK is Wealmoor, run by Leena and Anish Malde. They import fresh produce from different parts of the world, mainly Africa, and sell them in the UK mainly to large supermarkets. The Maldes play an active role in helping their suppliers in Africa through fair trade and local foundations, and have cultivated a high cultural intelligence in working with all kinds of stakeholders. It is natural for them to apply the principles of relationship business, though their customers may have different methods of operation and control. Leena and Anish often advise others about issues around culture and diversity as they are a rare success story in the industry. They take pride in their contact with farmers, and the supply of natural and healthy produce, whose largest consumers in the UK tend to be people from ethnic minority communities.

Faith in experts and science

If science and expertise are means of seizing power and elite control over society, then we need to be very careful and wary of its content and experts (Douglas 1992; Kay 2011; Beck 1992; Daly and Cobb 1994; Engelen *et al.* 2012). More research needs to be done about the history of finance as a discipline, and how its cultural assumptions got embedded and became used to hide selfish and even promote incorrect truths and wisdoms. There is a profound fallacy of misplaced concreteness (Kay 2011; Daly and Cobb 1994), where money has come to be treated as an objective fact, when in truth it is a social construct. How finance theory has come to influence global institutions and their embeddedness needs to be studied much more critically, especially from a cultural and ethical perspective. It is not enough to challenge just the ideas and theories, but also the role of core institutions, like universities and business schools, and also international organisations like the IMF and the World Bank in promoting a particular way of thinking, measuring, evaluating and behaving (Graeber 2014). As this has become more and more embedded, finance has conducted a direct war on democracy and democratic institutions.

Revelations about offshore secrecy jurisdictions and tax havens (including the Panama Leaks) are increasingly demonstrating that modern finance has become uprooted from any sense of social or public and environmental duty (Shaxson 2012). The rich are often everywhere and nowhere – even though they use state infrastructures and services to operate, they minimise their tax payments and move their assets to these offshore secrecy havens (Palan *et al.* 2010; Tax Justice Network 2015). In the UK, many are classed as 'non-dom' – that is not domiciled here for legal or tax purposes. As a result, instead of a trickle-down of wealth, we have a trickle-up of wealth and power, with fewer and fewer people controlling more and more of the world's resources and assets (Piketty 2014). When the values and institutions of finance are theorised and justified in a way that encourages accumulation and greed, the consequences can be very serious (Shefrin 2000; Daly and Cobb 1994). If this 'culture' spreads globally, we should not be surprised if it is the 'faithless' and unethical who rise to wealth, power and influence.

'Faithless' finance and its consequences

There are a few very large global financial institutions which serve the rich and the elites – international banks like JP Morgan Chase, Goldman Sachs, Citibank, Barclays, UBS, RBS, HSBC, IMF and World Bank; international accounting firms like KPMG, PWC, Deloitte and EY; and international law firms like Linklaters, Freshfields Bruckhaus Deringer, Eversheds, and Simmons & Simmons. Rarely in such organisations do we see proactive discussions and policies around faith, cultural diversity and ethics, including monitoring and enforcement mechanisms for employees and leaders should they breach fundamental values like independence, integrity and sincerity (Shah 2015b). This is further evidence of how contemporary finance has become detached from ethics. Sadly, professional firms too seem to have imbibed the 'everywhere and nowhere' transactional culture of modern finance, which may serve their clients well, but is not good for the long-term sustainability of society and our environment.

In addition, the rootedness of Jain firms within local communities also means that they support local charities and institutions and share their wealth in different ways. In Antwerp, the Jains have sponsored and manage a beautiful marble temple which is open to visitors, and regarded as a major cultural icon of the city. The same is true in London, where there is one very large 80-acre temple complex (Oshwal Centre) which is managed by the community and funded by business and professional families. The same is true of New York, Los Angeles or Singapore, and there are thousands of Jain temples and community centres in India today. These are places to which Jains go regularly to renew their vows, seek forgiveness for any misdemeanours, and engage with the whole cross-section of the community. Vices like greed and arrogance can seep in easily with success and power, and such 'checks' and regular practices play an important role in curbing the excesses. To ignore or marginalise faith in textbooks of finance is to imply that none of this is relevant to success and sustainability in finance, when the opposite is true. They do make a difference to leadership, growth and endurance in finance.

What is clear from the examples cited above is that personal conscience and behaviour matters a lot, especially for leaders and managers. Where that conscience comes from a culture which understands profoundly the limits of finance, and is able to see beyond present life and principles like ownership and possession, it offers us hope for an ethical future. This is a kind of self-regulation which has been shown to be effective in many different industries and contexts, giving a better chance for sustainable business, communities and futures.

9 Conclusion

Jainism's implications for finance research

Atul Shah

Writing this book has been a fascinating journey. Two people from very different cultural backgrounds, but with similar values, came together to share with a suspicious and sceptical contemporary audience a seemingly timeless philosophical and faith tradition, with ancient roots yet highly pertinent to the modern world. One of the biggest challenges we faced, and will continue to face, is the misunderstanding of Dharma as religion rather than an ethical and scientific system. Dharma is a living science and culture, one which is holistic, and at the same time deeply concerned about social and environmental sustainability. Social scientists all over the world are missing out on a huge wealth of wisdom when they ignore this science in their theories and research. All Indic traditions, Hindu, Buddhist, Sikh, Zoroastrian and Jain, have a Dharmic philosophy at heart. They have never divided science or nature and animals with humanity, nor have they tried to use it to conquer or control the planet.

There is a vast opportunity for the social sciences to draw from these philosophies and faith traditions, given the significant global challenges of biological, environmental and mental health crises, and the need for holistic science as opposed to 'siloed' thinking (Tett 2015). This book aims to open the horizons in finance by showing what can be learnt when we explore one such holistic philosophy and living culture. It seeks to add to the growing literature on these themes, such as the pioneering work of Ekins *et al.* (1992), Daly and Cobb (1994) and Elkington (1999) exposing the fallacies of narrow economic science and the seemingly oblivious attitude it often adopts towards the conflicts and crises of the 'real' world (Donaldson 1984).

In many parts of the world, faith and culture are deeply entwined (Armstrong 2006). It is therefore impossible to draw a boundary between the two. Economists and finance scholars unashamedly and ignorantly draw this boundary, at huge cost to society and learning. In examining human behaviour and psychology, the influence of faith is very important, and even studies in behavioural finance ignore faith perspectives to their peril. This book entwines behaviour, culture and faith, and makes no distinction between normative and positive ethics. It has been motivated by values of care and compassion for a fair and equal world, one which is sustainable and unselfish, and definitely not anthropocentric.

At root, money and finance are social constructs, requiring trust, relationships, ethics and confidence to exist and sustain their value and usefulness. Contemporary finance has lost touch with these fundamentals, and led science and society astray, with devastating public, economic and environmental consequences. Even after the 2008 crash, the reform of theory and education has been lacklustre at best, with no radical transformation in the research and teaching agenda. This study tries to bring finance back to its roots. By exploring Jain science and values, we have been able to uncover a range of different ideas, concepts and perspectives which will enrich the study and practise of finance. The fact that the Jains are not just a living philosophy and culture, but a well-connected and organised global professional community, with vast amounts of social capital, has given us added material to study the links between culture and financial sustainability. Contemporary finance teaching and education ignores both cultural and social capital, so the findings here open a variety of engaging possibilities for future research. The purpose of this book is to expose what we lose when we forget the roots of finance, and the fact that at its base it is a service and servant industry, not a master or controller. Finance does not make anything, but it supports the making of products or services. As a result, its culture needs to embrace compassion, humility and service.

Contemporary topics in finance such as risk, investment, growth, performance measurement, debt and leverage, agency and contracts, have been covered through the Jain lens. In the process, new dimensions or ways of researching and teaching these themes have been revealed. New topics such as Aparigraha (non-possessiveness), Ahimsa (non-violence), Anekant (pluralism), organic finance, the relationship between faith and business practice, community capital, intimate investment, meditation and reflexivity have been introduced. Many of these are, in reality, old themes, but have been obscured at the academic level by the compartmentalisation of subject areas and, in particular, by the study of business and finance with insufficient reference to historical and cultural influences. A sense of what it means to trust and to value and sustain relationships is demonstrated, we hope, and this should help readers understand the meanings of phrases like integrity and self-discipline in finance. The ideals and heritage have made Jains to be self-regulating, thereby helping them to be trusted by their neighbours. As a result, their relationships have grown and flourished over time, enhancing their brand and reputation. This also explains why their businesses have often survived many generations, as there is seldom if ever a rush to make quick money or grow for the sake of greed or profit maximisation. There is a far greater understanding of interdependence, and a respect for financial transactions to be win-win and not win-lose.

Finance is a relatively young discipline, starting in the US in the 1970s as an offshoot of economics (Mackenzie 2006), but then very quickly growing in reach and influence. Accounting is an older discipline (West 2003), but is often seen as a technical craft rather than a science, and its intellectual importance has been overshadowed by the growth of corporate finance and the influence of financial markets and instruments. In every business school, finance is now a key discipline and hence the reach and influence of its theory and practical application has grown exponentially with globalisation. Although there have been critics of this theory and science, it has somehow managed to weather the storm, and even survived the 2008 financial crisis with little change in its underlying logic. Mackenzie (2006) has shown that its growth has been an engine not a camera, fuelling the creation of new financial instruments, markets and risks. This book has tried to look at this discipline from a very different Jain lens, which is at once personal, cultural, social and ecological, and in the process has opened up new ways of studying and developing the discipline.

Unlike mainstream finance or even writings in ethical finance, this book does not offer solutions or magic formulae for success. It does not tell students that if you study this book, you will increase your earnings by this much, or make this much profit. Instead, it shares a different way of thinking and doing finance, which has been tested by history and societies over hundreds of years. True life cases and stories are shared to show how it is that Jains practice a responsible, cultured and generous finance. Such examples help us to understand how theory and practice are interwoven in everyday life and actions. The book provides readers with a way to think compassionately and creatively about finance, as it introduces a completely different culture and mindset, which most people would be unfamiliar with. Its nature is inter-disciplinary because when we negotiate life and everyday struggles we do not choose the subject from which our solution comes – we think, adapt and cope as whole beings.

Humans consciously and unconsciously weave different ideas and experiences to make choices and decisions. Studying the Jains offers us useful insights (whether we are of Jain heritage or not), as so little is written and known about this living community and the reasons for their sustained success in finance. In fact, the very detachment of cultural studies from finance has meant that the very idea that living cultures and their wisdoms and experiences can contribute to knowledge has been suppressed. It is up to the reader to draw what messages and lessons are applicable to themselves in carving out their own finance futures. The principles, stories and case studies we have used hope to inspire and reflect on the relevance to their own finance practice, as opposed to providing any pre-packaged solution. In this sense, we hope readers have found this book and its tone to be open-minded, as they are free to draw their own interpretations and conduct their own investigations. It is very difficult to convey a culture through words, as cultures have so many dimensions like stories, poetry, customs, rituals, art, faith, festivals and the best way to study and learn about culture is through direct personal experience and engagement.

The research does not easily follow common western norms of experimentation, falsification, statistical data analysis and empiricism, hypothesis testing, and even a 'rigorous' and comprehensive literature review. In the

Feyerabend (1975) sense, it is not fixated on the notion of method as science, but instead on a sincere quest for truth and objectivity, revealing the ethics and values of the authors in the process, honestly allowing readers to judge and evaluate the science. Our subjectivity and love for the Jain tradition is also not denied in this study. However, we still feel that the analysis and case studies demonstrate concepts and principles which have wide ramifications for the study of business ethics, economics and finance.

In particular, this study exposes the benefits of immersion in an ancient culture and looking outside at what is being taught and researched in contemporary finance, opening up new horizons and possibilities to resolve current financial and ethical crises. Given that so little is known about finance in eastern – or indeed any non-western – cultures, and how even books on global economics and finance write mainly about European and American histories (Finel-Honigman 2010; N. Ferguson 2012), the gaps in knowledge are wide open for us to fill. What motivates us is the hidden cultural bias in finance, which is rarely exposed and discussed by the experts who perpetuate it.

Life and purpose have been given clarity within the global Jain community, offering its members a sense of goal and direction. For most Jains, there is a very clear sense of purpose and destiny, which they have applied in their approach to business and finance. This method of what we would now call 'self-regulation' had the effect over time of helping them to build a track record of honesty, integrity and reliability. These values and character made the Jains naturally fit for a finance occupation, and also endowed them with sustainable success. In a business world where 'trust' is a rare quality, the Jains are a widely respected and trusted community. Individuals and families became proud of their culture and heritage, and continued to practise it and learn more about it through their engagement with male and female ascetics. Success in finance helped the Jains to invest in community institutions to help retain their culture and values and pass them to future generations.

There is a constant emphasis on self-discipline and self-perfection in Jain philosophy. When Jains achieved success in finance through these practices, the success also was more palatable and digestible, as they shared it widely with their community and society, including animals and the environment. Such engagement reminded them of the nature of money and wealth, and the limits to its ownership and possession. They also practised prudence and organic growth, as they were reluctant to take financial risks for their own sake, and not greedy to expand and multiply at any cost. Financial engineering and fakery is not a part of the moral compass of Jains. Effortless finance through clever arbitrage was never an aspiration – work was seen as an opportunity to serve and to help others. It is a source of joy and meaning in life.

In an age of globalisation, business studies has to engage with cultural diversity and not shield itself by pretending to a 'cultural neutrality'. Understanding the concept of multiple truths and Anekant opens many new horizons and possibilities for the development of finance. It also can challenge some of the very foundations and assumptions underlying a discipline. The mindset and fundamentalism of contemporary theory needs to open to help understand the wider impact of finance conduct, actions and behaviour, and to allow the active listening of diverse cultures and viewpoints about the meaning of finance. Interdependence in finance is often understood as the technical interactions between asset prices and risks, rather than the variety of peoples and cultures which occupy this planet and their different world views, characters and belief systems. Much more research needs to be done to help develop an open finance theory where different cultures are allowed a voice, and their attitudes to money and wealth given the due respect.

Jains are also students of business and educationists all over the world – for example the SP Jain Business School is a global educational institution founded and run by a Jain family. Similarly, the Jain International Trade Organisation (JITO) is an international network of Jain enterprises with a strong cultural and social ethic. We hope that such a book will help Jain students access their own knowledge and values in their education and development. When this book enters the business curriculum, it will enrich the experience of all students, and in the process also empower the Jain students to retain their culture and values, and take pride in their ethical inheritance. For entrepreneurs (Jain and non-Jain), this study can help them understand the wider link between culture and business.

Contemporary corporate finance education tends to place an excessive emphasis on limited liability companies, large corporations and financial markets, implying that these are the main locations for studying the practice of finance. It virtually ignores owner-managed family businesses which play a huge role in economies all over the world, and can sometimes be the same size or larger than many listed companies. It also takes greed, profit and wealth maximisation as a given. In so doing, it removes the diverse cultures and contexts in which people live and behave, and their different attitudes to money, profit and wealth. Worse, in assuming greed and theorising selfish behaviour, it spreads greed through the large footprint of business schools all over the world, and their student numbers and cohorts. Science has been used to justify and globalise a cultural dogma, with adverse social and environmental consequences. The business of finance education needs to take social and environmental responsibility, and stop cocooning itself from the real world. Many students may not realise that in signing up to study business, they are also signing up to a particular cultural and ethical outlook, which may end up damaging their own culture and values. In our view, the fundamental base of what is researched and taught as modern finance is often misleading, and this needs to change. This book therefore seeks to transcend critique and provides an example of what a different corporate finance can and does look like.

Modern financial institutions, like international banks, financial markets, hedge funds, private equity, investment banking, foreign currency and derivatives trading have come to dominate jobs and recruitment. New terms and language have developed to enhance the sophistication and complexity of high finance. Phrases like activist investors, asset-stripping, leveraged buy-outs, two-and-twenty, have become accepted jargon, conveying a 'cool' image of intelligence and success, disguising the aggression and greed. In contrast, the Jain language and character is much more non-violent, careful, reflective and contented. It rarely seeks profile or publicity. Ours is a caring finance, one which sees and feels the pain of others, and does not brush it aside in the name of efficiency or value-creation. There is no rush to squeeze time, and discount the sacrifices of future generations, or to ignore the inequality that finance can perpetuate. There is a profound understanding of the limits of money, growth and material success. The purpose of finance is never exaggerated, and its vocation is seen as a means to a more ethereal and sustainable end. In particular, wealth is not seen as an end in itself, but a means to a higher spiritual goal.

The example of the Jains demonstrates that there are other assumptions and values which may prevail, and they result in different goals and ideas about success and wealth. Such analyses also expose the vast difference in mindsets and behaviours that arise from such endeavours. It exposes different nuances in understanding about fundamental ideas like the nature and purpose of business, the responsibility to society and the environment, the role and limits of finance, the importance of risk and its management, and finally how trust and relationships lead to financial success and sustainability. It also shows the limits of a formulaic, impersonal and institutional approach to finance, which can easily lead to greed and excess. A personal type of finance enables people to feel and experience the consequences of their decisions and actions. This is as important as calculating the cheapest methods, or the highest value-generating investments, or the lowest risks.

One core theory in finance is that the value of an asset is equivalent to the discounted present value of all the future cash flows generated by the asset. Mathematically, there are tools to collapse the future into the present, and value future income streams. However, the process of doing so also opens questions about intergenerational transfers and equity, questions which are very moral, but often ignored by finance. For example, the valuation of internet start-ups like Uber or Facebook were huge in spite of the fact that they were initially loss-making. The founders became billionaires virtually overnight. Is this a good thing or a bad thing? How will future generations pay for such high valuations? Who wins and who loses, and is this fair and just? Such questions need to be asked if we are concerned about balance and equality, and also about excessive wealth and its consequences. The Jain philosophy can provide a moral compass for evaluating such dilemmas.

A subtle, tolerant yet actively engaged faith tradition such as Jain Dharma can help curb excesses and recklessness. It may give purpose and meaning to a financial enterprise, which has the capacity to give it a lasting success and sustainability. It often results in self-policing and self-regulation of conduct, character and behaviour. Faith helps people to build and value relationships as opposed to pure arms-length transactions, devoid of humanity. Stripping faith out of finance has social consequences, and if instead faith is placed in the fiction of money and wealth, the consequences of excessive faith can and have been devastating. Faith can help to make finance more 'palatable', help people face and understand human frailty and death, so that they may come to understand the limits of money and wealth. Faith helps to curb human greed and selfishness, and instead make social and environmental responsibility innate to business actions, instead of being a formula or marketing exercise.

Given that success in finance often catapults people into leadership positions and responsibilities, it is very important to study how leaders in finance behave, and the culture and values they inspire in others. When we study the Jains, we see a kind of 'servant leadership' where there is little arrogance and hubris, and instead there is simplicity and humility, with little desire for fame and publicity. More research needs to be done to understand alternative approaches to finance leadership, and the links between these styles and sustained success in finance. For Jains, it seems that serving the wider community is regarded as a very high honour, and a source of joy and inspiration. Rather than wealth creation, it is often giving and philanthropy that are seen as measures of success.

It is fascinating to observe the ways in which Jains have globalised, and adapted their culture and values to different countries and markets, including North America where the modern discipline of finance was largely shaped. Communities with strong roots and cultures may be perceived by many to be insular and selfish, but instead, the Jains have adapted to different contexts, while still retaining and sharing their values and culture. They have even created global businesses from their family networks and roots. The resilience and adaptability of this community has been truly remarkable, giving us yet another reason to study their methods and success formulae. When orthodox finance specialists talk about globalisation, they tend to use terms like 'economy' and 'efficiency' to justify business expansion and growth. Studying the Jains gives us an added ingredient of globalisation – the culture and resilience of a people, and their ability to operate and trade cross-culturally, without losing their character and values.

Contentment and sufficiency of profit and wealth are personal characteristics. So is happiness. The Jain philosophy of Aparigraha explains the different dimensions of this relationship, the attachments and bondage it can create, and how these can limit financiers from attaining true freedom and liberation. Surprisingly, the philosophy has also enabled Jains to attain great wealth and success in finance, in spite of their simplicity and values, or maybe because of it. This may sound paradoxical, but the learning from this experience and history is that the more business leaders can understand the personal context of money, wealth and its limits, the more they are likely to succeed and sustain this success. When vast fortunes and wealth are attained in business, the Jains have developed a method of retaining this success, and not become overwhelmed by it. They have also seen the sharing of wealth as a key part of financial success, not a sideshow or something to do when one retires from business and wealth creation. It has been a regular and ongoing activity, a practice which the Jains have used to nourish their personal relationship with wealth, and remind them of its limits and the consequences of excessive indulgence. In fact the very meaning of philanthropy for the Jains is very different, encouraging them to thank the recipient for helping them part with their money and share in their success.

Once we personalise finance, then all kinds of new dimensions open up, like how to think about finance holistically, and understand its wider economic, social, political and environmental context. Present mainstream approaches to finance often incapacitate such holistic thinking through their depersonalisation of theory and research. The student is separated and marginalised from the science in the quest for objectivity, even though finance is fundamentally a social science. In fact, some have argued that contemporary finance and its institutions have become a curse on society (Shaxson and Christensen 2013), especially where its global markets and institutions are heavily concentrated in cities like New York and London. It is possible that if students are taught this wider perspective and if research engages with this wider context, then the outcomes of finance teaching and behaviour would be very different. Instead of causing booms and crashes, finance could play an important role in building a sustainable planet and cultivating social and economic cohesion. For this to happen, our discussion of learning to think like Jain (see Chapter 2) reveals interesting dimensions to building a holistic and inclusive framework for considering business and finance. Students should be exposed to such frameworks and their possibilities.

The links between personal health and finance are completely ignored by the discipline of finance. However, given the mental health crises of modernity, there is more and more evidence emerging of how finance is intimately connected with mental health (Lewis 2016), and a cause of severe personal and family crises. Financial literacy is the key to navigating modern life, given the huge complexity of finance, and the high levels of greed among financial advisers. In fact, even when people 'succeed' in finance, they often suffer from mental health problems, because of the challenges of 'Affluenza' (James 2007).

The cases and examples set out in this book have in different ways shown how intimacy in finance can be applied, and the results it can give. Instead of detaching finance from people, emotions and society, the Jains have come to understand how to adapt and live with it, and what to do when they obtain too much financial success. Their approach to building and maintaining trust and relationships can provide fresh insights into how we can make finance more intimate, and therefore more responsible and accountable. It is important that we reduce the distance between the practice of finance and the human being responsible for its transactions and decision-making. The detachment of the financial act from the 'finance person' is problematic if we are to develop a humane and sustainable finance.

Notions of ethical investment are largely absent from contemporary finance research and education, primarily because of a theoretical framework which assumes that the best way for business to be a positive force is to focus on profit and wealth maximisation. Such theories do not consider the impact on people and society from such aggressive behaviour, and assume money is the root of all happiness and social progress. In contrast, the cases and examples illustrated in this book show that the Jains place ethics at the centre of their approach to finance, often without shouting out loud or any explicit spin or pronouncements. Their strong family and community values often lead them to think long term and even intergenerationally, ensuring that the business and institutions they build become resilient enough to last several generations. How many modern finance businesses have such longevity? The fact that we have had at least one global financial crash in each of the last four decades, means that many businesses have had surprisingly short shelf lives, including large institutions like Lehman Brothers, Bear Stearns and even HBOS or RBS.

Risk is a key aspect of the study and teaching of finance. However, it has become a technical field, where even the assumptions underlying its calculation often get forgotten or ignored, and the limits of calculation, and the highly political nature of risk management, are virtually denied (Beck 1992; Power 2007: Shah 2015a). It has become a field captured by experts and expertise, resulting in bias, miscalculation, misrepresentation, moral hazard, and the endorsement of excessive greed and risk-taking for the pursuit of private gain. Social and public purses have been raided by financial risk, and its expert endorsement and encouragement. In stark contrast, the personal understanding and approach to risk, however unsophisticated, has given Jains a more intimate understanding of its measurement and management, and there has been no hurry or thirst for risk for its own sake. By its very nature, a family business is a shared business, and helps spread the intimate experience of risk, encouraging careful conduct. Family and community have often helped in cushioning risk-taking, and shared lending and borrowing have helped to support infant business enterprises. Prudent conduct has led to a containment of debt and leverage in Jain businesses, in stark contrast to the modern preaching of borrowing as a root to wealth creation. In fact, the prudence has resulted in organic growth, something which is much more manageable and sustainable than debt fuelled growth, which so often has spiralled out of control.

The globalisation of business and industry has also introduced new dimensions of risk, which include cross-cultural sensitivity and understanding as a key finance skill. Contemporary finance education is silent on this risk, although the Jains have shown through lived experience how important it is to have cultural understanding to succeed. A holistic upbringing and world view which includes respect for all life, has given them a 'skill set' in this arena. Their strong family bonds and community networks have enabled them to build global businesses in a short time. Jain self-belief and resilience have given them the confidence to travel to new climates and countries and set up operations from scratch. For example, in a previously unfamiliar country and culture such as Belgium in the mid-twentieth century, Jains have become leading players in the diamond polishing industry, without generating any hostility, and permeating wider society and institutions without losing their culture and identity. They understand how to create value and give value to customers, whilst managing their financial risk at the same time.

The Jain philosophy of Anekant or many-sidedness has a number of implications for the future of finance theory and research. Firstly, any attempt at searching for a single theory or unified theory of finance is doomed to fail. Finance fundamentalism must be abandoned. Instead of being singular and reductive, finance should be much more open and inclusive in its theorising and research. It should appreciate that different and maybe even divergent truths can co-exist. The denial of intuition, intimacy and personal reflexivity in the practice of financial decision making also has consequences for the applicability of finance learning in business schools. Pluralism of thinking should be encouraged, in both finance research and teaching.

The grounded nature of Jain culture and lifestyle has helped financiers to maintain humility, and contain their excesses. Through community engagement and participation, they can directly experience the impact of their behaviour and actions on others. They do not shut themselves off into a bubble of rich people, extravagant parties and holidays, and private clubs and networks where they meet more of the same elites. The community networks are open and welcoming to both rich and poor, enabling them to mingle and see the resourcefulness and creativity of people who may not have financial wealth. Jains value very much this community membership and participation, and have often seen in community leadership, the highest aspiration of success. Many successful financiers have also been important community leaders or patrons. Communities convey a living experience of equality, not just a theoretical concept or idea. They help the rich and the 'successful' to keep their feet firmly on the ground and not get carried away by their wealth and power into arrogant conduct.

The difference between ownership and trusteeship is elaborated throughout this book. Whilst contemporary finance takes shareholder ownership as a given, and a master to whom financiers should serve for maximum rewards, the Jains have always understood ownership to be a temporary phenomenon. There is a profound understanding of human fallibilities, and the absolute reality of death, and the limits of greed and materialism. There is also a Dharmic understanding of the science of interdependence, which leads to a humble sense of trusteeship as opposed to an arrogant attitude to ownership and control. We are but passers-by on this planet, and must leave it at least as good as we found it, doing a minimum of damage and a maximum of good, say the Jains. And finance theory and practice should stem from such an attitude, if we are to protect the planet and not destroy it. At the very least, finance theory and education should take responsibility for the actions that result, and understand the profound flaws in the concept of shareholder ownership and their wealth maximisation as an over-riding objective. Where owners have delegated their responsibilities to managers, they fail to act as planetary carers and trustees.

We hope this research empowers students and scholars from all over the world to study and examine their own cultural approaches to finance, without fearing the formulaic and technical finance academy which thrives on impersonality. Public finance is a key component for providing social and economic infrastructure all over the world, and the separation of its study from corporate finance is also a subtle denial of the importance of government as a business stakeholder. In fact, this has played a key role in legitimising corporate tax avoidance and tax minimisation as an economic good for businesses. We feel that public finance needs to be taught to help business students build a holistic understanding of the nature of finance and its limits and possibilities. Similarly, the worlds of charity and social enterprise play a very important role in helping to nurture social and environmental harmony, and their finances are therefore equally worthy of study and reflection. In fact, by studying these different elements together, scholars and students will be able to enrich their knowledge and wisdom in finance and see its wholeness and interdependence.

Outside the communities in question, there has been very little research into Sikh, Hindu, Buddhist and Zoroastrian attitudes towards business and finance, despite vast evidence of their success in commercial spheres combined with thriving social and community lives. We hope that this intensive Jain analysis will inspire others to do likewise with different philosophical and faith traditions outside the western paradigm. In the process they will, we hope, reveal and share with the world how non-western cultural and ethical practices can enlighten and enrich the global business and finance conversation. Small and large global businesses alike have been deeply inspired by these faith traditions, and there are case studies compiled of some of the leaders and their cultural and ethical basis for business success (see Lala 2007 on the Tatas and Zoroastrian cultural influence). More such cultural analyses would, from my perspective as a Jain, also reveal the benefits of participation in living faith communities for honesty, transparency and sustainability in business and finance. Where there is a faith-based approach, or a secular philosophy based on social justice and respect for the individual, it would provide finance leaders with a sense of grassroots connection and humility, which may lead to different outcomes in terms of their behaviour, decisions and actions.

As the aim of this book was theoretical and conceptual, we were only able to share a few case studies about Jain finance practices by way of example. Given that there are at least one million Jain finance professionals living and working in various parts of the world, we hope that students will be inspired to research and write more case studies about their knowledge, practices and achievements. In particular, there is no specific study of the accounting practice of Jains, even though they are probably the largest per capita community of accountants in the world. Research which explores their professional conduct and ethics, client relationships and financial advice, would help significantly in understanding how their culture and values influence the practice of accounting.

Global financial institutions and businesses are being increasingly questioned about their culture, conduct and behaviour. One response has been to compile ethical codes and make them transparent. Often little evidence is provided of the policing and enforcement processes, and the codes are written in a very open-ended general way, becoming meaningless templates. This study demonstrates that in formulating such codes, diverse wisdoms and cultures can also provide unique insights – in fact, one could argue that given the enduring Jain history of success in finance, its ethics may be uniquely valuable to financial institutions in guiding their conduct and behaviour. Such cultures and traditions need to be consulted in the development of cultural and ethical guidance, especially for global financial and corporate institutions. More generally, to develop such codes in a 'culturally neutral' or 'acultural' manner shows the extent of the lack of awareness about the links between faith, culture and behaviour, and how transactional businesses are even when they write about people and their values. Instead of recognising the upbringing and heritage of their staff and building upon these, firms seek to impose a new set of 'neutral' values, further supressing their cultural identity.

The regulation of finance is a massive global industry, operating within both the public and private sectors. Sound accounting and accountability are crucial for good corporate reporting and governance. The Big 4 accounting firms (PWC, Deloitte, EY, KPMG) play a leading role in advising corporate clients about the implementation of regulation, whilst at the same time auditing them and helping them practice tax avoidance. For decades, the study of financial regulation was not considered 'cool' or important – finance courses focussed on risk, valuation, markets, products and investment appraisal and regulation was hardly taught. There was a strong ideology of efficient self-regulating markets, in spite of regular experiences of financial frauds and institutional and market failures. Instead of teaching about regulation, finance courses taught about derivatives and regulatory arbitrage – how firms could profit from gaps in regulation and remove 'imperfections in the markets'.

Ethics and regulation are closely entwined, but the tendency in finance has been towards rule-based regulation, rather than the policing of personal and corporate culture and behaviour. More research is still to be done on the culture and behaviour of finance regulators, and their moral compasses. We need to know how proud they are to be public servants, and how willing they are to challenge and question fearlessly the tide of corporate power and abuse. There is a lot of research which exposes the huge conflicts of interest of the global Big 4 accounting regulators – but little has changed in their practices. Where there has been an emphasis on people and conduct, the enforcement of such regulations has been weak and patchy (Admati and Hellwig 2013).

There is also a politicisation of regulatory processes, with the result that its effectiveness is compromised (Germain 2010; Shaxson 2012).

This study also aims to provide a new perspective on ethics-based regulation, such as the self-regulation within communities and the important role played by members of faith communities in cultivating an ethical conscience. Behaviour should be policed and monitored. Regulation and enforcement become much easier when people police their own conduct and behaviour, and seek to apply stringent ethical standards. More research on how finance leaders could be encouraged to develop a social conscience and engage with it would be very valuable. There is very little research about the conduct and behaviour of ethical accountants, who do not help their clients to minimise taxes at any cost or avoid regulatory compliance. We need to study them to understand what motivates them, and how their professional advice and services influence the practice of corporate finance. Systems and processes could be designed to help organisations develop an internal ethical conscience and regularly monitor and engage with it. The active denial of personal and organisational conscience by the finance industry should be challenged. Words like honesty and integrity only have meaning when conscience prevails and its role is acknowledged.

Reflecting on the core content and messages of this book, we cannot ignore the possibility of connections between racism and finance theory and expertise. Moore (2001) conducts a wide-ranging analysis of American society and shows that a lot of its thinking and institutions are dominated by white men. If we examine the core global institutions in finance, from the big international banks, to the regulators, the International Monetary Fund (IMF) and the World Bank, to the global accounting and legal firms, and even influential accounting and finance academics, this would not be far from the truth. Most prominent faces we see tend to be white and male. Research in other fields such as law, politics and sociology has shown that race has a key influence on the content of the subjects and the social science curriculum in higher education (Dixson and Rousseau 2006).

When I wrote *Celebrating Diversity* (Shah 2007a) my aim was to help Britain harness the huge strengths of its diversity, through cultural understanding and pluralism. A similar process of intellectual interrogation may legitimately be applied to the disciplines of accounting, business studies and finance throughout the Global North to determine whether or not there is a specific but disguised ethical and cultural bias in these curricula. Rather than merely complain about racism, we have shown in this book that there are positive new possibilities for approaching and embracing cultural differences in ways that can enrich scholarship in these areas and influence the development of new paradigms for business practice. By looking at the Jains in detail, this book has shown that finance from alternative cultural perspectives can be both insightful and revealing, holding up a critical mirror to the hegemonic financial culture. If unconscious cultural bias – or indeed conscious cultural prejudice – exists within the academic disciplines associated with finance, then such attitudes need to be challenged. The values associated with financial education, and the business practices to which they give rise, have a critical bearing on the environments in which we live and work, as well as the balance of political and economic power on our planet. Therefore, it is clear that nothing less than an inclusive or 'many-sided' approach to financial education will suffice.

Glossary

Jain culture has a rich vocabulary, drawn from the classical Sanskrit language and the vernacular Prakrit, known to linguistic scholars as Ardhamagadhi Prakrit. This list is not intended to be exhaustive, but covers the expressions and ideas used throughout this book. It represents with approximate equality the devotional and philosophical or scientific aspects of Jain culture. In the interests of clarity, we have not applied accents or diacritical marks either here or in the main text. These are used only in the Bibliography when included in the titles of published works. Where possible, we have taken account of variant spellings, although it should be noted that Jain vocabulary is diverse, reflecting new developments in thought and practice, the influence of modern Indian languages such as Gujarati and the presence of Jain communities in many regions of the world.

Acharya Spiritual master.
Ahimsa Non-violence, non-injury, avoidance of harm.
Ajiva Inert matter, insentient object without jiva (life monad or 'soul').
Akasa Space.
Aloka-Akasa Unoccupied space.
Alparambhi Requiring minimum violence or harm; used mainly for occupations and trades.
Anekantavada Principle of 'many-sidedness' (of reality), pluralism or 'multiple viewpoints' (also Anekant, Anekanta, Anekantvada).
Anga(s) Central Jain texts (literally 'limbs').
Anu Infinitesimal or subatomic particle.
Anuvrata(s) Five Lesser Vows undertaken by lay men and women.
Aparigraha Principle of non-possessiveness.
Asrava Beginning of 'karmic bondage' (Bandha), influx of karmic particles.
Asteya (sometimes called Achaurya) 'Non-stealing', avoidance of theft or taking what is not given.
Astikya Implicit understanding of the nature of reality.
Avasarpini Regressive half-cycle of time and the universe; *see* Utsarpini.
Avidya Ignorance, lack of knowledge or perception.
Bandha Karmic bondage.

Brahmacharya   Celibacy (for ascetics), fidelity and avoidance of promiscuity or exploitative relationships (for lay men and women).

Chopda Pujan   Ritual taking place every Diwali (q.v.), especially associated with businesspeople; new account books (chopda) are opened with the blessing of a priest to mark the New Year and new beginnings.

Dana   Charity, giving.

Darshana   Perception, (clear) vision.

Dharamshala   Religious guest house, lodging house for pilgrims.

Dharma   Universal law or cosmic order.

Digambar (or Digambara)   One of the two main schools of Jainism; literally means 'sky-clad' because the most senior male ascetics are naked.

Diwali   'Festival of Lights' celebrated in the autumn (or spring in the Southern Hemisphere) by Hindus, Jains, Sikhs and some Buddhists.

Ekant (Ekantika)   One-sidedness, doctrinaire viewpoint.

Gupti   Restraint.

Himsa   Violence, harm, destructive power.

Irya-Samiti   Principle of Careful Action. Also care in movement or walking.

Jai Jinendra   'Honour to [the] Jina', 'Hail to the Conqueror(s)', popular Jain greeting.

Jain-ness (Jainness)   Cultural sensibility of the Jains.

Jina   Spiritual victor, omniscient spiritual teacher; *see* Tirthankara.

Jiva   Life monad or 'soul', living being.

Jiva Daya   Sympathy or identification with all sentient beings.

Jnana   Knowledge.

Karma (in Jain thought)   Subtle matter composed of karmic particles, attracted to the jiva by yoga (activity) and preventing full self-knowledge, omniscience and transcendence of samsara (the cycle of birth, death and rebirth).

Karmon (pl. Karmons)   Karmic particles (modern scientific adaptation of traditional Jain concept by Professor Kanti V. Mardia).

Kasaya   Passion(s), usually negative, such as anger, fanaticism or material greed.

Kshama   Forgiveness, patience, tolerance.

Lokakasa   Inhabited universe, occupied space.

Mahavrata(s)   Five Greater Vows undertaken by ascetic men and women.

Maya   Deceit, illusion.

Mithyatva (Mithyadarsana)   False consciousness, distorted world view.

Moksha   Spiritual liberation, (moment of) enlightenment, acquisition of omniscience.

Muni   Ascetic man or woman.

Namo   (I) bow down and respect. Namokara Mantra is recited while meditating.

Naya   Viewpoint.

Nirjara   Breakage, shedding, falling away of karma/karmic particles.

Nirvana   Full enlightenment.

Nyaya Sampanna Vaibhava   Honestly earned wealth/possessions, motivation to earn wealth honestly. Sometimes Nyaya Sampanna Vibhava.

Panjrapoor   Animal hospital or sanctuary.

Papa   Negative, destructive or 'heavy' karma.

Parasparopagraho Jivanam   Concept of interconnectedness. Philosophical translation: all life is bound together by mutual support and inter-dependence. Religious translation: souls (jiva) render service to one another.

Parigraha   Possessiveness.

Pujan (or Puja, Pooja)   Prayer, religious ceremony or ritual.

Punya   Positive, benevolent, creative or 'light' karma.

Ratnatraya (sometimes Triratna)   Three Jewels or 'Triple Gems' of Jainism: Samyak Darshana (Right Vision or Viewpoint); Samyak Gyana (Right Knowledge) and Samyak Charitra (Right Action).

Sadhana   Spiritual development.

Sadharmi(k)-Vatsalya   Love for one's faith community, community dinner with devotional purpose.

Samiti   Watchfulness, care.

Samsara   Cycle of birth, death and rebirth, process of cyclic change.

Samvara   Stoppage of karmic influx (through awakening consciousness).

Samyak Charitra   Right Action; *see* Ratnatraya.

Samyak Darshana (sometimes Samyaktva)   Right Vision or Viewpoint; *see* Ratnatraya.

Samyak Gyana (sometimes Jnana)   Right Knowledge; *see* Ratnatraya.

Sarvodaya   Principle of 'compassion to all' (popularised by Gandhi).

Satya   Truth, truthfulness, honesty.

Seva (Sewa)   Community service, service to humanity.

Shraddha   Educated faith, intuition reinforced by knowledge and reason.

Shuksha   Education.

Sutra   Collection of spiritual aphorisms or teachings, usually in verse form ('thread' or 'string' in Sanskrit).

Svetambar (or Svetambara)   One of the two main schools of Jainism: literally means 'white-clad' because male and female ascetics wear white robes.

Swadeshi   Principle and practice of economic self-sufficiency or self-reliance (popularised by Gandhi and not exclusive to Jains).

Syadvada   System of logic based on qualified definition.

Syat   Maybe, perhaps, expression of possibility.

Tattva, Tattva(s), Nine Reals   Aspects of reality or 'things'.

Tirthankara   Ford-maker or guide to enlightenment, omniscient spiritual teacher.

Upashraya   Lodging house for ascetics.

Utsarpini   Progressive half-cycle of time and the universe; *see* Avasarpini.

Vrata(s)   Vow, vows.

Yoga   Activity or activities of body, mind and speech.

Bibliography

Adams, I. (2001) *Political Ideology Today*, 2nd edn, Manchester: Manchester University Press.

Admati, A. and Hellwig, M. (2013) *The Bankers' New Clothes*, Princeton: Princeton University Press.

Alrifai, T. (2015) *Islamic Finance and the New Financial System: An Ethical Approach to Preventing Future Financial Crises*, Singapore: John Wiley & Sons.

Amar Muni with Bothara, S., tr. (1999) *Acharanga Sutra* Books 1 and 2, New Delhi: Padma Prakashan.

Angelides, P. (2011) 'The Financial Crisis Enquiry Report', New York: Financial Crisis Inquiry Commission.

Armstrong, K. (2006) *The Great Transformation: The World in the Time of Buddha, Socrates, Confucius and Jeremiah*, London: Atlantic Books.

Arnold, P. (2009) 'Global financial crisis: The challenge to accounting research', *Accounting, Organisations and Society*, no. 34.

Babb, L. (1996) *Ascetics and Kings in a Jain Ritual Culture*, New Delhi: Motilal Banarsidass.

Bagchi, A.K. and Chatterjee, A. (2014) *Marxism: With and Beyond Marx*, New Delhi: Routledge India.

Bakan, J. (2004) *The Corporation: The Pathological Pursuit of Profit and Power*, New York: Free Press.

Barclay, H. (1982) *People Without Government: An Anthropology of Anarchism*, London: Kahn & Averill with Cienfuegos Press.

Beck, U. (1992) *Risk Society: Towards a New Modernity*, London: Sage.

Bentley-Hart, D. (2013) *The Experience of God – Being, Consciousness, and Bliss*, New Haven: Yale University Press.

Beyer, S.V. (2009) *Singing to the Plants: A Guide to Mestizo Shamanism in the Upper Amazon*, Albuquerque: University of New Mexico Press.

Blacker, C. and Loewe, M., eds. (1975) *Ancient Cosmologies*, London: George Allen & Unwin.

Boatright, J. (1999) *Ethics in Finance*, Oxford: Blackwell.

Boyer, R. (2005) 'From Shareholder Value to CEO Power: The Paradox of the 1990s', *Competition and Change*, no. 9, pp.7–47.

Brady Report (1988) *The October 1987 Market Break*, New York: Division of Market Regulation, United States Securities and Exchange Commission.

Brealey, R., Myers, S. and Allen, F. (2014) *Principles of Corporate Finance*, 11th edn, New York: McGraw-Hill.

Burke, E. (1968) *Reflections on the Revolution in France*, 1st Penguin edn, London: Penguin Books.

Chakrawertti, S. (2004) 'Literacy Rate: Jains Take the Honours', *The Times of India*, Mumbai (7 September 2004 edition). Also available at: http://timesofindia.indiatim es.com. Accessed 22 September 2016.

Chapple, C.K., ed. (2002) *Jainism and Ecology: Nonviolence in the Web of Life*, Cambridge, MA: Harvard University Press.

Chaucer, G. with Wright, D., tr. (2008) *The Canterbury Tales*, Oxford: Oxford University Press.

Clayton, E. (2016) 'As I See It – Dr Atul K. Shah', *Economia* (May 2016 issue).

Coggan, P. (2011) *Paper Promises – Money, Debt and the New World Order*, London: Penguin.

Cohan, W. (2011) *Money and Power: How Goldman Sachs Came to Rule the World*, New York: Penguin.

Cort, J.E. (2001) *Jains in the World: Religious Values and Ideology in India*, Oxford: Oxford University Press.

Cramme, O. and Diamond, P., eds (2012) *After the Third Way: The Future of Social Democracy in Europe*, London: I.B. Tauris & Co.

Crouch, C. (2011) *The Strange Non-Death of Neo-Liberalism*, Cambridge, UK: Polity Press.

Daly, H.E. (1991) *Steady-State Economics*, 2nd edn, Washington, DC: Island Press.

Daly, H.E. and Cobb, J. (1994) *For the Common Good: Redirecting the Economy toward Community, Environment and a Sustainable Future*, 2nd edn, Boston: Beacon Press.

Das, S. (2011) *Extreme Money: The Masters of the Universe and the Cult of Risk*, London: Pearson (Financial Times Series).

Devall, B. (1990) *Simple in Means, Rich in Ends: Practicing Deep Ecology*, London: Green Print.

Devall, B. and Sessions, G. (1985) *Deep Ecology: Living as if Nature Mattered*, Layton, UT: Gibbs Smith.

Diamond Empowerment Fund (2016) 'Our Mission'. Available at: www.diamondemp owerment.org/our-history-and-mission/. Accessed 28 July 2016.

Dixson, A. and Rousseau, C. (2006) *Critical Race Theory in Education*, Abingdon: Routledge.

Dobkin de Rios, M. (1992) *Amazon Healer: The Life and Times of an Urban Shaman*, Bridport: Prism Press.

Dobson, A. (2007) *Green Political Thought*, 4th edn, Abingdon: Routledge.

Donaldson, P. (1984) *Economics of the Real World*, 3rd edn, London: Penguin Books.

Doogar, R., Das, N. and Llewellyn Jones, R., eds. (2014) *Murshidabad: Forgotten Capital of Bengal*, Mumbai: Marg Publications.

Douglas, M. (1992) *Risk and Blame*, London: Routledge.

Douglas, M. and Wildavsky, A. (1982) *Risk and Culture*, Berkeley, CA: University of California Press.

Dundas, P. (2004) 'Beyond Anekāntavāda: A Jain Approach to Religious Tolerance', in Sethia, T., ed. *Ahimsā, Anekānta and Jainism*, New Delhi: Motilal Banarsidass, pp.123–137.

Eales, B. (1994) *Financial Risk Management*. London: McGraw-Hill.

Economist, (2015) 'Going Global – Secrets of the World's Best Business People', 16 December 2015 edition. London.

Ekins, P., Hillman, M. and Hutchison, R. (1992) *Wealth Beyond Measure: An Atlas of New Economics*, London: Gaia Books.

Elkington, J. (1999) *Cannibals with Forks: The Triple Bottom Line of 21st Century Business*, London: Capstone.

Engelen, E., Erturk, I., Froud, J., Johal, S., Leaver, A., Moran, M., and Williams, K. (2012) 'Misrule of experts? The financial crisis as elite debacle', *Economy and Society*, vol. 41, no. 3, pp.360–382.

Erturk, I., Froud, J., Johal, S., Leaver, A. and Williams, K. (2007) 'Against Agency: A Positional Critique', *Economy and Society*, no. 36, pp.51–77.

Ferguson, C. (2014) *Inside Job: The Financiers Who Pulled off the Heist of the Century*, UK: One World.

Ferguson, C. (director) (2010) *Inside Job*, [Documentary Film], USA: Sony Pictures Classics.

Ferguson, N. (2012) *The Ascent of Money – A Financial History of the World*, New York: Penguin Books.

Feyerabend, P. (1975) *Against Method: Outline of an Anarchist Theory of Knowledge*, London: Verso.

Finel-Honigman, I. (2010) *A Cultural History of Finance*, London: Routledge.

Fleming, P. and Jones, M. (2012) *The End of Corporate Social Responsibility: Crisis and Critique*, London: Sage.

Fortey, R. (1998) *Life: An Unauthorised Biography,* 2nd edn, London: Flamingo.

Frankfurter, G. and McGoun, E. (2002) *From Individualism to the Individual: Ideology and Inquiry in Financial Economics*, Farnham: Ashgate Publishing.

Fraser, I. (2015) *Shredded: Inside RBS – The Bank that Broke Britain*, Edinburgh: Birlinn.

Friedman, M. (1970) 'The Social Responsibility of Business is to Increase its Profits', *New York Times Magazine* (13 September 1970 edition).

Froud, J., Johal, S., Leaver, A. and Williams, K. (2006) *Financialization and Strategy: Narrative and Numbers*, London: Routledge.

Gendron, Y. and Smith-Lacroix, J. (2013) 'The Global Financial Crisis: Essay on the Possibility of Substantive Change in the Discipline of Finance', *Critical Perspectives on Accounting* (2013 edition).

Germain, R. (2010) *Global Politics and Financial Governance*, London: Palgrave Macmillan.

Glasenapp, H. von (1999) *Jainism: An Indian Religion of Salvation*, New Delhi: Motilal Banarsidass.

Gombrich, R. (1975) 'Ancient Indian Cosmology', in Blacker, C. and Loewe, M., eds. *Ancient Cosmologies*, London: George Allen & Unwin, pp.110–143.

Goux, J.J. (2001) 'Ideality, Symbolicity, and Reality in Postmodern Capitalism', in Cullenberg, S., Amariglio, J. and Ruccio, D., eds. *Postmodern Economics and Knowledge*, London: Routledge, pp.166–188.

Graeber, D. (2014) *Debt: The First 5000 Years,* 2nd edn, Brooklyn, NY: Melville House.

Griffin, S. (1984) *Woman and Nature: The Roaring Inside Her,* 2nd edn, Berkeley, CA: Counterpoint.

Hague, W. (2008) *William Wilberforce: The Life of the Great Anti-Slavery Campaigner*, London: Harper Perennial.

Hare, R.D. (1996) *Without Conscience: The Disturbing World of the Psychopaths Among Us*, New York: Guilford Press.

Harvard Business Review, special edition (2016) 'On Managing Across Cultures', Cambridge, MA: Harvard Business Review Press.

Hawken, P. (1994) *The Ecology of Commerce: A Declaration of Sustainability*, London: Phoenix.

Hendry, J. (2013) *Ethics and Finance: An Introduction*, Cambridge: Cambridge University Press.

Hertz, N. (2001) *The Silent Takeover: Global Capitalism and The Death of Democracy*, London: William Heinemann.

Hind, D. and Christensen, J. (2015) *The Greatest Invention: Tax and the Campaign for a Just Society*, Margate, UK: Commonwealth Publishing.

Hofmeester, K. (2013) 'Shifting Trajectories of Diamond Processing: From India to Europe and Back, From the Fifteenth Century to the Twentieth', *Journal of Global History*, vol. 8, no. 1, pp.25–49.

Hopkin, P. (2012) *Fundamentals of Risk Management*, London: Kogan Page.

Hopwood, A. (2007) 'Whither Accounting Research?', *The Accounting Review*, vol. 82, no. 5, pp.1365–1374.

Hopwood, A. (2009) 'Exploring the interface between accounting and finance', *Accounting, Organizations and Society*, no. 34, pp.549–550.

Horvath, P. (2014) 'Discovering Jainism for Business'. Available at: http://philiphorvath.com/discovering-jainism-business/. Accessed 27 July 2016.

Humphrey, C., Loft, A. and Woods, M. (2009) 'The Global Audit Profession and the International Financial Architecture: Understanding Regulatory Relationships at a Time of Financial Crisis', *Accounting, Organizations and Society*, vol. 34, nos. 6–7, pp.810–825.

International Finance Corporation (2014) 'Inclusive Business Case Study: Jain Irrigation Systems Limited'. Available at: www.ifc.org/inclusivebusiness. Accessed 30 May 2016.

Jain, K. (1998) *Aparigraha: The Humane Solution*, Varanasi, India: Parsvanath Vidyapeeth.

Jaini, P.S. (2001) *The Jaina Path of Purification*, 4th edn, New Delhi: Motilal Banarsidass.

Jaini, P.S. (2002) 'Ecology, Economics, and Development in Jainism', in Chapple, C.K., ed. (2002) *Jainism and Ecology: Nonviolence in the Web of Life*, Cambridge, MA: Harvard University Press, pp.141–159.

James, O. (2007) *Affluenza: How to be Successful and Stay Sane*, London: Vermillion.

Jensen, M. and Meckling, W. (1976) 'Theory of the Firm: Managerial Behaviour, Agency Costs and Ownership Structure', *Journal of Financial Economics*, no. 3, pp.305–360.

Kamdar, M. (2007) *Planet India: The Turbulent Rise of the World's Largest Democracy*, London: Simon & Schuster.

Karmali, N. (2016) 'Indian Farmers' Champion, Bhavarlal Jain, Dies at 78'. Available at: www.forbes.com. Accessed 26 February 2016.

Kay, J. (2011) *The Map Is Not the Territory: An Essay on the State of Economics*, Oxford: Institute for New Economic Thinking.

Kay, J. (2015) *Other People's Money: Masters of the Universe or Servants of the People?*, London: Profile Books.

Keating, M. and McCrone, D., eds. (2015) *The Crisis of Social Democracy in Europe*, reprint edn, Edinburgh: Edinburgh University Press.

Kets de Vries, M. (2012) *The Psychopath in the C Suite: Redefining the SOB*, Fontainbleau/Singapore/Abu Dhabi: INSEAD Working Paper no. 119.

Kettell, B. (2011) *Introduction to Islamic Banking and Finance*, Chichester: John Wiley & Sons.

Klein, N. (2008) *The Shock Doctrine: The Rise of Disaster Capitalism*, 1st edn, London: Penguin Books.

Klein, N. (2015) *This Changes Everything: Capitalism vs The Climate*, London: Penguin Books.

Koller, J.M. (2002) 'Jain Ecological Perspectives', in Chapple, C.K., ed. (2002) *Jainism and Ecology: Nonviolence in the Web of Life*, Cambridge, MA: Harvard University Press, pp.19–35.

Korten, D.C. (1995) *When Corporations Rule the World*, London: Earthscan.

Kothari, J. (2004) 'A Diamond is Forever', *Jain Spirit*, Issue 20 (September – November 2004), pp.48–50.

Lala, R.M. (2007) *The Creation of Wealth: The Tatas from the 19th to 21st Century*, New Delhi: Penguin Books India.

Lee, S. (2009) 'The Rock of Stability? The Political Economy of the Brown Government', *Policy Studies*, vol. 30, no. 1 (February 2009), pp.17–32.

Lewis, M. (2008) *The Big Short*, London: Penguin Books.

Lewis, M. (2011) *Boomerang: The Biggest Bust*, London: Penguin Books.

Lewis, M. (2016) 'Debt and Mental Illness are a Marriage Made in Hell – This is How to Cope', *Daily Telegraph*, London (5 April 2016 edition).

Lum, K. (2014, 16 October) 'The Rise and Rise of Belgium's Diamond Dynasties'. Available at: www.theconversation.com. Accessed 27 June 2016.

Luyendijk, J. (2015) *Swimming with Sharks: My Journey into the World of Bankers*, London: Guardian/Faber & Faber.

Mackenzie, D. (2006) *An Engine, Not a Camera – How Financial Models Shape Markets*, Cambridge, MA: MIT Press.

McDonald, L. and Robinson, P. (2009) *A Colossal Failure of Common Sense: The Incredible Inside Story of the Collapse of Lehman Brothers*, London: Ebury Press.

McFall, J. (2009) *Banking Crisis: Reforming Corporate Governance and the City*, London: House of Commons Treasury Committee, HC 519.

McGoun, E. (1995) 'The History of Risk Measurement', *Critical Perspectives on Accounting*, no.16, pp.511–532.

McGoun, E. (1997) 'Hyperreal Finance', *Critical Perspectives on Accounting*, no.18, pp.97–122.

McKenna, F. (2011) 'The Button-Down Mafia: How the Public Accounting Firms Run a Racket on Investors and Thrive While Their Clients Fail'. Available at: retheauditors.com. Accessed 20 May 2016.

McSweeney, B. (2009) 'The roles of financial asset market failure denial and the economic crisis: Reflections on accounting and financial theories and practices', *Accounting, Organisations & Society*, no. 34, pp.835–848.

Macy, J. (2013) *Greening of the Self*, Berkeley, CA: Parallax Press.

Mardia, K.V. (2007) *The Scientific Foundations of Jainism*, 4th edn, New Delhi: Motilal Banarsidass.

Mardia, K.V. and Rankin, A. (2013) *Living Jainism: An Ethical Science*, Winchester: Mantra Books.

Matilal, B.K. (2000) 'Anekānta: Both Yes and No', in Shah, N.J., ed. *Jaina Theory of Multiple Facets of Reality and Truth*, New Delhi: Motilal Banarsidass with Bhogilal Leherchand Institute of Indology, pp.1–17.

Meena Peters, M. (2014) 'The Remarkable History of the Diamond Trade', *Passage* (March – April 2014 edition), pp.12–13.

Mehta, M.L. (2002) *Jaina Psychology: An Introduction*, Varanasi: Parshvanath Vidyapeeth.

Mitchell, A. and Sikka, P. (2011) *The Pin-Stripe Mafia: How Accountancy Firms Destroy Societies*, Basildon, UK: Association for Accountancy & Business Affairs.

Modigliani, F. and Miller, M. (1958) 'The Cost of Capital, Corporation Finance and the Theory of Investment', *American Economic Review*, no. 48, pp.261–297.

Molissa, P. (2011) 'A Spiritual Reflection on Emancipation and Accounting', *Critical Perspectives on Accounting*, no. 22, pp.453–484.

Moore, M. (2001) *Stupid White Men*, London: Penguin Books.

Munishri Nyayavijayi, with Shah, N.J., tr. (1999) *Jaina Philosophy and Religion*, New Delhi: Motilal Banarsidass.

Murphy, R. (2015) *The Joy of Tax*, London: Transworld Publishers.

Naess, A. (author) with Drengson, A. and Devall, B., eds. (2010) *The Ecology of Wisdom: Writings By Arne Naess*, Berkeley, CA: Counterpoint.

O'Casey, S. (1998) *Three Dublin Plays*, London: Faber & Faber.

Palan, R., Murphy, R. and Chavagneux, C. (2010) *How Globalisation Really Works*, Ithaca, NY: Cornell University Press.

Parker, R. (2016, 4 March) 'How Stolen Treasure Kick-Started the Bank of England'. Available at: www.theconversation.com. Accessed 5 March 2016.

Peston, R. (2008) *Who Runs Britain? … And Who's to Blame for the Economic Mess We're In*, London: Hodder and Stoughton.

Piketty, T. (2014) *Capital in the Twenty-First Century*, Cambridge, MA: Harvard University Press.

Power, M. (2007) *Organized Uncertainty: Designing a World of Risk Management*, Oxford: Oxford University Press.

Prabhavananda, S. (1979) *The Spiritual Heritage of India: A Clear Summary of Indian Philosophy and Religion*, 2nd edn, Hollywood, CA: Vedanta Press.

Project Anveshan (2014) 'About the Project'. Available at: http://projectanveshan.com/about-the-project/. Accessed 28 July 2016.

Rajan, R. (2005) *NBER Working Paper no. 11728: Has Financial Development made the World Riskier?*, Cambridge, MA: National Bureau of Economic Research.

Rajan, R. and Zingales, L. (2003) *Saving Capitalism from the Capitalists*, New York: Crown Business.

Rand, A. (1957) *Atlas Shrugged*, New York: Random House.

Rankin, A. (2006) *The Jain Path: Ancient Wisdom for the West*, Winchester: O Books.

Rankin, A. (2010) *Many-Sided Wisdom: A New Politics of the Spirit*, Winchester: O Books.

Rankin, A. and Shah, A. (2008) *Social Cohesion: A Jain Perspective*, Colchester, UK: Diverse Ethics.

Rankin, A. and Mardia, K.V. (2013) *Living Jainism: An Ethical Science*, Winchester: Mantra Books.

Richman, B.D. (2006) 'How Community Institutions Create Economic Advantage: Jewish Diamond Merchants in New York', *Law and Social Inquiry*, vol. 31, no. 2, pp.383–420.

Robin, M.M. (2008) *The World According to Monsanto: Pollution, Corruption and Control of the World's Food Supply*, New York: New Press.

Roggi, O. and Altman, E., eds. (2013) *Managing and Measuring Risk: Emerging Global Standards and Regulation After the Financial Crisis*, Singapore: World Scientific Publishing Company (World Scientific Series in Finance, vol. 5).

Ross, S., Westerfield, R. and Jordan, B. (2012) *Fundamentals of Corporate Finance*, 9th edn, London: McGraw-Hill International.

Rousseau, J-J. with Cress, D.A. tr. (1987) *Basic Political Writings*, 2nd edn, Indianapolis, IN: Hackett Publishing Company.

Ruskin, J. (1985) *Unto this Last and Other Writings*, UK: Penguin Classics.

Said, E. (1994) *Culture and Imperialism*, London: Vintage Books.

Santoro, M. and Strauss, R. (2013) *Wall Street Values*, New York: Cambridge University Press.

Schumacher, E.F. (1993) *Small Is Beautiful: A Study of Economics as if People Mattered*, 2nd edn, London: Vintage Books.

Schwarz, W. and Schwarz, D. (1998) *Living Lightly: Travels in Post-Consumer Society*, Charlbury: John Carpenter.

Sessions, G., ed. (1995) *Deep Ecology for the 21st Century*, Boston: Shambhala Publications.

Sethia, T., ed. (2004) *Ahimsā, Anekānta and Jainism*, New Delhi: Motilal Banarsidass.

Shah, A. (1996a) 'Creative Compliance in Financial Reporting', *Accounting, Organisations and Society*, vol. 21, no. 1, pp.23–39.

Shah, A. (1996b) 'Corporate Governance and Business Ethics', *Business Ethics: A European Review*, vol. 5, no. 4, pp.225–233.

Shah, A. (1997) 'Regulatory Arbitrage Through Financial Innovation', *Accounting, Auditing and Accountability Journal*, vol. 10, no. 1, pp.85–104.

Shah, A. (2007a) *Celebrating Diversity: How to Enjoy, Respect and Benefit from Great Coloured Britain*, Stowmarket: Kevin Mayhew.

Shah, A. (2007b) 'Jain Business Ethics', *Accountancy, Business and the Public Interest*, vol. 6, no. 2, pp.115–130.

Shah, A. and Rankin, A. (2008) *Social Cohesion: A Jain Perspective*, Colchester: Diverse Ethics.

Shah, A. (2015a) 'The Political Economy of Financial Risk: A Case Study of HBOS' (Working Paper). Available at: www.academia.edu. Accessed 15 August 2016.

Shah, A. (2015b) 'Systemic Regulatory Arbitrage: A Case Study of KPMG' (Working Paper). Available at: www.academia.edu. Accessed 16 August 2016.

Shah, A. (2016) 'Q. What did Universities Learn from the Financial Crash? A. Nothing', *The Guardian*, London (2 February 2016 edition). Also available at: www.guardian.co.uk. Accessed: 3 February 2016.

Shah, A.M.P. (2016) 'A Family Office: In Its Own Words'. Available at: http://mtc-trust.com/News/A-Family-Office-In-its-own-words/. Accessed 28 July 2016.

Shah, B. (2016) Personal interview, 8 April 2016.

Shah, H. (2016) 'Lest We Forget – A Journey of Migration Across the Seas in Search of a Better Future'. Available at: www.amazon.co.uk. Accessed 9 August 2016.

Shah, N.J., ed. (2000) *Jaina Theory of Multiple Facets of Reality and Truth*, New Delhi: Motilal Banarsidass with Bhogilal Leherchand Institute of Indology.

Shambhu's Vegan Catering Services (2014) 'About Shambhu's'. Available at: http://shambhus.co.uk/about-shambhu-s/about-shambhus. Accessed 15 March 2016.

Shaxson, N. (2007) *Poisoned Wells: The Dirty Politics of African Oil*, New York: Palgrave Macmillan.

Shaxson, N. (2012) *Treasure Islands: Tax Havens and the Men who Stole the World*, New York: Vintage Books.

Shaxson, N. and Christensen, J. (2013) *The Finance Curse*, Chesham: Tax Justice Network.

Shefrin, H. (2000) *Beyond Greed and Fear: Understanding Behavioural Finance and the Psychology of Investing*, Cambridge, MA: Harvard Business School Press.

Shilapi, S. (2002) 'The Environmental and Ecological Teachings of Tīrthankara Mahāvīra', in Chapple, C.K., ed. (2002) *Jainism and Ecology: Nonviolence in the Web of Life*, Cambridge, MA: Harvard University Press, pp.159–169.

Shiller, R.J. (2012) *Finance and the Good Society*, Princeton: Princeton University Press.

Sigma Pharmaceuticals PLC (2014) 'About Sigma Pharmaceuticals plc'. Available at: www.sigmaplc.co.uk/aboutsigma.aspx. Accessed: 7 April 2016.

Sikka, P. (2008) 'Enterprise Culture and Accountancy Firms: New Masters of the Universe', *Accounting, Auditing and Accountability Journal*, vol. 21, no. 2, pp.268–295.

Sikka, P., Willmott, H. and Puxty, T. (1995) 'The mountains are still there – Accounting academics and the bearings of intellectuals', *Accounting, Auditing & Accountability Journal*, vol. 8, no. 3, pp.113–140.

Singh, R. (2000) 'Relevance of Anekānta in Modern Times', in Shah, N.J., ed. *Jaina Theory of Multiple Facets of Reality and Truth*, New Delhi: Motilal Banarsidass with Bhogilal Leherchand Institute of Indology, pp.17–135.

Singh, S.S. (2015) 'The Bankers of Bengal', *The Hindu Magazine*, Chennai (19 December 2015 edition). Also available at: www.thehindu.com. Accessed: 19 December 2015.

Singhvi, L.M. (1990) 'The Jain Declaration on Nature', in Chapple, C.K., ed. (2002) *Jainism and Ecology: Nonviolence in the Web of Life*, Cambridge, MA: Harvard University Press, pp.217–225.

Smith, A. (2012) *Wealth of Nations*, London: Wordsworth Editions.

Special Correspondent (2007) 'Jains's Contribution to exchequer "astounding"', *The Hindu Magazine*, Chennai (20 August 2007 edition). Also available at: www.the hindu.com. Accessed: 6 November 2016.

Standing, G. (2011) *The Precariat: The New Dangerous Class*, London: Bloomsbury.

Standing, G. (2014) *A Precariat Charter: From Denizens to Citizens*, London: Bloomsbury.

Strange, S. (1986) *Casino Capitalism*, Oxford: Basil Blackwell.

Subcommittee on Investigations (2011) *Wall Street and the Financial Crisis: Anatomy of a Financial Collapse*, Washington, DC: United States Senate Permanent Committee on Investigations.

Tatia, N. (1994) *That Which Is: Tattvārtha Sūtra (Umāsvāti)*, San Francisco: HarperCollins.

Tatia, N. (2002) 'The Jain Worldview and Ecology', in Chapple, C.K., ed. (2002) *Jainism and Ecology: Nonviolence in the Web of Life*, Cambridge, MA: Harvard University Press, pp.3–19.

Tett, G. (2010) *Fool's Gold: How Unrestrained Greed Corrupted a Dream, Shattered Global Markets and Unleashed a Catastrophe*, London: Abacus.

Tett, G. (2015) *The Silo Effect: The Peril of Expertise and the Promise of Breaking Down Barriers*, New York: Simon & Schuster.

Thaler, R.H. (2013) *Misbehaving: The Making of Behavioural Economics*, New York: Norton & Co.

Tharoor, S. (1997) *India: From Midnight to the Millenium and Beyond*, New York: Arcade Publishing.

Thompson, E.P. (2013) *The Making of the English Working Class*, London: Penguin Modern Classics.

Tobias, M. (1991) *Life Force: The World of Jainism*, Fremont, CA: Asian Humanities Press.

Tyrie, A. (2013) *Changing Banking for Good*, UK: House of Commons Treasury Committee Report HC 175–11.

Vadukut, S. (2008) 'Motilal Oswal – When everyone knows your name'. Available at: www.livemint.com. Accessed 2 April 2016.

Veerayatan (2015) 'Mission and Vision'. Available at: https://veerayatan.org/mission-vision/. Accessed 28 July 2016.

VegfestUK (2015) 'Nishma Shah Profile'. Available at: http://london.vegfest.co.uk/nishma-shah. Accessed 15 March 2016.

Vibhakar, D. (2013) 'Interview of [sic] Deepchand Gardi'. Available at: www.speakbindas.com. Accessed 3 April 2016.

West, B. (2003) *Professionalism and Accounting Rules*, Abingdon: Routledge.

Wilson, R. (2012) *Legal, Regulatory and Governance Issues in Islamic Finance*, Edinburgh: Edinburgh University Press.

Xu, L. and Zia, B. (2012) *Financial Literacy around the World: An Overview of the Evidence with Practical Suggestions for the Way Forward*, Washington, DC: World Bank, Policy Research Working Papers.

Zwan, N. (2014) 'Making Sense of Financialization', *Socio-Economic Review*, no. 12, pp.99–129.

Index